Blackstone's

Police Investigators' Workbook

Blackstone's

Police Investigators' Workbook

2022

Paul Connor

OXFORD
UNIVERSITY PRESS

OXFORD
UNIVERSITY PRESS

Great Clarendon Street, Oxford, OX2 6DP,
United Kingdom

Oxford University Press is a department of the University of Oxford.
It furthers the University's objective of excellence in research, scholarship,
and education by publishing worldwide. Oxford is a registered trade mark of
Oxford University Press in the UK and in certain other countries

© Oxford University Press 2021

The moral rights of the author have been asserted

First Edition published in 2021

Impression: 2

Public sector information reproduced under Open Government Licence v3.0
(http://www.nationalarchives.gov.uk/doc/open-government-licence/open-government-licence.htm)

Published in the United States of America by Oxford University Press
198 Madison Avenue, New York, NY 10016, United States of America

British Library Cataloguing in Publication Data
Data available

ISBN 978-0-19-284814-7

DOI: 10.1093/law/9780192848147.001.0001

Printed and bound by CPI Group (UK) Ltd,
Croydon, CR0 4YY

Acknowledgements

Thanks must go to all the Trainee Investigators who provided me with feedback about the content and style of the Workbook.

Many thanks to all the team at OUP, especially Jordan Burke, Stuart Johnson and Fiona Briden.

Contents

Contents

Contents

Introduction to the Workbook

This Workbook has been custom-written to assist candidates studying and revising for any of the National Investigators' Examinations (NIE) due to take place in 2022.

In order to make this publication as beneficial as possible, candidates studying for the NIE have examined each section of the Workbook and have provided feedback on the content and style of the material. The feedback received enabled the Workbook to be tailored to suit the needs of the NIE candidate.

The Workbook does not cover every single subject mentioned in the text of the *Blackstone's Police Investigators' Manual 2022* (the Manual). This is because subjects dealt with in the Workbook are approached in a different manner to that of the Manual. The Manual, by necessity, covers the entire syllabus of the NIE, whereas the Workbook is selective in its coverage. In order to ensure that you understand a subject, you will be asked to complete a variety of tasks such as completing written exercises, examining flowcharts and answering multiple-choice questions. This approach means that a subject dealt with in a matter of five pages in the Manual can take 20 pages to deal with in the Workbook. It should be noted that the Workbook relates to the NIE alone—there are no sections contained within the Workbook that relate to Parts V and VI of the Manual (relevant for candidates from the National Crime Agency and Immigration Enforcement only).

Before you begin, I must make two important points clear:

1. It is important that you do not use the subjects covered in the Workbook as a predictor of the content of the NIE. *Any* subject contained in the Manual can be tested in the examination and that subject might not be covered in the Workbook.
2. The questions you will answer in the NIE are based *solely* on the text contained in the Manual. If there is ever any contradiction between the Manual and the Workbook (or indeed any other text), remember: '*The Manual is always right.*'

A lot of effort has gone into writing this Workbook. I hope that you will benefit from that effort and that it makes a positive contribution to your study and revision.

Catalytic Learning—A System of Study Using this Workbook

Whether it is for an examination, an interview, a new skill at work or for any other purpose, we all have different approaches to learning. Because we are all so very diverse there is no set formula for study and revision that will suit us all. What works for me may not work for you.

For those who have successfully used a particular style or approach to study and revision in the past and believe that it will work when studying/revising for the NIE—stick with it. I am sure you will adapt the Workbook to suit your needs.

For those who do not fall into this category, you might want to try the following method to get the most out of the Workbook and any other resources at your disposal. Please remember that this is only a *suggested* way for you to use the Workbook and other resources. How you use them is a choice only you can make.

Essential Resources

You MUST have at your disposal:

– *Blackstone's Police Investigators' Manual 2022*
– *Blackstone's Police Investigators' Workbook 2022*
– Multiple-Choice Questions (MCQs) 2022

Methodology and Rationale

Below is a simple illustration of the Catalytic Model of Learning (CML).

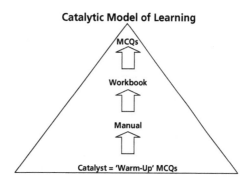

The CML consists of four distinct phases:

Phase 1—Catalyst
Phase 2—Information
Phase 3—Reinforcement
Phase 4—Test

Phase 1—Catalyst

Answer a small number of multiple-choice questions (MCQs) on the subject you are about to study (two or three at most). *The answers to the MCQs are unimportant—in fact, do not even look at the answers to the questions*. What is required is for you to have the experience of answering MCQs on a subject. Of course, you could use the questions that are contained within this Workbook but as you are likely to repeat this process on numerous occasions, another source of MCQs is an essential requirement.

Perhaps you could obtain additional MCQs from the Blackstone's *Police Investigators' Q&A Online Service* or from the Blackstone's *Police Investigators' Q&A*.

Phase 1 is essential as your perceptions about your knowledge of the law need to be challenged at an early stage. You may believe that your knowledge is of a good standard when in fact it is not. Unless this misconception is exposed immediately, and to the one person capable of doing something about it (you), it is easy to believe that your current knowledge and practical experience will be sufficient to get you through the exam—however, that will not be the case.

Phase 2—Information

Now read the *Investigators' Manual* on your chosen subject. Using the Manual at this stage provides you with 100 per cent coverage of the material that could be tested. You are also guaranteed to see the answers to the MCQs you have just answered. If the answer does not appear, then the MCQ must be invalid as ALL answers must be in the Manual. This discovery process underpins the legal points you examined in your MCQs.

Phase 3—Reinforcement

Now attempt the exercises in the Workbook (if there is an appropriate chapter). Remember that the Workbook is designed to assist you in your efforts to pass the NIE—it is not part of the NIE syllabus so you will not be tested on its contents. However, amongst other things it contains very useful charts, diagrams, mnemonics etc. that will augment your study. The written exercises will challenge you in terms of your application of your knowledge of the law.

Phase 4—Test

Now (if possible) answer *the same MCQs* you answered at the beginning of the process.

By answering the same small number of MCQs you can see what you have learnt. Did you change your mind when you gave your answer on this second occasion? Did your work serve to confirm what you believed in the first place?

In addition, using a new handful of MCQs each time allows you to return to the subject and be tested in new ways. This way you will not deplete your MCQ database (as so many candidates do) by answering dozens and dozens of the same MCQs time after time and think that this is 'learning'. The only thing such candidates are doing is 'learning' the answers to the MCQs and being fooled into thinking they are making good progress.

If you are still performing poorly after you have studied a subject for the fourth time, you know that you need to improve; if you are answering them correctly, this shows that you are well on your way.

An Example of the CML—'Theft'

Here is an example of the CML using 'Theft' as a subject for study.

1. Begin your work by answering several multiple-choice questions on 'Theft'.
2. When you have answered the multiple-choice questions, read the section on 'Theft' contained in the *Investigators' Manual*.

3. Now complete the 'Theft' section in the Workbook.
4. Return to the MCQs you attempted at the beginning of the process and make a second attempt at them. When you have finished, check your answers.

Some Options/Versions for the CML?

– After you have finished the Workbook section on the subject, you could return to the *Investigators' Manual* and read the section on 'Theft' for the second time.
– No Workbook section on the subject? Begin with some MCQs from your Q&A database/book, then read the Manual and then return to the same Q&As.

Conclusion

You might find, at first, that your performance is not what you would like it to be but do not give up because of this; it is quite normal. Your knowledge and ability will steadily increase as you move closer to the examination and as you complete more study and revision. I am confident that you will finish the process with a good level of knowledge. Remember that the Catalytic process will provide you with a good *foundation* of knowledge, but in order to maintain that level you should briefly revisit the subject from time to time.

PART 1

General Principles, Police Powers and Procedures

1 *Mens Rea* (State of Mind) and *Actus Reus* (Criminal Conduct)

1.1 Introduction

Examining state of mind and criminal conduct will provide you with valuable information that you can relate to ALL the offences you will study while studying and revising for your NIE. This is because every crime in your *Investigators' Manual* will involve some form of guilty knowledge and some form of action (there are no strict liability offences in your Manual). For that reason this section of the Workbook concentrates on three areas: (i) intention, (ii) recklessness and (iii) the chain of causation.

1.2 Aim

The aim of this section is to identify and explain some of the major issues regarding state of mind (*mens rea*) and criminal conduct (*actus reus*).

1.3 Objectives

At the end of this section you should be able to:

1. Explain how a court may infer intention.
2. Identify the differences between voluntary and involuntary intoxication.
3. Outline the meaning of recklessness.
4. Describe what is meant by the term 'chain of causation'.
5. Apply your knowledge to multiple-choice questions.

1.4 Intention

The word 'intent' is mentioned in many of the offences you will study and revise for the NIE.

1.4.1 Exercise—Definition of 'Intent'

What is the definition of 'intent'?

_____

_____

_____

EXPLANATION 1.4.1

Definition of 'Intent'

When you thought about this exercise you may have struggled to remember where you have read the definition of intent. That would not be surprising as there is no such definition. To keep things as simple as possible it is best to consider 'intent' from a common-sense point of view. If you intend to do something then you want it to happen and set out to see that it does; it is your purpose.

One of the reasons why it would be difficult to provide a definition of intent is that it is ever-changing according to the offence. The intention for murder is the intent to kill or cause grievous bodily harm, whereas for theft it is to act dishonestly, intending to permanently deprive.

Proving intention is not easy unless defendants provide an admissible confession, perhaps during interview, where they state that their intention was to bring about a certain result: *'I wanted him dead because he was having an affair with my wife.'* But what happens when such evidence is not available?

1.4.2 Exercise—Inferring Intent

Read the following scenario and answer the question that follows it.

DICKSON and STONE work with each other on a machine in a car factory. The machine presses metal into car parts and exerts high pressure on the metal in order to do so. The machine is extremely dangerous and both men are aware of this fact as there have been several serious accidents involving the machine in the past, one of which was fatal. An argument begins between the two men while they are operating the machine, culminating in DICKSON pushing STONE into the press which closes and crushes him to death. DICKSON is arrested for murder and during his interview he denies the offence. He maintains that he wanted to frighten STONE and teach him a lesson and that he did not intend to kill or cause him grievous bodily harm. He is charged with murder and the case goes to trial. There is no confession evidence to readily establish DICKSON's state of mind.

There are two ways that a jury may be able to infer intent from the circumstances. What are they?

1. _____

2. _____

EXPLANATION 1.4.2

Inferring Intent

The two ways that a jury may be able to infer intent are by way of:

1. case law; and

2. s. 8 of the Criminal Justice Act 1967.

We will deal with each of these methods in turn.

Case law states that *foresight of a probability of a consequence does not amount to an intention to bring that consequence about, but may be evidence of it.*

The jury/court considers:

- At the time of the criminal act was there a probability of a consequence?

- The greater the probability, the more likely it is that the defendant foresaw that consequence.

- If the defendant foresaw that consequence, the more likely it is that the defendant intended it to happen.

1.4.3   Exercise—Case Law and Inferring Intent

Now apply case law to the circumstances. How would case law assist a jury/court to infer DICKSON's intent?

_____

_____

_____

_____

_____

_____

_____

EXPLANATION 1.4.3

Case Law and Inferring Intent

It is best to deal with each word in turn and then consider its meaning in light of the evidence at your disposal.

Foresight = what did DICKSON see

Probability = was likely to happen

Consequence = as a result of the action

So *foresight of a probability of a consequence etc.* means you saw what was likely to happen as a result of your actions and, while it doesn't prove that you intended it, it may be evidence of it.

Think of these elements as a series of steps:

STEP ONE

At the time of the criminal act was there a probability of a consequence?

(When DICKSON pushed STONE into the machine, was it likely that he saw that STONE *would be killed or seriously injured*?)

↓

STEP TWO

The greater the probability, the more likely it is that the defendant foresaw that consequence.

(There was a very high chance of death or serious injury and therefore it is likely that DICKSON saw what the result of his actions would be.)

↓

STEP THREE

If DICKSON foresaw that consequence, the more likely it is that he intended it to happen.

(DICKSON knew what would happen—it is highly likely he intended it.)

Section 8 of the Criminal Justice Act 1967 states that a court/jury in determining whether a person has committed an offence:

(a) shall not be bound in law to infer that he intended or foresaw a result of his actions by reason only of its being a natural and probable consequence of those actions; but

(b) shall decide whether he did intend or foresee that result by reference to all the evidence, drawing such inferences from the evidence as appear proper in the circumstances.

Let's say that the following additional information was available to the police.

DICKSON and STONE have never got on with each other and have had several arguments. The relationship between the two men has been progressively worsening and last week the foreman of the factory had to step in to break up a fight between them when blows were exchanged in the factory canteen. Another worker at the factory, PARVIEW, overheard a conversation between DICKSON and another man in a pub several days ago. During the conversation, DICKSON was heard to say, *'Don't you worry, when the little shit's dead I'll make it look like an industrial accident.'*

1.4.4 Exercise—Section 8 of the Criminal Justice Act 1967

Using the additional evidence at your disposal, explain how s. 8 would assist to allow a court/jury to infer intent.

_____

_____

_____

_____

_____

_____

_____

_____

_____

EXPLANATION 1.4.4

Section 8 of the Criminal Justice Act 1967

What s. 8 of the Criminal Justice Act 1967 says is that pushing STONE into the press machine would quite obviously cause his death. However, just because this is obvious does not mean to say that the jury/court can infer that DICKSON intended to kill or cause GBH as a result. *However*, they can look at the evidence as a whole and by looking at that evidence infer intent if it appears proper to do so. The more evidence there is available that supports that inference, the more likely it is that DICKSON intended the result.

See *Investigators' Manual*, para. 1.1.3

1.4.5 Intoxication—Voluntary or Involuntary

When we say that someone is 'intoxicated', we are not describing someone who has had one too many sherries and is slightly tipsy or someone who has had one puff of a cannabis joint and feels a little light-headed! We are talking about someone who is so utterly intoxicated that their mind is not functioning and is preventing them from forming the necessary *mens rea* required to commit an offence. Think of all the coverage you have seen via TV or other media of the binge-drinking element of society in full flow—that is more like the situation we are thinking about.

Consider the person concerned as an intoxicated robot. Our intoxicated robot might have got itself into that state (*voluntary* intoxication) or maybe someone spiked the robot's tea with some LSD and *it is not the robot's fault* that it is in that state (*involuntary* intoxication).

Even when intoxicated, our robot can perform *basic* tasks (intoxicated robots can always get home, can't they?) but it cannot perform *specific* tasks (threading a needle is an impossible task).

Now think about that intoxicated robot, an offence of BASIC intent (example—s. 20 GBH) and an offence of SPECIFIC intent (example—murder).

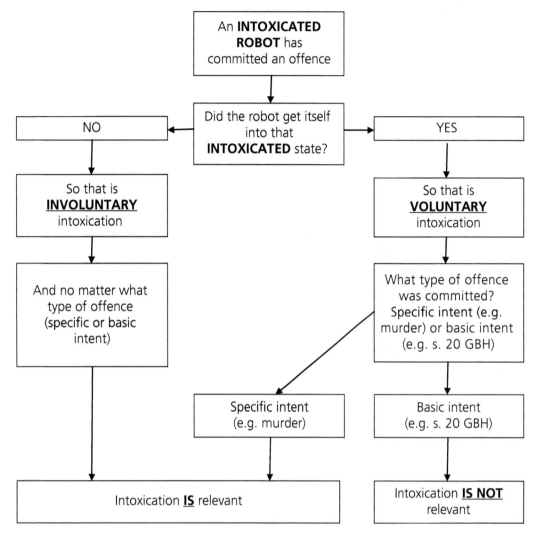

INVOLUNTARY INTOXICATION
Can be raised in answer to a charge of specific or basic intent
VOLUNTARY INTOXICATION
Can be raised in answer to a charge of an offence of specific intent *but not* basic intent

Points to Note

- Note that 'intoxication' is not all about being drunk (via alcohol)—'intoxication' can be caused by drink or drugs or a combination of the two (and the drugs do not have to be illegal).
- If a person misjudges the amount or strength of the intoxicant they take, this *will not* be regarded as involuntary intoxication.
- 'Dutch' courage would not amount to 'intoxication'. So if a defendant deliberately became intoxicated in order to gain false courage to go and commit a murder (a specific intent offence), they *will not* be able to rely on voluntary intoxication even though the crime is one of specific intent. This is because they have already formed the intent required and the intoxication is merely a means of plucking up 'Dutch' courage to carry it out.

See *Investigators' Manual*, para. 1.1.2.2

1.5 Recklessness

1.5.1 Exercise—What Does 'Recklessness' Mean?

You will see the word 'recklessness' in a large number of the offences you will study. Do not worry about a precise legal definition just yet; instead, write down what you think it means.

> **EXPLANATION 1.5.1**
> **What Does 'Recklessness' Mean?**
> There will be a wide variety of responses to this exercise. You may have included the following: acting without caution, an act marked by a lack of proper caution, without thought or care for the consequences of an action, an act marked by a lack of thought about danger or other possible undesirable consequences, doing something dangerous and not caring about the risks and the possible results, completely heedless of dangers or consequences, or rash.
> All of these (and more) would be a fair response to the question.
> Now that you have considered the word from a common sense perspective, you need to move on to consider it from a legal perspective.

1.5.2 Exercise—'Subjective' Recklessness

Examine the following scenario and see if you agree or disagree with the statement that follows it.

BAREHAM is hired to repair a large section of roof on a three-storey house. He needs to remove a large section of the existing roof before he can begin, and places a skip at the front of the house at ground level to throw roof tiles and other debris into as he demolishes the existing roof. BAREHAM does not bother to place a chute leading from the roof to the skip and realises that there is a slight chance that flying debris could injure someone. However, he believes that he is accurate enough to ensure that all the debris will land directly in the skip as he throws it from the roof. BAREHAM begins work, but the first tile he throws towards the skip misses and hits CASSWELL on the shoulder as she walks past the house. The blow breaks CASSWELL's collarbone.

In these circumstances, BAREHAM would be considered 'reckless' and could be convicted of a s. 20 assault. This is because the term 'recklessness' in assaults means *subjective recklessness*.

Do you agree or disagree with this statement?
Agree / Disagree
Why / Why not?

EXPLANATION 1.5.2

'Subjective' Recklessness

Recklessness is similar to intent insofar as it changes with the nature of the crime. This is illustrated in the above example and will be explained shortly. Following the decision in *R v G & R* [2003] 3 WLR 1060, the approach taken to the interpretation of the word 'reckless' is that it will be 'subjective'.

In the above scenario, BAREHAM would be considered to be 'reckless' in the subjective sense, i.e. BAREHAM saw there was a risk of harm but went on to take that risk anyway.

The simple approach to recklessness is this:

Recklessness is subjective. If the defendant *did not* see the risk, then he/she *is not reckless*.

See *Investigators' Manual*, para. 1.1.3

1.6 The Chain of Causation

1.6.1 Exercise—'But for' Test and Intervening Act

Read the following scenario and answer the questions that follow it, providing reasons for your answers where appropriate.

TULLAH and McDOWELL are involved in an argument inside a pub. Members of the pub door staff eject both men from the pub and the argument between the two men continues outside. The argument escalates and TULLAH punches McDOWELL in the face, intending to cause him actual bodily harm. The force of the blow knocks McDOWELL backwards and he trips on the kerb, causing him to fall over onto the pavement. McDOWELL's head hits the pavement and he loses consciousness. An ambulance is called to the scene and McDOWELL is taken to the Accident and Emergency (A&E) ward of a nearby hospital. The A&E ward is extremely busy as it is Saturday night and there have been a large number of serious incidents, adding pressure to the already overworked staff. A nurse quickly examines McDOWELL and, believing that he has sustained a very minor concussion, leaves him and goes to deal with another patient. In fact, McDOWELL has fractured his skull and has sustained life-threatening brain damage from the fracture. Thirty minutes later, McDOWELL dies without receiving any treatment. A post-mortem reveals that McDOWELL had a rare medical condition meaning that a slight blow to his skull could cause it to fracture and consequently cause his death. The blow that caused McDOWELL's skull to fracture would have left only bruising to the skull of the average person.

1. If you were dealing with this case, what offence(s) would you consider charging TULLAH with?

_____

Why?

_____

2. McDOWELL had a rare medical condition that contributed to his death. Did this affect your reasoning?
Yes / No
Why / Why not?

_____

3. McDOWELL received negligent treatment when he arrived at the A&E ward. Did this affect your reasoning?

Yes / No

Why / Why not?

EXPLANATION 1.6.1

'But for' Test and Intervening Act

1. You would probably charge TULLAH with murder or manslaughter, but how would you justify this charge based on the fact that TULLAH only intended to cause McDOWELL actual bodily harm?

   The chain of causation is all about cause and effect and is sometimes called the 'but for' test, e.g. 'but for the actions of the defendant this would not have happened'. A connection between the act(s) of the defendant and the final consequence must exist; this must be an unbroken chain of events. It is sometimes better to begin with the final link in the chain and work backwards.

   > McDOWELL is dead—*What was the cause of death?*
   > The cause of death was brain damage—*What caused the brain damage?*
   > A fracture to his skull—*What caused the fracture to his skull?*
   > His head hitting the pavement—*What caused his head to hit the pavement?*
   > He tripped on the kerb—*What caused him to trip on the kerb?*
   > A blow to the face that knocked him backwards—*Who struck the blow?*
   > TULLAH
   > **BUT FOR** *the fact that TULLAH struck McDOWELL, he would still be alive.*
   > *TULLAH is responsible for McDOWELL's death.*

2. The fact that McDOWELL has a rare medical condition meaning that his skull is exceptionally weak does not matter. Defendants must 'take their victims as they find them'. McDOWELL's thin skull may well have been a contributory factor leading to his death, but the reason it made a contribution was because of the chain of events that TULLAH set in motion by striking the blow.

3. Negligent medical treatment *will not normally* be regarded as an intervening act that will break the chain of causation. There are some rare exceptions to this rule, but it is best to consider these exceptions for what they are: 'exceptional'.

   See *Investigators' Manual*, paras 1.2.6 to 1.2.7

1.7 Conclusion

Having completed this section of the Workbook, you should be able to see how *mens rea* and *actus reus* connect to form part of nearly every crime you deal with. As such, the importance of these subjects should not be underestimated and you should remember to pay attention to other areas of the subjects that were not covered in this part of the Workbook, e.g. omissions and the DUTY mnemonic.

1.8 Recall Questions

Try and answer the following questions.

- What is an offence of 'specific intent'?
- Give two examples of offences of 'specific intent'.

- What is the difference between an offence of 'specific' and 'basic' intent?
- What can cause 'intoxication'?
- There is one offence contained in your syllabus that can be committed by 'negligence'. What is it?
- Summarise s. 8 of the Criminal Justice Act 1967.
- How does case law allow us to infer intent?
- What is the most important thing to remember about 'recklessness'?
- What two factors must you show when proving *actus reus*?
- What does the mnemonic DUTY stand for?
- What is the 'chain of causation' all about?
- What is the state of mind required of an accessory?
- Can a company commit a criminal offence?

1.9 Multiple-Choice Questions

Answers to these questions can be found in the 'Answers Section' at the end of the book. All explanations also include a reference back to the *Investigators' Manual 2022*.

1. JONSTON is drinking in a pub with ROBERTSON. JONSTON is drinking vodka and tonic and has only had one drink. JONSTON visits the toilets of the pub and, whilst he is away, ROBERTSON drops some LSD into JONSTON's drink. A few minutes later, JONSTON returns and drinks the vodka and tonic 'spiked' with LSD. The LSD has a terrible effect on JONSTON who loses control of his behaviour in the pub. He approaches WAREHAM and smashes a pint glass into WAREHAM's face causing WAREHAM extremely serious injury. JONSTON is later charged with a s. 18 wounding offence (contrary to s. 18 of the Offences Against the Person Act 1861) against WAREHAM.

Would JONSTON be able to rely on the fact that he was 'intoxicated' in answer to the s. 18 charge?

A No, because the intoxication was brought about by a drug and not by alcohol.

B Yes, but only because the intoxication was not self-induced.

C No, intoxication would not be relevant to a specific intent offence (and the s. 18 wounding is a specific intent offence).

D Yes, but the court will consider the known effects of the drug in deciding whether JONSTON had formed the required *mens rea* for the offence.

Answer _____

2. MERCER (an 11-year-old) and HOWDEN (a 14-year-old with the mental age of a 9-year-old) enter the back yard of a shop. They set fire to some newspapers and throw the papers underneath a plastic wheelie-bin before leaving the yard. MERCER and HOWDEN both believe that the newspapers will extinguish themselves on the concrete floor. However, the burning newspaper sets fire to the wheelie-bin, which spreads fire to the shop and some adjoining buildings, causing damage estimated at £1 million. MERCER and HOWDEN are arrested and state that they did not appreciate the risk that the wheelie-bin, let alone the shop and its adjoining buildings, would be destroyed or damaged by fire.

With regard to the meaning of 'recklessness', which of the following statements is correct?

A MERCER and HOWDEN could be prosecuted for an offence of arson as their state of mind would constitute recklessness.

B As MERCER and HOWDEN have failed to consider a risk that would be obvious to any ordinary person, their actions would be considered reckless.

C MERCER and HOWDEN were unaware that the risk existed or would exist, and would not be reckless in these circumstances.

D As MERCER is under 14 years of age, he will not be considered to be reckless. As HOWDEN is over 14 years old, he should have foreseen the consequences of his actions and will be considered reckless.

Answer _____

3. GRICE and LOVATT play for rival football teams. During a football presentation evening, a fight between the two men begins. In the course of the fight, GRICE stabs LOVATT twice with a knife. LOVATT is seriously injured and falls to the floor. GRICE picks LOVATT up and tries to carry him to a nearby hospital, but trips over several times during the short journey, dropping LOVATT onto the floor and further injuring him on those occasions. When LOVATT arrives at the hospital, a nurse examines him but misses the fact that one of the wounds has pierced a lung and caused a haemorrhage. The nurse gives LOVATT treatment that is negligent and affects his chances of recovery. LOVATT dies from his injuries a short time later. It is later established that the medical treatment LOVATT received was primarily responsible for his death.

Considering the law with regard to causal links and intervening acts, which of the following statements is correct?

A If the medical treatment which the victim is given results in his ultimate death, the treatment itself will not normally be regarded as an intervening act.

B GRICE is not responsible for LOVATT's death because the primary reason for his death was the poor medical treatment received from the nurse.

C Poor quality and/or negligent medical treatment will never break the chain of causation.

D The fact that LOVATT was dropped and injured several times during the journey to the hospital and was given poor medical treatment will break the chain of causation.

Answer _____

4. There is a significant amount of case law regarding what will and will not be seen as an 'intervening act' which breaks the chain of causation.

Which of the following comments is correct with regard to that case law?

A JERROM is a drug dealer who supplies heroin to REED, who later kills himself by taking an overdose of the heroin. JERROM is liable for the death of REED.

B WALTER stabs KERR during a fight. KERR requires a blood transfusion as a consequence but refuses this as he is a Jehovah's Witness. KERR bleeds to death from his injuries as a result. WALTER is not liable for KERR's death.

C FOSTER and STORK are passengers in a car being driven along a motorway by CURTIS. STORK tries to rape FOSTER, who jumps from the car to escape and is killed in the process. STORK is liable for FOSTER's death.

D BERESFORD is a pensioner who has a serious heart condition and is of a very nervous disposition. STATHAM robs BERESFORD of her handbag and, because of the fright caused by the incident, BERESFORD immediately has a heart attack and dies. STATHAM is not liable for BERESFORD's death.

Answer _____

2 | Incomplete Offences

2.1 Introduction

Offences involving encouraging crime, conspiracy and attempts all relate to the preparation undertaken by a defendant prior to the commission of a substantive offence. As the defendant moves closer to the commission of an offence, he/she may commit some or all of these offences. As it is not always desirable to allow an offence to take place, it is important to know at what stage an incomplete offence has been committed. For the purposes of your examination, you must be able to understand and distinguish between these types of offences.

2.2 Aim

The aim of this section is for you to comprehend the offences of conspiracy and attempts and their respective exceptions.

2.3 Objectives

At the end of this section you should be able to:

1. Outline the different stages leading to the commission of an offence.
2. Explain the differences between the offences under ss. 44, 45 and 46 of the Serious Crime Act 2007.
3. State what constitutes a statutory conspiracy (s. 1 of the Criminal Law Act 1977).
4. State what constitutes an attempt (s. 1 of the Criminal Attempts Act 1981).
5. List the exceptions to the offences of conspiracy and attempts.
6. Apply your knowledge to multiple-choice questions.

2.4 Stages Towards the Commission of a Crime

Incomplete offences deal with behaviour PRIOR to the commission of an actual crime. Consider them as a series of steps—each one gets you closer to committing the actual crime in question.

STEP 1
↓
Encouraging or Assisting a Crime
STEP 2
↓
Conspiring to Commit a Crime
STEP 3
↓
Attempting to Commit a Crime
STEP 4
↓
Committing a Crime

2.5 Encouraging or Assisting Crime

Sections 44 to 46 of the Serious Crime Act 2007 provides you with three ways in which this crime can be committed.

Actus Reus	The defendant must do an ACT CAPABLE of encouraging or assisting 'an offence' (ss. 45 and 46) or 'one or more of a number of offences' (s. 46)		
	s. 44	s. 45	s. 46
Mens Rea	Intending to encourage or assist	Believing an offence will be committed AND believing that the act will encourage or assist	Believing one or more offences will be committed AND believing that the act will encourage or assist

- These offences are triable in the same way as the anticipated offence.
- They attract exactly the same sentence as the anticipated offence.
- You can be convicted of more than one offence in relation to the same act.

What is an 'act'?
An act can take many forms—a course of conduct, a failure to discharge a duty and it may also involve making threats.
What does 'capable' mean?
The use of the word 'capable' is important—it means NO END RESULT IS REQUIRED.

The points below are worth noting:
- It does not matter if anyone *was in fact* encouraged or assisted to commit a crime.
- Nor does it matter if any anticipated offence is *ever* committed.
- Approaching an undercover police officer and encouraging the officer to commit a crime would amount to an offence.

Defence
It is a defence to ss. 44 to 46 if, in the circumstances he/she was aware of, or in circumstances he/she reasonably believed existed, it was reasonable to act as he/she did.

A person *cannot* be guilty of an offence under ss. 44 to 46 if the offence encouraged/assisted is a *protective* offence.

So if a 12-year-old girl encouraged a 40-year-old man to have sexual intercourse with her, the 12-year-old *would not* commit the encouragement offence in relation to 'child rape' (under s. 9 of the Sexual Offences Act 2003).

Why? Because the offence under s. 9 of the Sexual Offences Act 2003 was designed to *protect* a child under 13.

2.6 Statutory Conspiracy (s. 1 of the Criminal Law Act 1977)

Section 1 of the Criminal Law Act 1977 provides you with the definition of a 'statutory conspiracy'.

2.6.1 Exercise—Statutory Conspiracy?

Examine the following situations and decide whether they would constitute a statutory conspiracy. Give a short reason for your decision. (The explanations are given after the exceptions to the offence.)

1. HORNER and his wife plan to break into a pub. They recruit DAVIES to act as the get-away driver.
Statutory conspiracy?
Yes / No

2. GRISDALE agrees with SPENCER that they will damage FAULKNER's car, because FAULKNER has been sleeping with GRISDALE's wife. Before they damage the car, it is stolen, making the commission of the offence impossible.
Statutory conspiracy?
Yes / No

3. MAJOR asks his friend MOSS (who works in a breaker's yard) to crush his car so that he can claim for the car on the insurance; MOSS refuses.
Statutory conspiracy?
Yes / No

EXPLANATION 2.6.1

Statutory Conspiracy?

The definition of statutory conspiracy provides two points for you to consider:

1. Was there an agreement between at least *two* people and, if so,

2. If the agreement was carried out, would it lead to the commission of an offence by one or more of the parties?

If the answer is 'Yes' to both questions, then you have a statutory conspiracy. The fact that the commission of the offence is impossible is immaterial.

2.6.2 Exercise—Exceptions to Statutory Conspiracy

There are three instances where a defendant will not commit statutory conspiracy. There will be no statutory conspiracy where the only other party is:

1. _____

2. _____

3. _____

EXPLANATION 2.6.2

Exceptions to Statutory Conspiracy

There is no statutory conspiracy where the only other party is:

      H   His/her spouse (or civil partner)

      A   A person under 10 years of age

      T   The intended victim

Please note that:

- a husband and wife or civil partners can conspire if there is a third party involved in the conspiracy;

- if there are only two parties and one of them is an undercover police officer (who does not intend to go through with the agreement), the offence would not be committed as you would not have a 'meeting of minds';

- BUT—if there were three or more 'conspirators' and one of those was an undercover police officer, you would have a conspiracy—remove the mind of the undercover police officer and you still have a 'meeting of minds'.

Now, considering the questions in para. 2.6.1 we can offer a full explanation:

1. This is a statutory conspiracy. Although two parties to the conspiracy are husband and wife, a third party (DAVIES) is involved.

2. This is a statutory conspiracy. The fact that the car has been stolen, making the commission of the offence impossible, does not matter.

3. This is not a statutory conspiracy as there is no agreement between two or more parties.

See *Investigators' Manual*, para. 1.3.3.1

2.7   Attempts (s. 1 of the Criminal Attempts Act 1981)

2.7.1   Exercise—Considering 'Attempts'

When you consider 'attempts', what comes to mind?

EXPLANATION 2.7.1

Considering 'Attempts'

You may have answered the question using the words 'more than merely preparatory'. You may also have mentioned the fact that the *mens rea* required is an intent to commit an offence, that you can attempt the impossible and some of the exceptions to the offence.

2.7.2   Exercise—'More than merely preparatory'

LEE sacks PARK from his job as a security guard at a supermarket. To get revenge against LEE, PARK intends to burn down LEE's house. As the following sequence of events unfolds, decide if an attempt has been made by PARK and, if so, at what stage the attempt is made.

1. PARK makes some enquiries to find out where LEE lives.
2. PARK visits LEE's house to check if there are any security devices present.
3. PARK buys some rubber gloves to avoid leaving any fingerprints.
4. PARK puts a petrol bomb in his car.
5. PARK buys a lighter.
6. PARK drives to LEE's house.
7. PARK puts on the rubber gloves.
8. PARK picks up the lighter and petrol bomb and walks towards LEE's house.
9. PARK stands outside LEE's house with the petrol bomb in his hand.
10. PARK lights the petrol bomb and throws it at LEE's house. It smashes against the wall of the house but fails to ignite.

EXPLANATION 2.7.2

'More than merely preparatory'

Ask yourself two questions:

1. At any point, has the defendant embarked on the crime proper? If the answer is 'Yes' then,

2. At what point did the defendant go beyond mere preparation?

In the previous example, points 1 to 9 would be considered mere preparation. At point 10, PARK would be liable for an attempt. Whether the defendant has gone beyond mere preparation will be a question of fact for the jury/magistrate(s).

2.7.3   Attempting the Impossible

A defendant would be guilty of an attempt even if the facts were such that the commission of the offence is impossible. For example, a defendant decides to steal a wallet from a jacket left in a changing room. However, the fact is that there is no wallet in the jacket pocket. When the defendant puts his hand into the empty jacket pocket, he would still be guilty of attempted theft.

As ever, there are certain offences that cannot be attempted:

1. conspiracy;
2. aiding, abetting, counselling or procuring an offence; and
3. offences of assisting an offender and accepting or agreeing to accept consideration for not disclosing information.

You might remember these exceptions by remembering that you cannot attempt anything in SPACE:

You cannot attempt:

S	Summary only offences
P	Procure/Counsel/Aid/Abet an offence
A	Assist offender/Conceal relevant offence (Criminal Law Act 1967)
C	Conspiracy
E	Encourage/Assist suicide (Suicide Act 1961)

The general rule is that you *cannot* attempt to commit a summary only offence. The **EXCEPTION** to that rule is that you can attempt to commit 'Simple Damage' and Low-Value Shoplifting (summary only offences).

See *Investigators' Manual*, paras 1.3.4 to 1.3.5

2.8 Conclusion

Now that you have completed this section of the Workbook, you should be able to identify when an incomplete offence has been committed. You should see that although these offences are relatively straightforward, the exceptions to the rule could cause some difficulty.

2.9 Recall Questions

Try and answer the following questions.

- What are the differences between the offences under ss. 44 to 46 of the Serious Crime Act 2007?
- What is the common defence to offences under ss. 44 to 46 of the Serious Crime Act 2007?
- What are the two points you need to consider for an offence of statutory conspiracy?
- Who can't you conspire with? (Can you remember the mnemonic?)
- What are the two questions you need to ask yourself when considering an offence involving an attempt?
- Can you attempt to conspire?
- What offences cannot be attempted (SPACE)?
- Can you attempt the impossible?

2.10 Multiple-Choice Questions

Answers to these questions can be found in the 'Answers Section' at the end of the book. All explanations also include a reference back to the *Investigators' Manual 2022*.

1. JOHN BURCOTT plans to rob a bank. He asks his wife, ALISON BURCOTT, if she will assist him in the robbery and she agrees. He also asks SALE (who works as a security guard at the bank) to assist him and SALE agrees. ALISON BURCOTT and SALE do not know that each of them will play a part in the robbery.

  Would this constitute an offence of statutory conspiracy (contrary to s. 1 of the Criminal Law Act 1977)?

  A No, because BURCOTT's wife and SALE do not know of each other's existence.

  B Yes, but if the agreement is later abandoned the offence will not be committed.

  C No, because one of the conspirators is JOHN BURCOTT's wife.

  D Yes, but only between JOHN BURCOTT and SALE.

Answer _____

2. BLACKMAN decides he is going to break into a garden centre and steal gardening equipment. He goes out and buys a crowbar to force the lock on the store door. Late at night,

he goes out of his house wearing a pair of gloves and a balaclava. He climbs over the fence surrounding the garden centre and walks towards the store doors. He takes out the crowbar and tries to break the door lock but is disturbed by a security guard. BLACKMAN panics and runs home.

At what point, if at all, does BLACKMAN commit the offence of attempted burglary (contrary to s. 1 of the Criminal Attempts Act 1981)?

A When he leaves his house with the crowbar and wearing the gloves and balaclava.

B When he climbs the fence and walks towards the store doors.

C When he takes out the crowbar and tries to break the door lock.

D He does not commit an attempt in these circumstances.

Answer _____

3. MYCROFT goes to some garages at the rear of his house with an aerosol can containing orange spray paint. He intends to spray graffiti on several garage doors (belonging to his neighbours), causing a few pounds worth of damage. However, when MYCROFT tries to use the aerosol paint on a garage door, it does not work as the nozzle is blocked and therefore no damage is caused.

Which of the following statements is correct with regard to MYCROFT's activities?

A He commits the offence of attempted criminal damage.

B He cannot commit attempted criminal damage, as 'simple' criminal damage is a summary only offence and you cannot attempt a summary only offence.

C You cannot attempt the impossible; as the aerosol spray will not work, MYCROFT commits no offence.

D MYCROFT has not committed attempted criminal damage as he has not 'embarked on the crime proper'.

Answer _____

3 | General Defences

3.1 Introduction

The 'General Defences' chapter contains a number of defences that can be used in answer to a wide variety of charges. Apart from some limitations in relation to duress and duress of circumstances, a key point to note is that these defences can be used in answer to any charge.

Rather than provide you with a series of exercises to assist your knowledge and understanding, this chapter sets out to explain the law contained in your *Blackstone's Investigators' Manual* with the assistance of examples and flowcharts.

3.2 Aim

The aim of this section is for you to be able to explain the issues surrounding intoxication, inadvertence and mistake, duress, duress of circumstances and self-defence.

3.3 Objectives

At the end of this section you should be able to:

1. Summarise the issues relevant to defences of inadvertence and mistake.
2. Distinguish between the defences of duress and duress of circumstances.
3. Outline the central elements relating to the defence of self-defence.
4. Apply your knowledge to multiple-choice questions.

3.4 Inadvertence or Mistake

When either of these defences are used, the defendant is saying that when they did something it was done in error—*they* made a mistake in their mind that negates *mens rea*.

The mistake will be considered subjectively—it does not have to be a 'reasonable' mistake just an honest and genuine one.

EXAMPLE

KIFFIN and HALE are in a newsagents. KIFFIN picks up several bars of chocolate which HALE states he will pay for. KIFFIN walks out of the newsagents thinking HALE has paid for the chocolate—in fact, HALE has become distracted and is reading a magazine in the newsagents.

If KIFFIN were accused of theft he could say that he made a mistake in his mind—he honestly and genuinely thought the goods had been paid for and therefore was not acting dishonestly—the mistake in his mind negates the *mens rea* for theft.

Mistakes Must Be About FACTS

The mistake must be a mistake about a *fact* not a mistake about the *law*. So if a police officer is arresting me for a public order offence and I do not believe the officer has a power of arrest and I assault the officer, this *will not* provide me with a defence—I have made a mistake about LAW (the power of arrest). At this stage, it would be a good idea for you to read about the offence of assaulting a police officer (in the chapter dealing with Non-fatal Offences Against the Person, see *Blackstone's Investigators' Manual*, para. 2.7.14) and link this defence with that offence.

See *Investigators' Manual*, para. 1.4.2

3.5 Duress

If the only reason a person commits a crime is because they (or their 'loved ones') were threatened with death or serious injury, then they may have a defence of duress. Follow the flowchart below to see how this defence works.

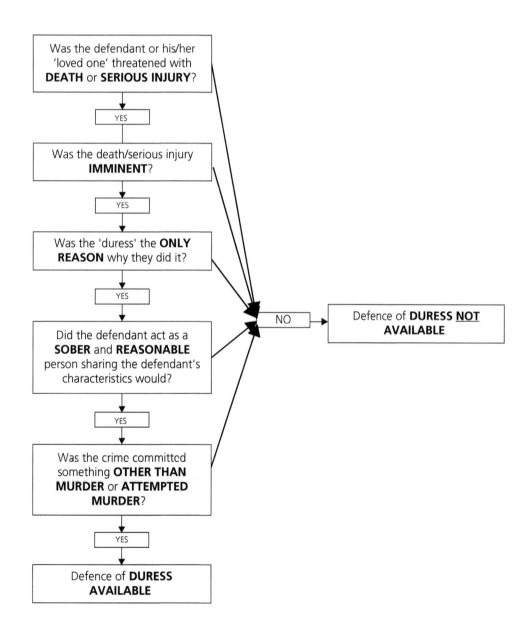

Points to Note

- Death or serious injury *does not appear* to include psychological injury.
- If the defendant can escape from the threat, it *is not* 'imminent'.

Duress (Gangs and Terrorist Organisations)

If you join a violent gang/terrorist organisation, you *did not do it* because they have a particularly efficient flower-arranging section did you? You *knew* what you were getting involved in so you *cannot claim duress* to any crimes you may go on to commit under threat of death or serious injury from another gang member/member of the terrorist organisation or rival of that gang/organisation.

However, if the purpose of the gang/organisation *is not* predominantly violent or dangerous (e.g. a gang of shoplifters), the defence of duress may be available in relation to offences committed while under threat of death or serious physical injury from other gang members.

See *Investigators' Manual*, para. 1.4.3

3.6 Duress of Circumstances

This is sometimes referred to as 'necessity' and the defence operates in *almost exactly the same way* as duress. The major difference being that in duress of circumstances, the person carries out a behaviour because of a *situation* that presents a risk of death or serious injury rather than a direct threat/demand from another person. If we put duress and duress of circumstances side by side in flowchart form, we can see the connections between them and the subtle differences.

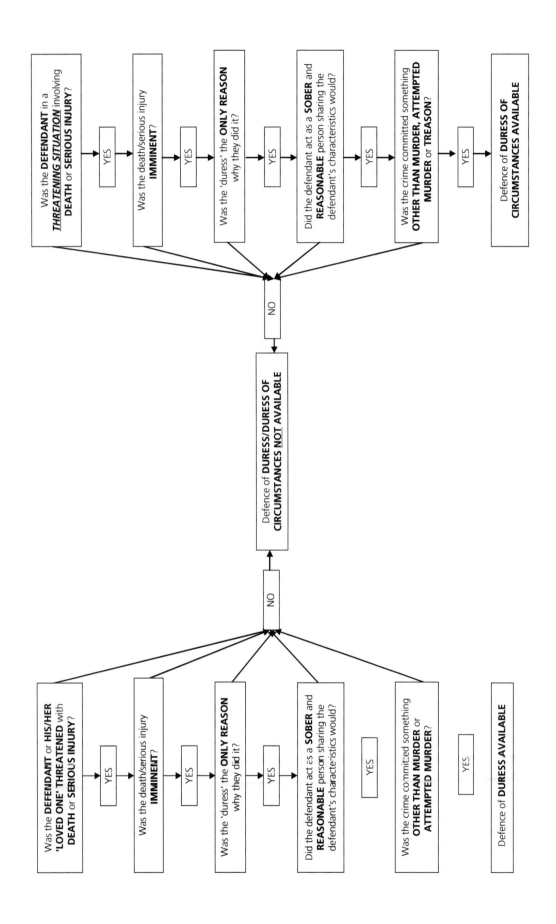

Was the **DEFENDANT** in a ***THREATENING SITUATION*** involving **DEATH** or **SERIOUS INJURY?** → YES → Was the death/serious injury **IMMINENT?** → YES → Was the 'duress' the **ONLY REASON** why they did it? → YES → Did the defendant act as a **SOBER** and **REASONABLE** person sharing the defendant's characteristics would? → YES → Was the crime committed something **OTHER THAN MURDER, ATTEMPTED MURDER** or **TREASON?** → YES → Defence of **DURESS OF CIRCUMSTANCES AVAILABLE**

NO → Defence of **DURESS/DURESS OF CIRCUMSTANCES NOT AVAILABLE**

NO

Was the **DEFENDANT** or **HIS/HER 'LOVED ONE' THREATENED** with **DEATH** or **SERIOUS INJURY?** → YES → Was the death/serious injury **IMMINENT?** → YES → Was the 'duress' the **ONLY REASON** why they did it? → YES → Did the defendant act as a **SOBER** and **REASONABLE** person sharing the defendant's characteristics would? → YES → Was the crime committed something **OTHER THAN MURDER** or **ATTEMPTED MURDER?** → YES → Defence of **DURESS AVAILABLE**

EXAMPLE

CAIN is walking past a block of flats when a siren sounds warning that the flats are about to be demolished by explosion. CAIN is desperate to escape death or serious injury so runs over to a car, smashes the car window and drives off in the car.

See *Investigators' Manual*, para. 1.4.4

3.7 Defence of Self, Others and Property

The law can be formulated very simply along the following lines (use the mnemonic SCALD):

A person may use reasonable force in the circumstances as he/she believed them to be for the purposes of:

S Self-defence/defence of another; or
C Crime prevention; or
A Another's defence; or
L Lawful arrest; or
D Defence of property.

Reasonable Force in Circumstances as He Believes Them To Be?

In other words, you did what you did because you thought it was the right response.

EXAMPLE

TAO is dressed as a character from a horror film and holding a chainsaw in his hands. He jumps out in front of MARTIN (a friend of TAO's) screaming that he is going to kill MARTIN (this is only done to frighten MARTIN for a joke). MARTIN believes he is going to be seriously injured by TAO and, acting in self-defence, he responds by punching TAO in the face and giving TAO a 'black eye'. In these circumstances, MARTIN could claim his actions were carried out in self-defence.

You might point out that MARTIN is mistaken in his belief—TAO was not going to hurt him and that this is just a friendly joke but the defence is available as MARTIN reacted to the circumstances as *he believed* them to be. The reasonableness of MARTIN's belief is relevant in deciding whether or not MARTIN held that belief (so the more unreasonable the belief, the less the court is likely to believe the person held it). If a court accepted MARTIN held that belief, the fact that TAO was not going to hurt MARTIN (a mistake made by MARTIN) would not affect MARTIN's ability to use the defence.

Does Drunkenness Impact on the Defence?

It does.

EXAMPLE

EAGAN is drunk and whilst walking along a street sees JOYSON walking towards him. EAGAN forms the mistaken opinion that JOYSON is going to attack him and punches JOYSON in the face.

The defence of 'self-defence' would not be available. You could not use this defence when the mistaken belief is due to voluntary intoxication.

Not Reasonable Force if Disproportionate

Force used *will not* be reasonable if it is disproportionate. When deciding whether the force used was reasonable in the circumstances, the court will take the following into account:

- that a person acting for the **SCALD** purpose may not be able to weigh to a nicety the exact measure of any necessary action; and
- that evidence of a person's having only done what the person honestly and instinctively thought was necessary for a legitimate purpose constitutes strong evidence that only reasonable action was taken by that person for that purpose.

So, for example, when MARTIN reacted to TAO's joke, the court may consider that his response was reasonable because he did not have time to sit down and think about whether this was a 'joke' or not and what would be a proportionate response to the situation. It happened in a split second and MARTIN honestly believed he was going to be attacked and responded instinctively.

'Householder' Cases

Disproportionate force is allowed when you are acting in self-defence (you or others) against trespassers in your HOME. The use of grossly disproportionate force *is not* allowed.

Point to Note

- The 'householder' approach extends to people who live and work in the same premises and armed forces personnel who may live and work in buildings such as barracks for periods of time.

Human Rights—Taking Life

Article 2 of the European Convention on Human Rights (Right to Life) states that force used should be no more than absolutely necessary.

Lethal force might be permissible when carrying out a **DARE**:

D   Defending ANY person from unlawful violence;

A   Arresting someone lawfully;

R   Riot/insurrection (action lawfully taken for the purpose of putting an end to the riot/insurrection);

E   Escape (preventing the escape of a person lawfully detained).

Point to Note

The taking of life in order to prevent crime is not mentioned in Article 2.

Use of Force to Protect Property

There is nothing wrong with using reasonable force in order to protect property. However, bearing in mind the earlier comments regarding disproportionate/grossly disproportionate force AND Article 2 of the European Convention on Human Rights, it might be difficult (to say the least) to justify taking the life of a human being in order to protect property (no matter how valuable that property is).

See *Investigators' Manual*, paras 1.4.5 to 1.4.5.5

3.8   Conclusion

Now that you have completed this section of the Workbook, you should be able to identify when certain general defences will or will not be available. Your examiners have been particularly keen on issues in relation to duress and duress of circumstances so these might be a priority area for you to study and understand.

3.9   Recall Questions

Try and answer the following questions.

- Mistakes can be made but only in relation to what?
- To what offences is the defence of 'duress' unavailable?
- What is the major difference between the defences of 'duress' and 'duress of circumstances'?
- What does the mnemonic SCALD stand for?
- In what circumstances might 'disproportionate' force being used be acceptable?

3.10   Multiple-Choice Questions

Answers to these questions can be found in the 'Answers Section' at the end of the book. All explanations also include a reference back to the *Investigators' Manual 2022*.

1. PC SULLIVAN visits a house owned by KHAN to arrest KHAN for an offence of theft which occurred two weeks ago in a shopping centre near KHAN's house. KHAN answers the door to the officer who asks KHAN's name. When KHAN responds and PC SULLIVAN places his hand on KHAN's shoulder and arrests him on suspicion of theft and also tells KHAN where and when the offence took place. KHAN is outraged as he knows that he is innocent as he only returned from a three-month holiday in India two days ago. A struggle develops during which KHAN assaults PC SULLIVAN. KHAN is never charged with the theft but he is charged with an offence of assault with intent to resist arrest (contrary to s. 38 of the Offences Against the Person Act 1861). He pleads 'not guilty' and the case goes to trial. KHAN states that PC SULLIVAN had no right to arrest him as he was innocent of the theft and the arrest was therefore unlawful.

Considering the law in relation to the defence of mistake, which of the following comments is correct?

A There are no circumstances where a genuine or honest mistake could provide a defence to an offence of assault with intent to resist arrest.

B KHAN had made a mistake of law (believing the officer had no power of arrest in the circumstances) which could form the basis for a defence of mistake to the charge of assault with intent to resist arrest.

C KHAN had formed the genuine but mistaken opinion that the arrest was unlawful which means he could use the defence of mistake in answer to the charge of assault with intent to resist arrest.

D Belief in one's own innocence, however genuine or honestly held, cannot afford a defence to a charge of assault with intent to resist arrest.

Answer _____

2. HIMLEY has been charged with an offence of attempted murder. The circumstances are that she pushed CARTER into the path of a bus driven by MANNION. MANNION just managed to brake and swerve but still struck CARTER causing him life-threatening injuries. HIMLEY states that the only reason she committed the offence was because her boyfriend, who was standing next to her when she committed the offence, there and then threatened to cause her serious physical injury if she did not do as he told her to and he demanded that she push CARTER into the path of the bus.

Would HIMLEY be able to raise the defence of 'duress' in these circumstances?

A Yes, as she was there and then threatened with serious physical injury.

B No, because the offence she is charged with is attempted murder.

C Yes, as the only restriction on this defence is that it cannot be used in answer to a charge of murder.

D No, as duress is not available to an offence where the victim suffers serious physical injury.

Answer _____

4   Entry, Search and Seizure

4.1   Introduction

In the course of an investigation you may take part in a search of premises utilising powers under the Police and Criminal Evidence Act (PACE) 1984 (although you may not have used all of the powers that will be discussed in this section). A good knowledge and understanding of these powers is essential as a great deal of crucial evidence could be lost if a search is carried out unlawfully. Knowing what you can and cannot do in respect of PACE searches will prevent this undesirable occurrence.

4.2   Aim

The aim of this section is to assist you to understand the powers of entry, search and seizure that derive from PACE 1984.

4.3   Objectives

At the end of this section you should be able to:

1. Distinguish between the powers under ss. 17, 18, 19 and 32 of PACE 1984.
2. Identify what an indictable offence is.
3. State your powers under s. 18 of PACE 1984.
4. Explain your powers under s. 32 of PACE 1984.
5. Outline your powers under s. 17 of PACE 1984.
6. State your powers under s. 19 of PACE 1984.
7. Demonstrate your knowledge by completing the exercises in this section.
8. Apply your knowledge to multiple-choice questions.

4.4   Distinguish Between the Powers Under ss. 17, 18, 19 and 32 of PACE 1984

Each of these four sections at your disposal under PACE 1984 provides you with different powers of entry, search and/or seizure. They also require a certain state of mind to exist on the part of the officer in order for the power to be executed. You must be aware of precisely *what* each section allows along with what you *need to be thinking* to enable the power.

4.4.1 Exercise—Powers Under ss. 17, 18, 19 and 32 of PACE 1984

What does each power allow you to do? Fill the boxes with a 'Yes' or 'No' where you believe appropriate.

Section	Power to Enter Premises?	Power to Search Premises for Evidence?	Power to Seize Evidence?	Power to Search Person?	Power to Seize Evidence from Person Searched?
17					
18					
19					
32					

EXPLANATION 4.4.1

Powers Under ss. 17, 18, 19 and 32 of PACE 1984

Your grid should look something like this:

Section	Power to Enter Premises?	Power to Search Premises for Evidence?	Power to Seize Evidence?	Power to Search Person?	Power to Seize Evidence from Person Searched?
17	YES	NO	NO	NO	NO
18	YES	YES	YES	NO	NO
19	NO	NO	YES	NO	NO
32	YES	YES	NO	YES	YES

In essence:

- Section 17 is a power of entry (for arrest—although you can search the premises to find the person you want to arrest).
- Section 18 is a power of entry, search and seizure.
- Section 19 is a power of seizure.
- Section 32 is a power of entry, search and seizure (but you can only seize items found while searching a person!).

4.4.2 Exercise—Suspect or Believe?

We will deal with the specific state of mind required for each power later but for now just consider whether the power requires an officer to *suspect* or *believe*.

Tick or cross the box you believe is appropriate for the particular power.

Section	Officer must suspect	Officer must believe
17		
18		
19		
32		

EXPLANATION 4.4.2

Suspect or Believe?

Your completed grid should look like the one below:

Section	Officer must suspect	Officer must believe
17		×
18	×	
19		×
32		×

Section 17 has been placed in the 'Officer must believe' column as the powers of entry and search conferred by s. 17 are exercisable if the constable has 'reasonable grounds for believing'. It should be noted that the single exception to this is when exercising the power under s. 17(1)(e)—entry and search to save life and limb does not require a state of mind.

REMEMBER that the only power that operates on an officer's 'suspicion' is s. 18.

4.5   Indictable Offence

Sections 18 and 32 of PACE 1984 require an arrest to trigger the powers—the arrest must be for an indictable offence.

4.5.1   Exercise—What is an Indictable Offence?

1. What is an indictable offence?

_____

_____

2. Based on your answer to Question 1 of this exercise, would the following offences potentially trigger powers of search and seizure under ss. 18 and 32 of PACE?

 i. An offence of s. 20 wounding?

Yes / No

 ii. An offence of burglary?

Yes / No

 iii. An offence of robbery?

Yes / No

EXPLANATION 4.5.1

What is an Indictable Offence?

1. The Interpretation Act of 1978, Sch. 1 defines what an 'indictable offence' is:

    An 'indictable offence' means an offence which, if committed by an adult, is triable on indictment, whether it is exclusively so triable (e.g. murder) or triable either way.

    In other words, an 'indictable offence' also includes offences that are 'triable either way' so unless the offence you have just arrested the person for is 'summary only', you can use your powers under ss. 18 and 32.

2. As a result of the above information, we can say that a s. 20 wounding (triable either way), burglary (triable either way) and robbery (triable on indictment only) are all offences that could trigger your powers under ss. 18 and 32 of PACE.

4.6   Section 18 of PACE 1984

4.6.1   Exercise—What Do You Know About s. 18 of PACE?

PC SIDAWAY arrests HARTELL at the scene of a rape in a park and escorts him to a designated police station. On arrest, HARTELL is wearing a distinctive green jacket. Checks on HARTELL reveal that the rape is highly likely to be the culmination of a series of sexual attacks on women in the park by an offender wearing a similar jacket. However, on the previous occasions the offender has also worn a clown mask and has sexually assaulted his victims after threatening them with a red handled flick-knife. PC SIDAWAY contacts the CID and DC KIRK takes charge of the case. DC KIRK establishes that HARTELL not only lives in a house near to the park but also rents an allotment backing on to the park. The allotment has a shed on it. DC KIRK is thinking about his powers under s. 18 of PACE.

1. Before DC KIRK can use his s. 18 PACE power, what must he have reasonable grounds to suspect?

---

2. Why could a search take place at HARTELL's home address?

---

3. Why could a search take place at the allotment shed rented by HARTELL?

---

4. Whose authority is required for this search to take place and how will it be recorded?

---

5. Could PC SIDAWAY have carried out a s. 18 search prior to taking HARTELL to the designated police station?

Yes / No

If 'Yes' then why and who would you inform? If 'No' then why not?

EXPLANATION 4.6.1

What Do You Know About s. 18 of PACE?

1. DC KIRK must have reasonable grounds for suspecting that there is evidence on the premises (other than items subject to legal privilege) that relates either to that offence (the rape) or to some other indictable offence which is connected with or similar to that offence (the sexual assaults are certainly connected to the rape but even if they were not, you could convincingly argue that they are similar to it).

2. A s. 18 search can take place at premises *occupied* by the arrested person.

3. A s. 18 search can take place at premises *controlled* by the arrested person.

4. The authority of an inspector is required. In these circumstances, the authority would be recorded in HARTELL's custody record.

5. Yes. PC SIDAWAY could have searched either of the premises (if he knew of them) and without the authority of an inspector. This can only take place if HARTELL's presence would be necessary at a place (other than a police station) for the effective investigation of the offence. For example, if PC SIDAWAY knew HARTELL's address and considered that evidence might be lost if a search was not carried out immediately, he could have taken HARTELL to his home and searched it. When the search was complete, PC SIDAWAY should inform an officer of the rank of inspector or above that he has completed it.

See *Investigators' Manual*, para. 1.6.5.3

4.7 Section 32 of PACE 1984

4.7.1 Exercise—What Do You Know About s. 32 of PACE?

TI GREEN is taking a witness statement in CRONIN's house. While CRONIN is making a cup of tea, TI GREEN looks out of the front window of the house and sees HALLARD walk out of the front door of a house exactly opposite CRONIN's. HALLARD walks along the footpath to the front gate and stops at the front gate. Moments later, LESTER approaches HALLARD and a drug deal takes place after which LESTER walks away. TI GREEN has witnessed the whole episode and leaves CRONIN's house and approaches HALLARD. As he approaches HALLARD, he witnesses HALLARD drop several wraps of white powder onto the ground. TI GREEN reaches HALLARD, picks up the wraps and arrests HALLARD on suspicion of supplying a controlled drug (triable either way offence).

Think about this situation in respect of s. 32 of PACE.

1. There are three reasons why TI GREEN could search HALLARD. What are they?
The officer has reasonable grounds for believing that:

  i. _____

_____

  ii. _____

_____

  iii. _____

_____

2. What three items of clothing could TI GREEN require HALLARD to remove in public?

i. _____

ii. _____

iii. _____

3. TI GREEN could search HALLARD's mouth under s. 32 of PACE.
True / False

EXPLANATION 4.7.1

What Do You Know About s. 32 of PACE?

1. The three reasons are:

   i. the arrested person may present a danger to him/herself or others; or

   ii. the arrested person has something concealed on his/her person which might be used to assist him/her to escape lawful custody; or

   iii. the arrested person has something concealed on his/her person which might be evidence relating to an offence.

2. The clothing TI GREEN could require HALLARD to remove consists of:

   i. outer coat;

   ii. jacket;

   iii. gloves.

3. True.

- Note that if a search of HALLARD's person is carried out for one of the above three reasons, then there is a power of seizure for anything that TI GREEN finds that falls into any of those categories.

4.7.2 Exercise—Extent of s. 32 Power

TI GREEN searches HALLARD but does not find any drugs on his person. He asks HALLARD where he lives and HALLARD replies that he lives in a flat several miles away from the scene of the arrest. TI GREEN thinks that there might be drugs in the house that HALLARD walked out of.

Could TI GREEN use s. 32 of PACE 1984 to search the house that he saw HALLARD come out of moments before the drug deal and subsequent arrest?
Yes / No
Why / Why not?

EXPLANATION 4.7.2

Extent of s. 32 Power

Yes. TI GREEN can enter and search any premises in which the person was when arrested or immediately before being arrested for an indictable offence (provided he has reasonable grounds to believe that there is evidence on the premises in respect of that offence, i.e. the supply of a controlled drug and NOTHING ELSE!).

> • Bizarrely, s. 32 DOES NOT provide a power of seizure of any item that he finds during the course of the search of the house—even if it is evidence of the offence for which he was arrested (see s. 19 of PACE for a power).
>
> See *Investigators' Manual*, para. 1.6.5.2

4.8 Section 17 of PACE 1984

In essence, s. 17 of PACE is a power of ENTRY, by force if necessary, for the purposes of making an arrest. That entry may well be to arrest for an indictable offence but there is a long list of other offences for which the power exists, e.g. to arrest a person for an offence under s. 4 of the Road Traffic Act 1988 (unfit to drive through drink/drugs) or to save life and limb.

Please note the following points regarding s. 17:

- Apart from when entry is to save life or limb, the officer MUST have reasonable grounds for believing that the person he/she is seeking is on the premises.
- When entry is to recapture a person unlawfully at large, the officer MUST be PURSUING that person.
- The power of entry is open to ANY officer (no uniform required) *apart from two offences*:
    i. offences under the Criminal Law Act 1977 (entering and remaining on property); and
    ii. an offence under the Criminal Justice and Public Order Act 1994 (failing to comply with an interim possession order).

Neither of these offences are on your syllabus so the rule of thumb should be that a UNIFORM IS NOT REQUIRED!

See *Investigators' Manual*, para. 1.6.5.1

4.9 Section 19 of PACE 1984

4.9.1 Exercise—What Do You Know About s. 19 of PACE?

Consider the situation that TI GREEN might find himself in if, once he gets into the house that HALLARD was seen walking out of, he searches and finds a large quantity of cocaine.

Can he seize this cocaine?
Yes / No
Under what power?

EXPLANATION 4.9.1

What Do You Know About s. 19 of PACE?

Yes, TI GREEN can seize the cocaine BUT NOT under s. 32 of PACE. He can seize it under the power provided by s. 19 of PACE.

You must now consider your powers under s. 19 of PACE.

4.9.2 Exercise—Extent of s. 19 Power

1. When can a constable exercise his/her powers under s. 19 of PACE?

_____

2. The constable may seize anything which is on the premises if he has reasonable grounds for believing that:

i. _____

or

ii. _____

3. The items may only be seized if the constable believes it is necessary to prevent the evidence from being:

i. _____

ii. _____

iii. _____

iv. _____

4. What would happen if the constable wanted to seize information stored on a computer, e.g. business accounts?

_____

_____

5. This power can be used if the constable is a trespasser.
True / False
6. Could a vehicle be seized under s. 19 of PACE?
Yes / No

EXPLANATION 4.9.2
Extent of s. 19 Power

1. Powers under s. 19 of PACE are exercisable when a constable is *lawfully* on the premises.

2. A constable may seize anything he/she has reasonable grounds for believing:

    i. has been obtained in consequence of the commission of an offence; or

    ii. is evidence in relation to an offence which he/she is investigating or any other offence.

3. The officer must believe it is necessary to prevent the item being:

    i. concealed;

    ii. altered;

    iii. lost; or

    iv. destroyed.

4. The officer can require the information to be produced in a form in which it can be taken away (e.g. a memory stick) and in which it is visible and legible (e.g. a print-out).

5. False—the constable must be on premises 'lawfully'. The moment he/she becomes a trespasser, the power is removed.

6. A vehicle can be seized, as can a tent, or indeed anything which is classed as 'premises'.

See *Investigators' Manual*, para. 1.6.8.1

4.10 Conclusion

You should now possess a good understanding of what you can and cannot do in respect of your powers to enter premises, search them and individuals and seize evidence under PACE 1984. There are other areas in respect of searches that have not been covered in this section of the Workbook and you are strongly advised to read them in the Manual.

4.11 Recall Questions

Try and answer the following questions.

- Which is the only power of search requiring an officer to 'suspect'?
- Who authorises a s. 18 PACE search?
- Could you search a garage under s. 18 of PACE if you suspected that a person controlled it?
- What does a s. 32 PACE search allow you to do?
- What can you seize in a s. 32 PACE search?
- If you are searching a bedsit using s. 32 of PACE, what other rooms/areas might you be able to search?
- Do you have to be in uniform to enter premises under s. 17 of PACE?
- Why might you seize an item under your s. 19 PACE power?
- What is an indictable offence?
- What is the difference between s. 17 of PACE and ss. 18, 32 and 19 of PACE?

4.12 Multiple-Choice Questions

Answers to these questions can be found in the 'Answers Section' at the end of the book. All explanations also include a reference back to the *Investigators' Manual 2022*.

1. WADDILOVE has been arrested for an offence of theft from his employer and is in custody at a designated police station. The property stolen consisted of several dozen Dyson vacuum cleaners (worth over £10,000) which were all recovered from a van WADDILOVE was driving when he was arrested. The officer in the case, PC LYNN, has reasonable grounds for suspecting that WADDILOVE may have electrical goods in his house that have come from other thefts from WADDILOVE's employer and wishes to search WADDILOVE's house for those goods.

Can PC LYNN use his powers under s. 18 of PACE 1984 to search WADDILOVE's house?

A No, PC LYNN cannot use his power under s. 18 of PACE as the property he is seeking does not relate to the offence for which WADDILOVE was arrested.

B Yes, PC LYNN can use his power under s. 18 of PACE if an officer of the rank of inspector or above authorises it.

C No, PC LYNN cannot use his power under s. 18 of PACE as the offence of theft is not an indictable offence.

D Yes, PC LYNN can use his power under s. 18 of PACE if he obtains authorisation from the custody officer.

Answer _____

2. DC AHMED wants to arrest LLOYD for an offence of burglary. He visits LLOYD's home address which is a bedsit inside a larger house. As DC AHMED approaches the front door of LLOYD's bedsit, it opens and LLOYD steps outside into the hallway holding some of the property stolen in the burglary in his hands. DC AHMED immediately arrests LLOYD for the burglary. DC AHMED now wishes to search LLOYD for anything that might be evidence of the offence as he has reasonable grounds to believe LLOYD has such evidence on his person. He is also considering searching LLOYD's bedsit and a communal lounge in the house as he has reasonable grounds to suspect that there is evidence relating to the burglary on those premises.

Considering s. 32 of PACE 1984 only, which of the following comments is correct?

A DC AHMED can only search LLOYD.

B DC AHMED can only search LLOYD and the bedsit he has just come out from.

C DC AHMED can search LLOYD, the bedsit he has just come out from and the communal lounge.

D DC AHMED cannot carry out any searches under s. 32 of PACE in these circumstances.

Answer _____

3. TI JACKSON (who is dressed in plain clothes) visits a house owned by LILLY to arrest her for an offence of robbery. TI JACKSON has visited LILLY's house before and knows that she lives alone. The officer rings the doorbell and steps back from the front door. As he does so, he sees a curtain move in an upstairs bedroom window causing him to believe that LILLY is inside the house. Several minutes later and after ringing the bell three more times and attempting to communicate with anyone inside the house, there is no answer at the door.

Taking into account TI JACKSON's powers under s. 17 of PACE 1984 only, which of the comments below is correct?

A TI JACKSON cannot force entry into the house to arrest LILLY as he is not in uniform.

B TI JACKSON can force entry into the house to search for and arrest LILLY.

C TI JACKSON cannot force entry into the house unless he has communicated with the occupier who has then refused him entry.

D Section 17 allows TI JACKSON to force entry into the house to search for and arrest LILLY and also to search for evidence relating to the robbery.

Answer _____

4. DC DYER is making house to house enquiries in relation to a murder where the victim was stabbed with a screwdriver. He visits NICKLIN who went to the aid of the victim and was covered in the victim's blood as a result. NICKLIN invites DC DYER into his house and into the lounge where the two talk about the offence. Several minutes later, NICKLIN says to DC DYER, *'That is enough for now, I want you to leave my house. You are no longer welcome.'*

On his way out of the lounge, DC DYER sees a bloodstained shirt hanging over a radiator in the lounge. DC DYER reasonably believes that the shirt is evidence of the offence of murder that he is investigating.

With regard to powers under s. 19 of PACE 1984 only, which of the following statements is correct?

A DC DYER can seize the bloodstained shirt as he has reasonable grounds to believe that it is evidence in relation to an offence he is investigating.

B Section 19 can only be used when the officer reasonably believes the item has been obtained as a consequence of an offence not as evidence of an offence.

C Section 19 allows DC DYER to seize the bloodstained shirt and to search NICKLIN's house for evidence relating to the offence he is investigating.

D DC DYER cannot use his powers under s. 19 of PACE 1984 because he has been told to leave and is no longer 'lawfully' on the premises.

Answer _____

5 Special Warnings

5.1 Introduction

A special warning permits a court to draw adverse inferences in certain circumstances. Understanding why a special warning should be given, when it should be given, who should give it and how it should be given will not only assist you in your preparation for the NIE, but should also provide you with useful practical information should the need arise to give a special warning during the course of an interview.

5.2 Aim

The aim of this section is to provide you with an understanding of special warnings.

5.3 Objectives

At the end of this section you should be able to:

1. Explain why a special warning can be given (under ss. 36 and 37 of the Criminal Justice and Public Order Act 1994).
2. Explain when a special warning should be given.
3. Explain who should give a special warning.
4. Explain what should be included in a special warning.
5. Apply your knowledge to multiple-choice questions.

5.4 Why Can a Special Warning be Given?

5.4.1 Exercise—Section 36 of the Criminal Justice and Public Order Act 1994

Examine the following scenario and answer the related questions.

HARDING is the victim of a serious sexual assault. In her statement she describes the person who attacked her as having a distinctive tattoo on his arm. She describes the tattoo as a rose with the words 'Mary Jane' written underneath it. Following a medical examination, samples of the offender's hair and semen are recovered from HARDING. HARDING also states that she scratched her attacker on the right-hand side of his face. Several days later, COOPER is arrested in connection with the offence.

A forensic examination confirms that the hair and semen samples recovered from HARDING match COOPER's DNA profile. COOPER has the tattoo on his right arm as described previously and also has scratches on the right-hand side of his face.

During his interview, COOPER refuses to answer any questions.

Which of the previous 'facts' may COOPER be specially warned for and why?

_____

_____

_____

_____

_____

_____

_____

_____

_____

Which of the previous 'facts' would not be the subject of a special warning and why?

_____

_____

_____

_____

_____

_____

_____

EXPLANATION 5.4.1

Section 36 of the Criminal Justice and Public Order Act 1994

There are a number of reasons why a special warning can be given under s. 36 of the Act. The reasons are in two parts: the 'physical' and the 'interview' parts. Both parts must be present for a special warning to apply.

The 'physical' part

Does the interviewing officer have any 'physical' evidence? If it helps you to remember, the mnemonic is PC FOPSOMM.

Where a person is arrested by a constable and there is on him/her:

P   Person or

C   Clothing or

F   Footwear or

O   Otherwise in his possession or

P   Place at time of arrest a

S   Substance

O   Object

M   Mark

M   Mark on an object

If PC FOPSOMM is present, the interviewing officer must then ask himself/herself, do I believe the presence of PC FOPSOMM may be attributable to the suspect having taken part in the offence?

If the answer to this question is 'Yes', then the interviewing officer must examine the second part.

The 'interview' part

Has the suspect failed or refused to account for the presence of PC FOPSOMM?

If the answer is 'Yes', then a special warning can be given.

In this scenario, there are several 'facts' for which you may have considered COOPER could be subject to a special warning. These should have included COOPER's distinctive tattoo, the hair and semen recovered from HARDING and the scratches to the right-hand side of COOPER's face.

Let's take these 'facts' one at a time and subject them to the previous reasoning.

COOPER's distinctive tattoo

The tattoo could be classed as a mark on COOPER's person. However, the presence of the tattoo on COOPER's arm is not due to his having committed the offence. It was on COOPER's arm before the offence was committed, i.e. the reason why COOPER has the tattoo is not because he committed the offence. Therefore, the tattoo cannot be the subject of a special warning.

The hair and semen that matches COOPER's DNA

These items were not found on COOPER's person, clothing, footwear, otherwise in COOPER's possession or at a place in which COOPER is at the time of his arrest. Therefore, the hair and semen (although excellent evidence) cannot be subject to a special warning.

The scratches on the right-hand side of COOPER's face

The scratches could be classed as a mark on COOPER's person. If the interviewing officer believes that the presence of the scratches is due to COOPER having committed the offence, then the 'physical' part is satisfied. As COOPER has refused to answer any questions during the course of the interview (a failure or refusal to account), then the 'interview' part is satisfied. Therefore, COOPER could be given a special warning in relation to the scratches.

5.4.2 Exercise—Section 37 of the Criminal Justice and Public Order Act 1994

Examine the following scenario and answer the related questions.

At 2 am an automatic alarm was activated at St Andrew's Junior School. PC KERR arrived at the scene and saw a youth jump from a window of the school and run off. The youth was chased by PC KERR but was lost in the dark. PC HARRIS (a dog handler) attended and searched the school grounds. PC HARRIS's dog tracked the youth to a store shed in the grounds of the school. At 2.10 am, the dog handler arrested the youth (TAYLOR) for the burglary. TAYLOR was searched and a screwdriver was found in his coat pocket. £100 cash was stolen from the school, but this has not been found anywhere. At 10 am, DC EVERTON interviews TAYLOR. TAYLOR refuses to give an explanation for his presence in the store shed, but states that he found the screwdriver in the school grounds. DC EVERTON thinks that TAYLOR is lying about the screwdriver.

Which of the previous 'facts' may TAYLOR be specially warned for and why?

Which of the previous 'facts' would not be subject of a special warning and why?

> **EXPLANATION 5.4.2**
>
> **Section 37 of the Criminal Justice and Public Order Act 1994**
>
> As with s. 36, the reasons for giving a special warning under s. 37 can be split into the 'physical' and the 'interview' parts and, again, both parts must be present for a special warning to apply.
>
> **The 'physical' part**
>
> The important fact to remember here is that the 'arresting' officer and the 'finding' officer *must be* the same person.
>
> The interviewing officer must ask himself/herself: was the arrested person found at a place at or about the time the offence was committed?
>
> If the answer is 'Yes', then the interviewing officer must then ask himself/herself: do I believe that the presence of the suspect at that place and time may be attributable to the suspect having taken part in the offence?
>
> If the answer to this question is 'Yes', then the interviewing officer must examine the second part.
>
> **The 'interview' part**
>
> Has the suspect failed or refused to account for their presence at that time and place?
>
> If the answer is 'Yes', then a special warning can be given.
>
> In this scenario, there are three 'facts' for which you may have considered TAYLOR could be subject to a special warning. These should have included TAYLOR's presence when he jumped out of the school window and his presence in the store shed (both under s. 37), and the screwdriver found in his coat pocket (under s. 36).
>
> As with the first scenario, we will take these 'facts' one at a time and subject them to the previous reasoning.
>
> *TAYLOR's presence when he jumped out of the school window*
>
> PC KERR 'found' TAYLOR at this point, but lost him and did not arrest him. The 'arresting' and 'finding' officer must be the same person and, as this is not the case, TAYLOR cannot be given a special warning for his presence at this location. If PC KERR had arrested TAYLOR outside the school window, then a special warning would be applicable if TAYLOR refused to account for his presence at the school.
>
> *TAYLOR's presence in the store shed*
>
> PC HARRIS 'found' TAYLOR in the store shed and arrested him. The 'arresting' officer and the 'finding' officer are one and the same. If DC EVERTON believes that TAYLOR's presence in the store shed is attributable to his participation in the offence, the 'physical' part is satisfied. TAYLOR has refused to account for his presence in the store shed, satisfying the 'interview' part. Therefore, a special warning could be given for this fact.
>
> *The screwdriver found in TAYLOR's coat pocket*
>
> The screwdriver is an object in TAYLOR's possession (PC FOPSOMM). If DC EVERTON believes that the presence of the screwdriver is attributable to TAYLOR having taken part in the offence, then the 'physical' part is satisfied. However, the 'interview' part is not satisfied. Regardless of DC EVERTON's beliefs, TAYLOR has given an account of why the screwdriver is in his possession. Therefore, a special warning is not applicable.
>
> Try using the flowchart at the end of this chapter to assist you to work out if a special warning is applicable.

5.5 When Should a Special Warning be Given?

5.5.1 Exercise—When Should a Special Warning be Given?

Read the following scenarios and follow the instructions you are given.

GIBSON seriously assaults MILES using a knuckleduster. PC CALCUTT arrests GIBSON a short distance away from the scene of the offence and finds a knuckleduster in GIBSON's pocket. PC CALCUTT cautions GIBSON, who remains silent. PC CALCUTT escorts GIBSON to his police station and custody block, where the circumstances of the arrest are related to the custody officer. GIBSON states that he does not require a solicitor. GIBSON is later interviewed by DC ROBERTS. As DC ROBERTS is explaining the interview procedure, GIBSON interrupts her and states, *I'm not answering any questions no matter what you say.'* DC ROBERTS continues the interview procedure and cautions GIBSON. During the interview, GIBSON does answer some of DC ROBERTS's questions, but remains silent when asked any questions relating to the knuckleduster.

At what point(s) could GIBSON be specially warned in relation to the knuckleduster?

_____

_____

_____

_____

_____

EXPLANATION 5.5.1

When Should a Special Warning be Given?

A special warning can only be given after caution. Although there is nothing in principle preventing a special warning being given by PC CALCUTT at the scene of the arrest, you should remember that requests for information under ss. 36 and 37 are a form of questioning and should take place at a police station. In interview, the suspect has to be given an opportunity to answer questions about the 'fact' the interviewer wishes them to account for, because you cannot fail or refuse to answer questions about something you have not been asked about. Therefore, GIBSON's interruption of DC ROBERTS would not mean he should receive a special warning at that stage. GIBSON should be specially warned about the knuckleduster in interview after he has been given the opportunity to answer questions and has failed or refused to answer those questions.

The fact that GIBSON does not have a solicitor present does not make any difference to the situation, as he has been given the opportunity to consult one. If this opportunity has not been given to the suspect, then no adverse inferences can be drawn from the suspect's failure or refusal to account for the object, etc.

5.6 Who Should Give a Special Warning?

There are a number of myths with regard to who should give a special warning to the suspect. These include that the special warning must be given by the officer who finds the object, mark etc. or by the officer who found the suspect at a place at or about the time of the offence. Quite simply, the interviewing officer gives the special warning.

5.7 What Should be Included in a Special Warning?

5.7.1 Exercise—What Should be Included in a Special Warning?

There are five points that must be covered when an interviewing officer gives a special warning to a suspect. What are they?

1. _____

_____

2. _____

_____

3. _____

_____

4. _____

_____

5. _____

_____

EXPLANATION 5.7.1

What Should be Included in a Special Warning?

PACE *Code 'C'* (para. 10.11) provides that the interviewing officer *must* tell the suspect in *ordinary* language:

- what offence is being investigated;

- what 'fact' he/she is asking the suspect to account for;

- that he/she believes the 'fact' may be due to the suspect's taking part in the commission of the offence;

- that a proper inference may be drawn if the suspect fails or refuses to account for the 'fact' about which he/she is being questioned; and

- that the interview is being recorded.

  In relation to ss. 36 and 37, the accused cannot be convicted solely on an inference drawn from a failure or refusal to respond. The court must first be satisfied that there is sufficient other evidence to establish a prima facie case to answer (s. 38(3)).

5.7.2   Exercise—Create a Special Warning

Using Exercise 5.4.2, write down the special warning you would give to TAYLOR.

1. _____

2. _____

3. _____

4. _____

5. _____

EXPLANATION 5.7.2

Create a Special Warning

The special warning you have written should be similar to the following:

1. 'I am investigating a burglary for which you are under arrest, in which St Andrew's school was broken into and £100 cash was stolen.'

2. 'You were arrested at 2.10 am this morning by PC HARRIS, who found you in the store shed contained within the grounds of the school.'

3. 'I believe that you were in that store shed because you had just broken into the school.'

4. 'I am going to ask you to explain why you were there and I must warn you that a court may draw their own conclusions if, from now on, you fail or refuse to account for why you were there.'

5. 'I must remind you that this interview is being recorded.'

See *Investigators' Manual*, paras 1.9.2.4 to 1.9.2.5

Try the same with the COOPER example in Exercise 5.4.1.

5.8 Conclusion

Now that you have finished this section of the Workbook, you should have a good understanding of special warnings. The correct application of the law relating to this subject will assist you in the NIE and will also ensure that you can carry out a professional interview, allowing a court the opportunity to draw an inference from a suspect's failure or refusal to account for a given fact. See the flowchart at the end of this chapter regarding the application of special warnings.

5.9 Recall Questions

Try and answer the following questions.

- Why could you give a special warning under s. 36 of the Criminal Justice and Public Order Act 1994? (Can you remember the mnemonic?)
- Why could you give a special warning under s. 37 of the Criminal Justice and Public Order Act 1994?
- When should you give a special warning?
- Who should give the special warning?
- What are the five points a suspect must be told when you give a special warning?

5.10 Multiple-Choice Questions

Answers to these questions can be found in the 'Answers Section' at the end of the book. All explanations also include a reference back to the *Investigators' Manual 2022*.

1. DOOLEY breaks into a house and steals an antique gold necklace. The police are alerted to the burglary and PC COOK chases DOOLEY from the house into an alleyway. DOOLEY throws the stolen necklace onto the ground just before PC COOK detains him. PC COOK recovers the necklace. DOOLEY is interviewed by DC NEVIN and remains silent when questioned about the necklace.

Can DOOLEY be given a special warning under s. 36 of the Criminal Justice and Public Order Act 1994 regarding the necklace?

A No, because the necklace was not found on DOOLEY's person.

B Yes, because it was found in a place in which he was at the time of his arrest.

C No, because it was not found in or on his clothing or footwear.

D Yes, but only if PC COOK gives DOOLEY the special warning.

Answer _____

2. A warehouse in DC HACKWORTH's area is totally destroyed by an arson attack. DC HACKWORTH has evidence that SINGH, who has previous convictions for arson, is responsible for the offence. DC HACKWORTH arrests him at his home address and brings him into the custody block. SINGH declines the services of a solicitor. PC FELLOWS overhears DC HACKWORTH relating the circumstances of the arrest and speaks to the officer. He tells DC HACKWORTH that he saw SINGH outside the warehouse two days before the arson attack. During his interview, SINGH answers 'no comment' to all the questions that are put to him.

Could DC HACKWORTH give SINGH a special warning in these circumstances?

A Yes, SINGH has failed to account for his presence near the scene of the crime.

B No, special warnings do not apply to 'no comment' interviews.

C Yes, but only if SINGH has a solicitor present in the interview.

D No, SINGH was not found at the crime scene at or about the time of the offence.

Answer _____

3. JACKSON is arrested for an offence of robbery. During the course of the subsequent interview regarding the offence (and in the presence of his solicitor), JACKSON is correctly given a 'special warning' under s. 36 (failure to account for objects, substances and marks) and also s. 37 (failure to account for presence) of the Criminal Justice and Public Order Act 1994. JACKSON fails to answer any of the questions put to him after the 'special warnings' are given.

With regard to those 'special warnings', which of the following is true?

A An inference can be drawn from JACKSON's failure to answer the relevant questions at a magistrates' court and/or a Crown Court.

B An inference can only be drawn from JACKSON's failure to answer the questions at a Crown Court.

C An inference can be drawn at a magistrates' court from JACKSON's failure to answer questions when given a 'special warning' under s. 36 but not s. 37.

D An inference can be drawn by any court and JACKSON could be convicted solely on such an inference.

Answer _____

Special Warnings Flowchart

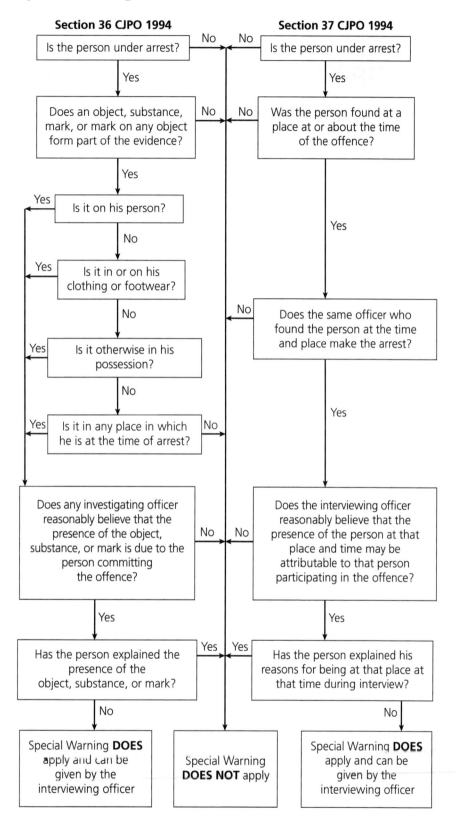

Section 36 CJPO 1994

Section 37 CJPO 1994

Is the person under arrest? — No — No — Is the person under arrest?

Does an object, substance, mark, or mark on any object form part of the evidence? — No — No — Was the person found at a place at or about the time of the offence?

Is it on his person? — Yes

Is it in or on his clothing or footwear? — Yes

Does the same officer who found the person at the time and place make the arrest? — No

Is it otherwise in his possession? — Yes

Is it in any place in which he is at the time of arrest? — Yes — No

Does any investigating officer reasonably believe that the presence of the object, substance, or mark is due to the person committing the offence? — No — No — Does the interviewing officer reasonably believe that the presence of the person at that place and time may be attributable to that person participating in the offence?

Has the person explained the presence of the object, substance, or mark? — Yes — Yes — Has the person explained his reasons for being at that place at that time during interview?

Special Warning **DOES** apply and can be given by the interviewing officer

Special Warning **DOES NOT** apply

Special Warning **DOES** apply and can be given by the interviewing officer

47

6 The Regulation of Investigatory Powers Act (RIPA) 2000

6.1 Introduction

The Regulation of Investigatory Powers Act (RIPA) 2000 governs the way in which the police and other public authorities utilise their ability to carry out surveillance and use Covert Human Intelligence Sources (CHIS). Apart from the Act itself, there are specific Codes of Practice that relate to RIPA 2000, guidelines produced by the Investigatory Powers Commissioner's Office and the practices and policies of individual forces to consider. Consequently, RIPA 2000 is a complex piece of legislation to deal with in practice. However, in this section of the Workbook you will only be dealing with the Act. This chapter provides a simple outline of how this legislation works. For particular issues, you should seek guidance from your force specialist departments.

6.2 Aim

The aim of this section is to provide you with an understanding of the issues surrounding the use of CHIS and surveillance.

6.3 Objectives

At the end of this section you should be able to:

1. Outline the purpose of RIPA 2000.
2. Describe what a CHIS is.
3. State the authorisation levels related to CHIS activity.
4. Describe what intrusive surveillance is.
5. Describe what directed surveillance is.
6. State the authorisation levels related to surveillance activity.
7. Demonstrate your knowledge by completing the exercises in this section.
8. Apply your knowledge to multiple-choice questions.

6.4 The Purpose of RIPA 2000

You may consider that RIPA 2000 does not affect you in your day-to-day duties but it is incredibly easy to find the Act having some kind of involvement in your investigations. RIPA 2000 is not necessarily just about surveillance relating to major investigations—in fact, it is the opposite as it relates to ordinary run-of-the-mill investigations on a regular basis. Therefore, it is important that you know what the Act regulates along with the consequences of breaching the Act.

6.4.1   Exercise—Basic Principles of RIPA 2000

1. What three types of activity does RIPA 2000 apply to?

  i. _____

  ii. _____

  iii. _____

2. Would the Act apply to a journalist working for a private company (e.g. *The Sun* newspaper)?
Yes / No
Why / Why not?

  _____

3. Breaching RIPA 2000 will have three potential consequences—what are they?

  i. _____

  ii. _____

  iii. _____

EXPLANATION 6.4.1

Basic Principles of RIPA 2000

1. The type of police activity the Act regulates is:

    i. Covert Human Intelligence Sources (CHIS);

    ii. intrusive surveillance; and

    iii. directed surveillance.

2. The Act would not apply to a journalist—this is because the Act only applies to *public authorities* and not to private companies or private individuals.

3. Breaching the Act will have three consequences:

    i. evidence obtained may be excluded by any court or tribunal;

    ii. a breach may give rise to proceedings under police conduct regulations;

    iii. a person may take a claim to the Investigatory Powers Tribunal.

    See *Investigators' Manual*, paras 1.12.1 to 1.12.2

6.5   CHIS

You have already come across this acronym several times in this section so you should be aware that CHIS stands for:

C   Covert
H   Human
I   Intelligence
S   Source

That is what CHIS stands for but *what exactly* is a CHIS?

6.5.1   Exercise—Key CHIS Behaviour

1. Is the activity of the CHIS carried out in an open fashion for everyone to see?

_____

2. What does a CHIS establish or maintain?

_____

3. With whom?

_____

4. For what purpose?

_____

EXPLANATION 6.5.1

Key CHIS Behaviour

1. Of course not, what would be the point? A CHIS carries out his/her activity in secrecy—their activity is _covert_.
2. A CHIS establishes or maintains _a relationship_.
3. The relationship is with _another person_.
4. For the covert purpose of obtaining information/providing access to information or covertly disclosing information obtained by the use of such a relationship.

6.5.2   Exercise—Identifying a CHIS

1. What is a covert purpose?

_____

2. RAFER is walking his dog when he sees BOYD dealing drugs outside a school. He telephones the police to inform them of BOYD's activities.
Is RAFER a CHIS?
Yes / No

3. PESSLEY is a window cleaner. On his round, he is cleaning LAKE's bedroom windows when he sees over 50 boxes containing computer equipment in LAKE's bedroom. PESSLEY thinks they are stolen and contacts the police to inform them.
Is PESSLEY a CHIS?
Yes / No

4. If you believe that neither RAFER nor PESSLEY are CHIS, consider what it would take to change that opinion.

_____

EXPLANATION 6.5.2

Identifying a CHIS

1. A purpose is covert if the relationship (and subsequent disclosure) is conducted in a manner calculated to ensure that one of the parties is unaware of that purpose (it is a secret purpose).

2. No. There is *no relationship* between RAFER and BOYD so RAFER cannot be a CHIS.

3. No. Once again, there is *no relationship* between PESSLEY and LAKE.

4. If the police direct the actions of either person then they could become a CHIS. For example, RAFER contacts you about BOYD. You note the information provided and then ask RAFER if he will approach BOYD the next time he sees him to find out what he is selling and for how much. It might not seem a great deal to ask, but what you are doing is 'tasking' RAFER. Imagine that RAFER does as you ask and then reports back that BOYD is selling cannabis for £20.00 per bag. Consider the following:

    i. Has RAFER established a relationship with BOYD? The answer is 'Yes'.

    ii. Was it for the covert (hidden) purpose of obtaining information? The answer is 'Yes'.

    iii. Is one of the parties (BOYD) unaware of RAFER's true purpose, i.e. to provide information to the police. The answer is 'Yes'.

RAFER is now a CHIS

See *Investigators' Manual*, paras 1.12.3 to 1.12.3.1

6.5.3 Exercise—Authorisation for CHIS Activity

One area that may cause problems for police officers is trying to remember who authorises CHIS activity and for how long.

1. What is the relevant rank for CHIS authorisation in normal circumstances?

___

2. In normal circumstances, how is that authorisation given?

___

3. In normal circumstances, how long will that authorisation last?

___

4. DC JAMES is contacted by DAVIS who tells him that he can provide information about drug smuggling. DAVIS states that a shipment of cocaine is arriving at an airport in one hour's time and wants to know if he should try to find out more about the shipment. DC JAMES needs to obtain urgent authorisation for DAVIS to act as a CHIS.
(a) Who are the two officers who could provide this authorisation?

    i. ___

    ii. ___

(b) How could this authorisation be given?

    i. ___

    ii. ___

(c) For how long?

i. _____

ii. _____

5. The next day DC JAMES is contacted by MARSTON (aged 16 years) who tells the officer that he can provide information about the same gang of drug smugglers. Can juveniles become CHIS?
Yes / No

6. If 'Yes' who could authorise this?

_____

7. For how long?

_____

8. What is the difference between DAVIS and MARSTON?

_____

EXPLANATION 6.5.3

Authorisation for CHIS Activity

1. In normal circumstances, an officer of the rank of superintendent or above.

2. In normal circumstances, it is given in writing.

3. In normal circumstances, authorisation lasts for 12 months (beginning on the day it was granted).

4. (a) i. A superintendent or above.

   ii. An inspector may give the relevant authorisation.

   (b) i. A superintendent could give the authorisation in writing or orally,

   ii. An inspector may give the authorisation but ONLY in writing.

   (c) i. and ii. The time limit for an urgent authorisation is the same for both authorising ranks—72 hours (three days).

5. Yes.

6. ONLY an officer of the rank of assistant chief constable/commander can authorise a juvenile to become a CHIS.

7. The authorisation time limit for a juvenile CHIS is reduced from 12 months to four months.

8. Juvenile CHIS activity can only be authorised by an officer of the rank of assistant chief constable/commander and for four months not 12. An inspector COULD NOT provide urgent CHIS authorisation for a juvenile.

6.5.4　Exercise—Restrictions on CHIS Authorisation

An inspector cannot give oral authorisation in any circumstances and cannot authorise the activity of a juvenile CHIS.

What other restriction is placed on an inspector's authorisation?

_____

EXPLANATION 6.5.4

Restrictions on CHIS Authorisation

Inspectors cannot give authorisation for any type of CHIS activity where the CHIS may obtain confidential material (this is material subject to legal privilege, confidential personal material or confidential journalistic material).

You should refer to your *Blackstone's Investigators' Manual 2022* where you will find a set of tables clearly setting out the authorisation procedures relating to CHIS activity.

See *Investigators' Manual*, para. 1.12.3.2

6.5.5 Why Can a CHIS Be Used?

The designated person (superintendent or inspector) must believe that CHIS activity is *necessary* for the following reasons:

- **C** Crime and Disorder Prevention
- **H** Health and Tax
- **I** Interests of National Security
- **S** Specified by Secretary of State

and that an authorisation is *proportionate* to what is sought to be achieved.
See *Investigators' Manual*, para. 1.12.3.1

6.6 Surveillance

Before you examine intrusive and directed surveillance, you must consider exactly what the term 'surveillance' means.

6.6.1 Exercise—What is 'Surveillance'?

What do you consider the term 'surveillance' to mean?

EXPLANATION 6.6.1

What is 'Surveillance'?

Like CHIS activity, any type of surveillance must be *covert* (carried out in a manner that is calculated to ensure that people subject to it are unaware that it is (or might be) taking place). You may have included other terms when answering the question such as the use of cameras or recording equipment and watching people from observation posts. You would not be wrong as the actual term 'surveillance' encompasses activities such as:

i. monitoring, observing, listening to and recording people and their conversations, activities and communications;

ii. recording anything monitored, observed or listened to in the course of surveillance; and

iii. surveillance by or with the assistance of a surveillance device.

See *Investigators' Manual*, para. 1.12.4

6.7   Intrusive Surveillance

Before you examine what directed surveillance is, it is best to examine what intrusive surveillance is. This is because the definition of directed surveillance refers to intrusive surveillance. Start with the exercise at para. 6.7.1 (Intrusive Surveillance? You Decide) and deciding whether or not the activity considered by the officer would be intrusive surveillance. An explanation for this exercise is given at the end of the exercise and explanation at para. 6.7.2.

6.7.1   Exercise—Intrusive Surveillance? You Decide

DC FARMER is considering carrying out the following activities to obtain intelligence on the activity of CARMEN, a known handler of stolen goods. Decide whether the potential activities would be considered intrusive surveillance or not.

1. DC FARMER wants to place a recording device in the sitting room of CARMEN's house to record conversations he has with his criminal associates who visit him there.
Is this intrusive surveillance?
Yes / No

2. DC FARMER also wants to place a recording device in a small storage unit that CARMEN rents to store goods.
Is this intrusive surveillance?
Yes / No

3. CARMEN is known to meet his criminal associates in a room at a hotel near to his house. DC FARMER wants to place a listening device in the hotel room that CARMEN uses.
Is this intrusive surveillance?
Yes / No

4. DC FARMER wants to attach a 'tracker' device to the underside of CARMEN's car. This device will only provide the police with the geographical location of CARMEN's vehicle.
Is this intrusive surveillance?
Yes / No

5. DC FARMER also wishes to place a recording device inside CARMEN's car to monitor his conversations.
Is this intrusive surveillance?
Yes / No

6. DC FARMER wishes to use a hand-held recording device to monitor CARMEN's conversations when he visits his brother's house. Although the device will be held by DC FARMER and used some 30 feet from the house, the device will provide sound recordings of the same quality as if the device were actually in the house.
Is this intrusive surveillance?
Yes / No

6.7.2   Exercise—Defining 'Intrusive' Surveillance

Complete the following definition (some clues have been provided for you):

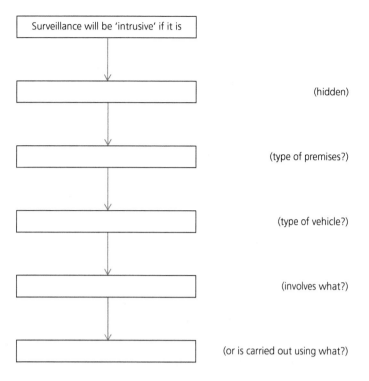

Surveillance will be 'intrusive' if it is

(hidden)

(type of premises?)

(type of vehicle?)

(involves what?)

(or is carried out using what?)

EXPLANATION 6.7.2
Defining 'Intrusive' Surveillance

Your answer should have looked something like the following:

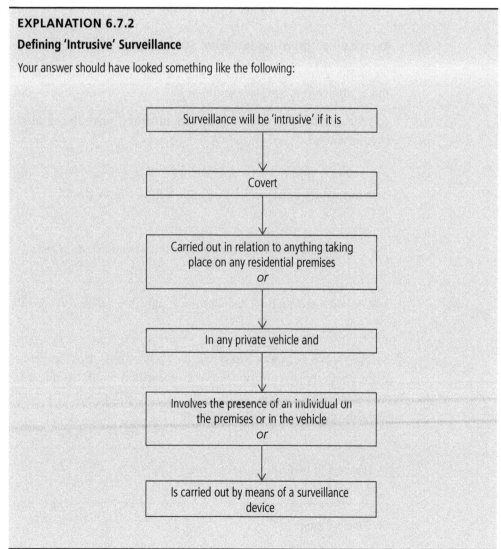

Now, considering the definition of 'intrusive surveillance', let's return to the exercise at para. 6.7.1 (Intrusive Surveillance? You Decide).

EXPLANATION 6.7.1

Intrusive Surveillance? You Decide

1. Yes—intrusive surveillance (CARMEN's home is residential premises).

2. No—not intrusive surveillance (the storage unit is NOT residential premises or a private vehicle).

3. Yes—intrusive surveillance (this is because hotel bedrooms are considered residential premises at all times).

4. No—not intrusive surveillance (the surveillance is taking place ON not IN CARMEN's private vehicle. But even if the device were placed INSIDE CARMEN's vehicle, surveillance carried out by means of a device purely to provide information about the location of the vehicle is NOT intrusive.)

5. Yes—intrusive surveillance (the device is inside the vehicle but is different to example 4 as it is recording/ monitoring conversations).

6. Yes—intrusive surveillance (although the device is outside the house it is providing recordings of such quality that it *might as well be in the house.* As such it is intrusive surveillance).

Remember—residential premises and private vehicles!

See *Investigators' Manual,* para. 1.12.4.2

6.7.3 Exercise—Authorising Intrusive Surveillance

Like CHIS authorisations, this is another potentially problematic area and therefore one that is often questioned by examiners.

1. What is the relevant rank for an intrusive surveillance authorisation in normal circumstances?

---

2. In normal circumstances, how is that authorisation given?

---

3. In normal circumstances, how long will that authorisation last?

---

4. Who else needs to be told about the application before it is actually approved?

---

5. BRAWN has been kidnapped and it is believed his life is in danger. The incident room dealing with the investigation receives information that KING might be responsible. The SIO in charge of the investigation wishes to carry out urgent intrusive surveillance in KING's house.
  i. Who could provide this authorisation?

---

ii. How could this authorisation be given?

---

iii. For how long?

EXPLANATION 6.7.3

Authorising Intrusive Surveillance

1. Chief constable/commissioner or designated deputy.

2. In normal circumstances, it is given in writing.

3. In normal circumstances, authorisation will last for three months.

4. The authorisation will not go 'live' until the Surveillance Commissioners have been notified of the application (after approval by the chief constable/commissioner the Surveillance Commissioners is notified of the application). When it approves the application and that approval is received in the office of the chief constable/commissioner, the intrusive surveillance can begin.

5. i. The chief constable/commissioner or his/her designated deputy.

   ii. The chief constable/commissioner or his/her designated deputy can give the authorisation in writing or orally.

   iii. The time limit for an urgent authorisation is 72 hours (three days).

Where the authorisation from the chief constable etc. is of an urgent nature, the surveillance may begin when he/she approves it. The application is still sent to the Surveillance Commissioners for their approval afterwards. Should the Surveillance Commissioners refuse the application, any surveillance activity must cease (an extremely rare occurrence).

Intrusive surveillance may not take place unless the authorising office believes that it is necessary and proportionate and:

- in the interests of national security;

- for the purpose of detecting or preventing 'serious crime';

- for the purpose of safeguarding the economic well-being of the United Kingdom.

You should refer to your *Blackstone's Investigators' Manual 2022* where you will find a set of tables clearly setting out the authorisation procedures relating to intrusive surveillance.

See *Investigators' Manual*, para. 1.12.4.2

6.8 Directed Surveillance

Now that you have dealt with intrusive surveillance, you come to the final RIPA 2000 category covered in your Manual—directed surveillance. Start with the exercise in para. 6.8.1 (Directed Surveillance? You Decide) and decide whether or not the activity considered by the officer would be directed surveillance. An explanation for the exercise at para. 6.8.1 is given at the end of the exercise and explanation in para. 6.8.2.

6.8.1 Exercise—Directed Surveillance? You Decide

1. An overt CCTV system in a town centre which displays signs around the town centre telling shoppers they are subject to surveillance would not be caught by the provisions of RIPA 2000.
True / False

2. PC KALSI is on uniform foot patrol and sees what he believes to be a drug deal taking place. He takes off his high-visibility clothing and watches the suspected drug dealer for several minutes. This is directed surveillance.
True / False

6.8.2 Exercise—Defining 'Directed' Surveillance

Complete the following definition (some clues have been provided for you):

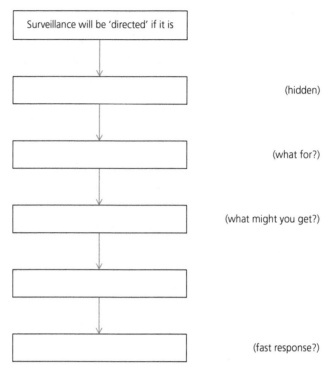

Surveillance will be 'directed' if it is	
	(hidden)
	(what for?)
	(what might you get?)
	(fast response?)

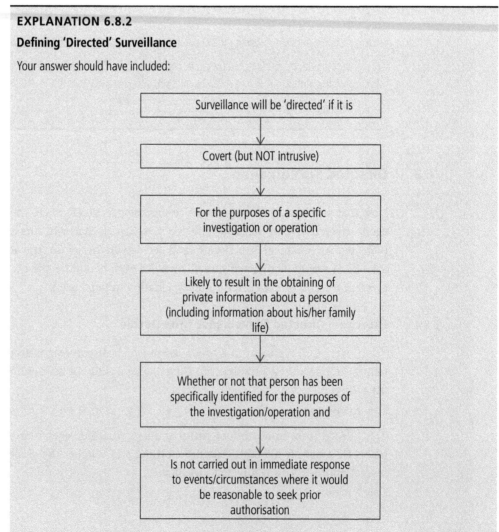

EXPLANATION 6.8.2

Defining 'Directed' Surveillance

Your answer should have included:

Surveillance will be 'directed' if it is

Covert (but NOT intrusive)

For the purposes of a specific investigation or operation

Likely to result in the obtaining of private information about a person (including information about his/her family life)

Whether or not that person has been specifically identified for the purposes of the investigation/operation and

Is not carried out in immediate response to events/circumstances where it would be reasonable to seek prior authorisation

Some points to note:

- Covert but NOT intrusive—which is why you must know what 'intrusive' surveillance is. Remember that one surveillance activity cannot be both types of surveillance, e.g. placing a device inside a car cannot be directed and intrusive surveillance—it must be one or the other (intrusive).
- Private information is an extremely far-reaching term. The contents of your shopping basket as you leave a supermarket, the fact you are there, what time it is and who you are with all constitute private information about you.
- An operation does not have to target a specific individual or individuals. Observations on a supermarket car park for unknown offenders who are robbing shoppers would be a good example.
- Immediate response—how long can an officer observe in immediate response before it is no longer an immediate response and is activity requiring authorisation? The courts and Surveillance Commissioners have not addressed this thorny problem and so your examiners will have to avoid it other than in the most basic terms.

EXPLANATION 6.8.1

Directed Surveillance? You Decide

Based on the information you have been provided with, we can state the following:

1. True. The cameras are OVERT (the signs). CCTV normally falls outside the Act. BUT if the cameras were used for a specific operation, e.g. to target drug dealers outside a pub covered by the system, then it becomes *directed surveillance*. This is because the use of the cameras is no longer 'general' but specific. The drug dealer at the door of the pub has a camera specifically focusing on him—do those signs tell the drug dealer that fact? They do not. The use of the cameras in this fashion is COVERT and the rest of the definition is satisfied.

2. False. See the previous definition and points to note.

   One last point on specific situations—the use of a 'tracker' device (as per the example in para. 6.7.1(4)) whilst not intrusive surveillance IS directed surveillance.
   See *Investigators' Manual*, paras 1.12.4.1, 1.12.4.2

6.8.3 Exercise—Authorising Directed Surveillance

There are some similarities with the authorisations for intrusive surveillance but be careful not to confuse the two.

1. What is the relevant rank for a directed surveillance authorisation in normal circumstances?

---

2. In normal circumstances, how is that authorisation given?

---

3. In normal circumstances, how long will that authorisation last?

---

4. Information is received that VAN DURLING will be selling drugs in a warehouse in the next few hours. DC GOUGH wants to carry out urgent directed surveillance at the warehouse.

(a) Who are the two officers who could provide this authorisation?

i. _____

ii. _____

(b) How could this authorisation be given?

i. _____

ii. _____

(c) For how long?

i. _____

ii. _____

EXPLANATION 6.8.3

Authorising Directed Surveillance

1. An officer of the rank of superintendent or above.

2. In normal circumstances, it is given in writing.

3. In normal circumstances, authorisation will last for three months.

4. (a) i. An officer of the rank of superintendent or above.

       ii. An officer of the rank of inspector or above.

   (b) i. The superintendent can give the authorisation in writing or orally,

       ii. The inspector can give the authorisation but ONLY in writing.

   (c) i. and ii. The time limit for an urgent authorisation is the same for both authorising ranks—72 hours (three days).

With surveillance authorisations, REMEMBER that INSPECTORS can only authorise activity in URGENT cases and it MUST ALWAYS BE IN WRITING.

• One last point to note on authorisation levels. If the material sought by the directed surveillance is confidential material then the authorisation level for the activity is raised to chief constable.

You should refer to your *Blackstone's Investigators' Manual 2022* where you will find a set of tables clearly setting out the authorisation procedures relating to directed surveillance activity.

See *Investigators' Manual*, para. 1.12.4.1

6.9   Conclusion

As you have discovered, there is a great deal to RIPA 2000; its importance cannot be underestimated. The grounding you have given yourself by reading the Manual and this Workbook will assist you to deal with some of the issues that will present themselves to you in the NIE.

6.10 Recall Questions

Try and answer the following questions.

- What are the three potential consequences of breaching RIPA 2000?
- What is a CHIS?
- In normal circumstances, who would authorise CHIS activity and for how long?
- What does the mnemonic CHIS stand for? (Why can a CHIS be used?)
- What is the definition of directed surveillance?
- What is the definition of intrusive surveillance?
- Who can authorise intrusive surveillance in urgent circumstances?

6.11 Multiple-Choice Questions

Answers to these questions can be found in the 'Answers Section' at the end of the book. All explanations also include a reference back to the *Investigators' Manual 2022*.

1. BARKER (who works as a cashier for a building society) is looking out of her window when she sees WIDDOWS acting suspiciously on a street corner outside her house. As BARKER watches WIDDOWS, it becomes plain that he is dealing in drugs. BARKER contacts the police and speaks to DC GAMER and tells him about what she has seen. The next day, BARKER observes WIDDOWS when he enters the building society where she works and places a large amount of cash into an account in the name of JOHN OGDEN. Once again, BARKER speaks to DC GAMER and tells him what she has seen. DC GAMER asks BARKER to keep a close eye on the 'JOHN OGDEN' account and to keep a note of when WIDDOWS enters the building society and with whom he enters, if anyone.

   At what point, if at all, does BARKER become a Covert Human Intelligence Source (CHIS)?

A When she provides information to DC GAMER about WIDDOWS dealing drugs on the street outside her house.

B When she provides information to DC GAMER about WIDDOWS entering the bank and placing money into the 'JOHN OGDEN' account.

C When DC GAMER asks her to keep an eye on the 'JOHN OGDEN' account and WIDDOWS's activities when he enters the building society.

D BARKER does not become a CHIS in these circumstances.

Answer _____

2. DC MADDALENA receives information that GARDEN is selling drugs from inside a small factory unit that he rents. DC MADDALENA wants to set up a surveillance operation that will involve placing a video camera inside GARDEN's factory unit to watch and record what is going on.

   With regard to RIPA 2000, which of the following statements is correct?

A This activity would be classed as intrusive surveillance because the activity is taking place inside premises.

B This activity would be classed as directed surveillance.

C This activity would be classed as intrusive surveillance as the operation is using a video camera to watch and record GARDEN's activities.

D This activity would not be covered by the Act as it does not involve the presence of an individual on the factory premises to watch GARDEN's activities.

Answer _____

3. TI BUCK wishes to carry out an operation involving directed surveillance against MENDIS in relation to offences of handling stolen goods. The surveillance required is of a non-urgent nature.

In respect of the authorisation for such an activity, which of the following statements is correct?

A An officer of the rank of superintendent or above should give the authorisation; the duration of the authorisation will be for three months beginning on the day it was granted.

B An officer of the rank of superintendent or above should give the authorisation; the duration of the authorisation will be for one month beginning on the day it was granted.

C An officer of the rank of superintendent or above should give the authorisation; the duration of the authorisation will be for 72 hours beginning on the day it was granted.

D An officer of the rank of inspector or above should give the authorisation; the duration of the authorisation will be for three months beginning on the day it was granted.

Answer _____

RIPA Flowchart—Authorisation Levels

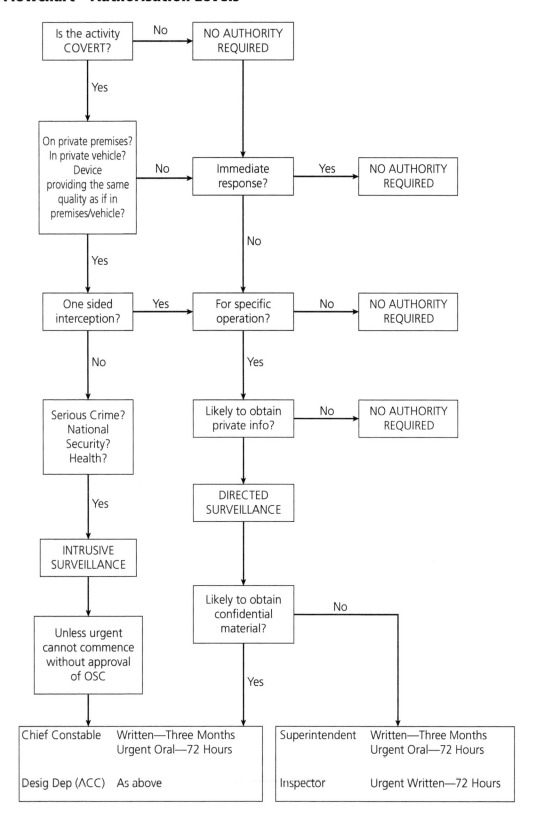

PART 2

Serious Crime and Other Offences

7 Homicide

7.1 Introduction

Although homicide only accounts for a small percentage of all recorded violent crime, you will be aware of the requirements that investigating even the simplest of these offences makes. Thankfully these offences are rare (in terms of crime statistics), but just because they are not as commonplace as offences of burglary or criminal damage does not mean they will not be questioned in your examination.

7.2 Aim

The aim of this section is to give you an insight into the offences of murder and manslaughter.

7.3 Objectives

At the end of this section you should be able to:

1. Define the offence of murder.
2. Outline the circumstances in which one of the 'special defences' to murder could be advanced.
3. Distinguish between offences of voluntary and involuntary manslaughter.
4. Describe the different types of manslaughter.

7.4 Murder

7.4.1 Exercise—What Do You Know About It?

Write down anything that you can recall about the definition of murder under common law.

_____

_____

_____

_____

EXPLANATION 7.4.1

What Do You Know About It?

Your answer should have included the following elements:

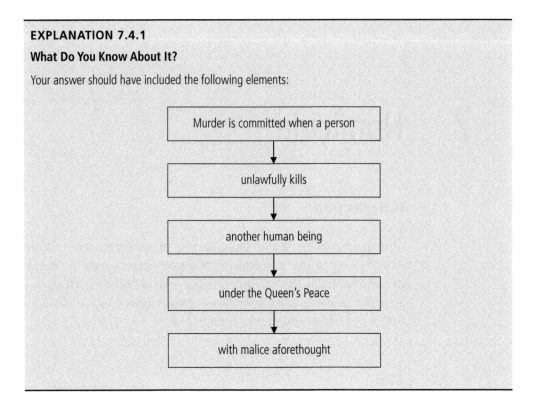

Murder is committed when a person

↓

unlawfully kills

↓

another human being

↓

under the Queen's Peace

↓

with malice aforethought

7.4.2 Case Study

Read the following case study. You will use the information presented to you to complete exercises in this section of the Workbook.

RAY is 26 years old and works on a fish counter in a large department store. His common-law wife, QUIRK, works at the same store on the checkout tills and is seven months pregnant. RAY is at work when he accidentally overhears two colleagues talking about QUIRK having an affair with HUGHES, who is RAY's supervisor. RAY had suspected that the two were having an affair for some time but had never had proof. Having heard this, he decides that QUIRK is carrying HUGHES's baby and not his. He listens to the conversation and hears that QUIRK and HUGHES had been seen kissing each other in a nearby pub called 'The Fox'. RAY decides that he will catch QUIRK and HUGHES at the pub, kill them both and in the process kill the unborn child.

The next day, RAY contacts a criminal associate and obtains a revolver to commit the crime.

Several days later, QUIRK tells RAY that she is going out for a drink with some friends and will not be back until the early hours of the morning. RAY pretends that he is not bothered but, an hour after QUIRK has left, he loads the revolver and drives to 'The Fox' pub intending to kill QUIRK and HUGHES if he finds them together. RAY runs into the pub and sees QUIRK and HUGHES sitting together in a small alcove. He walks up to the couple and pointing the revolver at HUGHES says, *'I hope she was to die for because that's exactly what you're going to do!'* RAY shoots HUGHES in the head, killing him instantly. He points the revolver at QUIRK's stomach and she tries to move away as RAY pulls the trigger. QUIRK is shot in her left side causing her serious injury but not, as RAY had intended, her death. RAY sits down at the table and shouts out, *'Call the police, I've done what I had to!'* The police arrive and RAY is arrested.

QUIRK is rushed to hospital and, although her injuries are serious, they are not life-threatening. However, the trauma causes QUIRK to go into labour and although the baby is born alive it dies several hours later. The cause of the death of the baby is directly connected to RAY's attack on QUIRK.

A murder incident room is set up and DCs HEXTALL and FARRELL are seconded to the enquiry. This is the first time either officer has been part of a murder investigation and after the first briefing they are driving to see a possible witness. During the journey they discuss the offence and the circumstances of the incident.

7.4.3 Exercise—Care to Comment?

The officers make a number of comments during their conversation. Answer the following questions about those comments and provide reasons for your answers where appropriate.

1. DC HEXTALL says, *'If RAY is found guilty of this he'll definitely get life.'* Is DC HEXTALL right?
Yes / No
Does a judge have any discretion regarding the sentence for an offence of murder?
Yes / No

2. DC FARRELL says, *'Why did they bother saying "unlawfully kills", surely all killing is "unlawful"?'*
What does the term 'unlawfully kills' actually mean?

Give an example of when killing someone might be 'lawful'.

3. DC HEXTALL says, *'He'll get done for the murder of HUGHES, the attempted murder of QUIRK and murder of the baby.'*
Is DC HEXTALL right in relation to:
HUGHES? Yes / No
QUIRK? Yes / No
The baby? Yes / No
What is the required mens rea for the offence of murder?

What is the required mens rea for an offence of attempted murder?

4. At what point would QUIRK's baby become 'another human being'?

5. RAY did not shoot the baby; he shot QUIRK. Could RAY be prosecuted for the murder of QUIRK's baby?

Could RAY be charged with the manslaughter of the baby?
Yes / No

6. DC FARRELL says, *'Yes, he'll get done for murder but only if we can prove that it was premeditated.'*
Does this offence require premeditation?
Yes / No

EXPLANATION 7.4.3

Care to Comment?

1. DC HEXTALL is right. The offence of murder is punishable with a life sentence. A judge has no option but to sentence a defendant to life imprisonment if found guilty as this is a mandatory sentence (the sentence for manslaughter is also life, except that a judge has discretion where sentencing is concerned).

2. The term 'unlawful killing' means causing the death of an individual without justification and includes situations where someone has failed to act after creating a situation of danger. An example of a 'lawful' killing could be when a police officer uses lethal force to protect life or when a person acts in self-defence.

   It also includes occasions where somebody fails to act after creating a situation of danger. In the DUTY mnemonic in the chapter on criminal conduct (chapter 1.2 of the *Investigators' Manual*), the **D** stood for Dangerous Situation. The example given was about a person who accidentally started a fire and did nothing about it. Imagine the person who accidentally started the fire in that house was not the only person there—someone else was in the house and they did not get out when the house burnt down. That would be an unlawful killing by the person who did nothing about the fire they started.

3. DC HEXTALL is right in relation to HUGHES (the *mens rea* for murder is the intention to kill or the intention to cause grievous bodily harm). DC HEXTALL is also right in relation to QUIRK (but note that the required *mens rea* for attempted murder will be an intention to kill only). The officer is not right in relation to the baby (see Answer 5 in this Exercise).

4. Trainee Investigators often worry about this point, but your Manual is clear and states that 'another human being' includes a baby who has been born alive and has an existence independent of its mother. If it helps, there is no need for the umbilical cord to have been cut, but the baby must have been totally expelled from the mother's womb.

5. No—RAY cannot be prosecuted for the murder of the baby in these circumstances. If RAY intended to kill or cause serious injury to the mother (as RAY did of course), that intention cannot support a charge of murder in respect of the baby if it goes on to die after being born alive. RAY could be prosecuted for manslaughter.

6. Premeditation is not required for this offence.

See *Investigators' Manual*, paras 2.1.2 to 2.1.2.2

7.4.4 Exercise—Special Defences

There are three 'special defences' available to a charge of murder. What are they?

1. _____

2. _____

3. _____

EXPLANATION 7.4.4

Special Defences

Your answer should have included:
1. Diminished responsibility.

2. Loss of control.

3. Suicide pact.

There are a host of general defences to a criminal charge, such as insanity, intoxication or mistake. What makes these defences special is the fact that they can only be used in defence to a charge of murder and murder alone. If one of these defences is used successfully, it allows a conviction for voluntary manslaughter as opposed to murder.

What follows is an outline of these special defences using a two-question approach to consider the issue.

7.4.5 Diminished Responsibility

Ask yourself these questions:

1. Was the defendant suffering from an abnormality of mental functioning?
2. Did it substantially impair his/her mental responsibility for his/her acts?

7.4.6 Loss of Control

Ask yourself these questions:

1. Did the defendant lose control and kill because of a 'qualifying trigger'?
2. Would a person of the same age and sex as the defendant, with a normal degree of tolerance and self-restraint, have done the same?

7.4.7 Suicide Pact

Ask yourself these questions:

1. Was there a suicide pact (i.e. an agreement to kill each other)?
2. Did the defendant have the settled intention of dying at the time the killing took place?

7.4.8 Exercise—A Special Defence?

Let's return to DCs HEXTALL and FARRELL and the case study. Their conversation continues—answer the questions regarding their conversation.

DC HEXTALL says, *'Of course RAY will probably come up with some defence to get him off.'*

Using the two-question approach, do you think that RAY could use one or more of the special defences in answer to:

A charge of murder with regard to HUGHES?
Yes / No
If 'Yes', what special defence and why, and if 'No', why not?

_____

_____

A charge of manslaughter with regard to QUIRK's baby?
Yes / No
If 'Yes', what special defence and why, and if 'No', why not?

_____

A charge of attempted murder with regard to QUIRK?
Yes / No
If 'Yes', what special defence and why, and if 'No', why not?

_____

EXPLANATION 7.4.8

A Special Defence?

The special defence of a suicide pact is obviously not available, so you are left with diminished responsibility and loss of control. At no stage in the case study has it been mentioned that RAY was suffering from an abnormality of the mental functioning that substantially impaired his mental responsibility; therefore, that defence (diminished responsibility) would not be available to any of the charges. Loss of control may have caused you to think a little more about the circumstances. The murder of HUGHES, the manslaughter of QUIRK's baby and the attempted murder of QUIRK were brought about by RAY's reaction to the news that QUIRK was having an affair with HUGHES. This could possibly form the basis for a loss of control as someone in this position could become extremely angry as a consequence. However, RAY spent several days planning the attack (e.g. the purchase of the revolver), so the attack could not be considered anything but one motivated by revenge. The Coroners and Justice Act 2009 limits the availability of the special defence of 'loss of control' and specifically states that the defence is NOT available when the defendant acted in a 'considered desire for revenge' so any attempt to use this defence would therefore fail. In addition, remember that the special defences would never be available to the charge of manslaughter (of the baby) and attempted murder (of QUIRK).

   It must be stressed that this is a basic approach to special defences and you should refer to your Manual for a full explanation.

   See *Investigators' Manual*, paras 2.1.3 to 2.1.3.3

7.5 Manslaughter

At this stage of the Workbook, you have examined murder and voluntary manslaughter. The final category in the Homicide section is *involuntary manslaughter*.

   The critical difference between the offences of murder and voluntary manslaughter and the offence of involuntary manslaughter is that the latter requires *no* mens rea *to kill or cause grievous bodily harm*.

7.5.1 Exercise—Categories of Manslaughter

There are two categories of manslaughter examined in your Manual. What are they?

1. _____

2. _____

EXPLANATION 7.5.1

Two Categories of Manslaughter

You may have mentioned:

1. Manslaughter by unlawful act.

2. Manslaughter by gross negligence.

7.5.2 Exercise—Manslaughter by Unlawful Act

Examine the following scenarios and decide if the person concerned has committed an offence of manslaughter by unlawful act and provide a short reason for your answer.

1. PARKS has an argument with MOORE. The argument becomes heated and PARKS punches MOORE, and causes him a serious injury. MOORE falls over and hits his head on a kerbstone. MOORE receives serious head injuries and dies as a result.
Would this constitute manslaughter by unlawful act?
Why / Why not?

_____

2. HUDSON is sacked from his job as a train driver. To get revenge against his employer, he decides to cause damage to some signalling and safety equipment. As a direct consequence of his actions, a goods train is derailed and the driver of the train is killed.
Would this constitute manslaughter by unlawful act?
Why / Why not?

_____

3. FISHER steals a warning sign indicating that a footbridge is weak and should not be used. ACFORD crosses the bridge, which collapses and ACFORD falls to her death.

Would this constitute manslaughter by unlawful act?
Why / Why not?

_____

When you are considering whether or not this offence has been committed, you must ask three questions:

1. Has an inherently unlawful act been committed?

(Do not limit yourself to offences where physical harm is a natural consequence. Theft and criminal damage are inherently unlawful acts.)

2. Would the general public consider that the consequences of this act involve a risk of someone being harmed?

(There must be a risk of harm and that risk is judged objectively. An objective judgement takes no account of what the individual who carried out the act thought; that is irrelevant. What is relevant is what a group of onlookers (the jury?) would think.)

3. Did the defendant have the required *mens rea* for the unlawful act?

(All you are concerned with is if the defendant had the *mens rea* for the original unlawful act, nothing more.)

You might want to try and remember these questions in the following format:

R Risk of harm (objective)?
U Unlawful act (inherently)?
M *Mens rea* for the act?

In light of this information, you should return to the previous scenarios and ensure that your understanding of the subject is correct.

EXPLANATION 7.5.2

Manslaughter by Unlawful Act

In all three scenarios, the offence has been committed. Putting the three questions to each scenario and using the acronym would lead you to the following:

1. (R) Risk of harm (objective)? Yes, it seems obvious that all the acts involve a risk of someone being harmed.

2. (U) Unlawful act (inherent)? Yes, assault/criminal damage/theft.

3. (M) *Mens rea* for the act? Yes, in all three cases.

7.5.3 Manslaughter by Gross Negligence

The title of this offence tells you a great deal about it. Where an individual has died due to the *gross negligence* of another, there may be criminal liability. A good example of this offence was *R v Adomako* [1995] 1 AC 171, where an anaesthetist had failed to notice (for six minutes) that a patient's oxygen supply had become disconnected from a ventilator during an operation. As a result, the patient suffered a cardiac arrest and died.

7.6 Conclusion

You should now possess a good knowledge of the offences of murder and manslaughter and you should be able to differentiate between the types of offences and liability that can possibly occur when an individual dies. If you are still unsure, you might want to examine the homicide flowchart that takes you through the offences.

7.7 Recall Questions

Try and answer the following questions.

- What is the sentence for murder/manslaughter?
- What is the definition of the offence of murder under common law?
- What does 'the Queen's Peace' mean?
- What is the *mens rea* for murder and attempted murder?
- What happens if a victim of an attack dies more than three years after the attack?
- What are the 'special defences' relating to murder?
- What are the questions you must ask when considering those 'special defences'?
- What is the difference between voluntary and involuntary manslaughter?
- What are the three questions you should ask when considering an offence of manslaughter by unlawful act?
- What is the acronym for manslaughter by unlawful act?
- What is gross negligence manslaughter all about?

7.8 Multiple-Choice Questions

Answers to these questions can be found in the 'Answers Section' at the end of the book. All explanations also include a reference back to the *Investigators' Manual 2022*.

1. ADRIAN MILLER lives with his wife JOAN who is eight months pregnant by ADRIAN. They have a volatile relationship and one night during an argument ADRIAN stabs JOAN in her side with a kitchen knife. When ADRIAN stabbed JOAN he intended to cause her grievous bodily harm; he accomplishes his aim but in the process he also injures the unborn foetus in JOAN's womb. JOAN is taken to hospital suffering from severe shock and a deep wound to her side. The shock causes her to go into labour and after 12 hours the baby is born. The baby has a separate existence from the mother (JOAN) but dies six hours after being born as a result of the knife injury received whilst in the womb.

Which of the following statements is correct with regards to the criminal liability of ADRIAN MILLER?

A He is guilty of the murder of the baby, as he intended to commit grievous bodily harm to JOAN and the baby died as a result of his actions.

B He is guilty of the manslaughter of the baby in these circumstances.

C He has no criminal liability for murder or manslaughter in these circumstances.

D He would be guilty of the murder of the baby, owing to the doctrine of transferred *mens rea*.

Answer _____

2. ANDREW and DIANE TAYLOR (husband and wife) are going through a bad time in their relationship because DIANE keeps accusing ANDREW of having an affair. Her accusations are unfounded. ANDREW is working hard trying to set up a new business and one night he arrives home late, having just won a large contract. DIANE accuses him of arriving late because he was meeting his lover. This accusation is the 'last straw' for ANDREW and, suddenly losing all self-control, he picks up a nearby stainless steel rolling pin and hits DIANE across the head with it, intending to kill her. Although DIANE's injuries are substantial she survives the attack.

Which of the following statements is correct?

A ANDREW TAYLOR would be guilty of the attempted murder of his wife as his intention was to kill her.

B ANDREW TAYLOR would be guilty of the attempted murder of his wife, but could use the 'special defence' of 'loss of control'.

C ANDREW TAYLOR would be guilty of the attempted murder of his wife, but in the circumstances he could raise the 'special defence' of 'loss of control' and this would reduce the offence to one of a s. 18 wounding.

D ANDREW TAYLOR would be guilty of the attempted murder of his wife, but could use the 'special defence' of 'loss of control' with the permission of the DPP.

Answer _____

3. CLARKE and SUMPTER are chatting in CLARKE's house. They are very good friends and they are not drunk. CLARKE goes upstairs and brings down his father's army pistol to show to SUMPTER. He points the gun at SUMPTER who is not at all scared by this action as CLARKE is his friend. When CLARKE points the gun at SUMPTER, he has no intention to cause him to apprehend the immediate and unlawful use of violence; he is not even reckless as to the fact. CLARKE pulls the trigger believing that it will not fire, but there is a 'live' round in the chamber and the gun goes off, killing SUMPTER.

Considering the offence of manslaughter by unlawful act only (and that the only possible unlawful act in these circumstances is one of assault), which of the following statements is correct?

A CLARKE is guilty of manslaughter by unlawful act and could be sentenced to life imprisonment for this offence.

B CLARKE is guilty of manslaughter by unlawful act because he had no intention to kill SUMPTER or to cause him grievous bodily harm.

C CLARKE is guilty of manslaughter by unlawful act for which there is a mandatory 10-year prison sentence.

D CLARKE is not guilty of the offence because he does not have the required *mens rea* for an offence of assault.

Answer _____

Homicide Flowchart

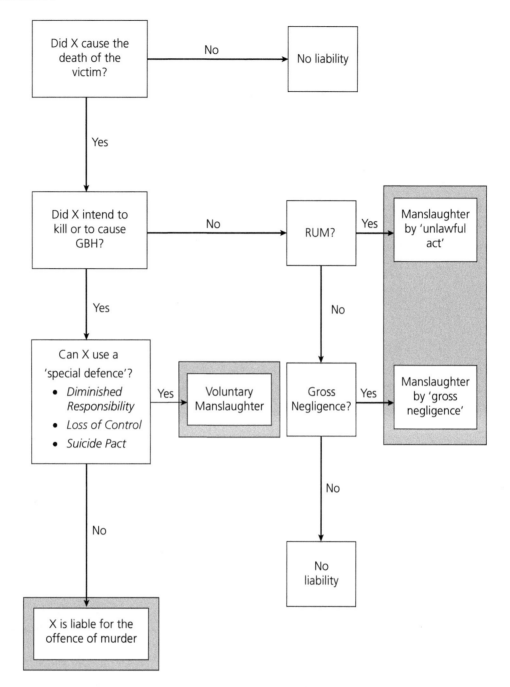

8 | Misuse of Drugs

8.1 Introduction

The Misuse of Drugs Act 1971 is the mainstay of legislation regulating drugs offences. Although the abuse and illegal distribution of controlled drugs create crimes in their own right, you will be aware of the effect that drug-related crime has on society in general. This section of the Workbook concentrates on several of the main offences as well as basic terms and defences available under the Act.

8.2 Aim

The aim of this section is to explain some of the offences and defences under the Misuse of Drugs Act 1971.

8.3 Objectives

At the end of this section you should be able to:

1. State the meaning of the term 'possession'.
2. Identify the points to prove for the offence of possession of a controlled drug contrary to s. 5(2) of the Misuse of Drugs Act 1971.
3. Identify the points to prove for the offence of possession with intent to supply a controlled drug contrary to s. 5(3) of the Misuse of Drugs Act 1971.
4. Identify when an offence of supplying a controlled drug contrary to s. 4(3) of the Misuse of Drugs Act 1971 has been committed.
5. Outline the defences available under s. 5 of the Misuse of Drugs Act 1971.
6. Outline the defences available under s. 28 of the Misuse of Drugs Act 1971.
7. Summarise the elements of s. 8 of the Misuse of Drugs Act 1971 (occupiers).
8. Identify the ingredients required for a Travel Restriction Order to be made.
9. State the powers of the police under s. 23 of the Misuse of Drugs Act 1971.
10. Describe the requirements of the offence of obstruction under s. 23(4) of the Misuse of Drugs Act 1971.
11. Apply your knowledge to multiple-choice questions.

8.4 Possession

8.4.1 Exercise—Possession or Not?

Examine the following scenarios and provide an answer based on whether or not the named person has 'possession'. Do not concern yourself with whether an offence has been committed. Think about *possession* alone.

1. WHITE is a drug dealer who keeps a large quantity of cannabis hidden under his bed at his home address. WHITE is out of his house and dealing in drugs when he is arrested. When WHITE is arrested, does he have possession of the cannabis hidden under his bed?
Yes / No

2. THORLEY approaches a drug dealer and asks to buy some heroin. The dealer tells THORLEY that he has some heroin in his car parked 100 metres away. THORLEY gives the dealer £100 and asks him to go to his car and get the drug.
Does THORLEY have possession of the heroin when the cash exchanges hands?
Yes / No

3. SHENTON has arranged for his drug dealer to send him 50 LSD tablets through the post. SHENTON leaves his house to go to work and, 30 minutes later, a postal worker puts the letter containing the drugs through SHENTON's front door letterbox.
Would SHENTON be in possession of the LSD tablets once they had been posted through his front door?
Yes / No

4. PULCELLA lives in a block of flats. The front door of his flat is insecure and, without PULCELLA's knowledge, his neighbour (who is a drug dealer) hides several hundred Ecstasy tablets inside a settee in PULCELLA's living room.
Does PULCELLA have possession of the Ecstasy tablets once the drug dealer has hidden them inside his settee?
Yes / No

5. LARTER has been suffering from headaches in the afternoon. He picks up several aspirins from a flatmate's bedside table and goes to work. The tablets are in fact Ecstasy tablets.
When LARTER picks up the Ecstasy tablets thinking they are aspirin, does he possess the Ecstasy?
Yes / No

6. JILBERT is a delivery driver. He parks outside an address and removes a parcel with the words 'Fragile—Contains Glass' printed on it, to deliver to the address. The parcel actually contains a large amount of cannabis resin.
When JILBERT delivers the parcel, does he have possession of the cannabis resin?
Yes / No

7. FERGUSON owns a flat where she and her boyfriend live. FERGUSON's boyfriend has a friend who is a drug dealer. The drug dealer visits the flat regularly and uses cannabis while he is there. FERGUSON realises that the drug dealer is highly likely to bring drugs into her house. The police raid the flat and find some cannabis in a drawer in the kitchen. There is no proof that the cannabis actually belongs to FERGUSON.
Does FERGUSON possess the cannabis in these circumstances?
Yes / No

EXPLANATION 8.4.1

Possession or Not?

Possession has been described as a neutral concept. When you are considering possession *alone* it might be better to think of it as the 'tough luck' principle. To prove possession you need:

1. physical control of it; and

2. knowledge of its presence.

So if you have something (and that means anything) in your physical control and you know that you have that something, then it's tough luck if it turns out to be a drug and you didn't know that. Do not worry about whether the person who possesses it is innocent or not, that is what the defences under this Act are for. This approach will help solve some of the previous scenarios, but you also need to know what 'physical control' actually means.

1. Tough luck, WHITE—you have possession. Actual physical custody of the drug is not required but physical control is. WHITE has physical *control* of the drugs at his home address. Think about the situation where a dealer is arrested and then a search of the dealer's house is carried out later on; if he/she was the only occupant and you found drugs there, you would charge him/her with an offence in relation to those drugs because he/she has possession of them.

2. THORLEY does not have possession. This is because THORLEY does not have physical control over the drug as yet. At this stage, only the drug dealer has possession.

3. Tough luck, SHENTON—you have possession. Normally you cannot possess something unless you are aware that you have control over it. This is an exception to that rule because even though SHENTON is unaware that the LSD has arrived, it was delivered to his address in *response to a request from him* (*R v Peaston* (1978) 69 Cr App R 203 (CA)).

4. PULCELLA does not have possession. As explained in the SHENTON scenario, you cannot have possession if you are unaware that you have control over it. The drugs have been placed in PULCELLA's flat without his knowledge so he cannot be aware that he has control over them. The same reasoning would apply if drugs were placed in someone's pocket, car etc. without their knowledge—they are unaware of their presence—they do not have possession.

5. Tough luck, LARTER—you have possession. LARTER has physical control over the tablets and he knows of their presence. It is *TOTALLY IRRELEVANT* that he does not know that what he has is in fact a controlled drug.

6. Tough luck, JILBERT—you have possession for the same reason as LARTER.

7. FERGUSON does not have possession. This follows the ruling in *Adams v DPP* [2002] EWHC 438 (Admin), where the court stated that where knowledge of possession of the drug was limited to the fact that a visitor had brought drugs into the defendant's home intending to take them, that was not sufficient evidence from which it was appropriate to infer that she had control over the drugs.

There is only one other issue in relation to possession:

Quantity—if the quantity is 'visible, tangible and measurable' it can be possessed. If it is too small to even know about it, it cannot be possessed.

See *Investigators' Manual*, paras 2.2.3 to 2.2.3.6

Having established what possession actually is, you will now examine three chief offences relating to the concept.

8.5 Possession of a Controlled Drug

You should now be in a position to say that you understand the concept of 'possession'.

If that is the case then you only need to add one factor to be able to identify the points to prove for the offence of possession of a controlled drug.

Possession (as explained previously)

+

The defendant knows that he/she is in possession of something which is, in fact,
a prohibited or controlled substance

The only other factor that should be considered is sentencing. A clue to the sentencing comes from the section itself.

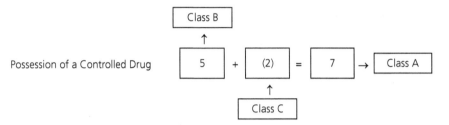

See *Investigators' Manual*, para. 2.2.3.7

8.6 Possession with Intent to Supply

Now you understand the offence of possession of a controlled drug, you only need to add one factor to be able to identify the points to prove for the offence of possession of a controlled drug with intent to supply.

Possession of a controlled drug/substance (as explained previously)

+

The intention that he/she will supply that drug/substance to another

8.6.1 Exercise—Possession with Intent to Supply Scenarios

The offence of possession with intent to supply is more complex than mere possession. Examine the following scenario and answer the questions that follow it.

PC CLOUGH takes part in a drugs raid and during the raid she finds a large amount of cannabis resin hidden in a wardrobe. PC CLOUGH places a small amount of the cannabis resin in a drugs bag and secretes the rest in her jacket. This is because PC CLOUGH is also a drug dealer who has been taking drugs from other searches and from those she has arrested for drugs offences to sell on the streets. PC CLOUGH arrested FLINT for possession of a controlled drug some time ago and after he witnessed her removing the majority of his drugs for herself, he informed the police about what he saw. An undercover operation has been mounted to obtain evidence of PC CLOUGH's drug dealing activities. DC JOY (an undercover police officer) has made contact with PC CLOUGH in her drug dealing capacity and PC CLOUGH has told him that she can supply him with £10,000 worth of cannabis resin. The night before the deal is due to take place, the police raid PC CLOUGH's home address and arrest her for possession with intent to supply (amongst other offences). Her house is searched and the police recover approximately £10,000 worth of cannabis resin. A search of the room where the resin was stored reveals the following:

i. a large amount of clingfilm;
ii. several sets of scales;
iii. a book containing details of who PC CLOUGH sells drugs to and the quantities they buy;
iv. a large amount of tin foil;
v. a dozen 'Rizla' cigarette paper packs;
vi. £15,000 in various note denominations; and
vii. bank account details showing that PC CLOUGH has over £50,000 placed in three different bank accounts in her name.

When PC CLOUGH is interviewed she states that as a police officer she has lawful possession of the drugs and that the arrest is unlawful.

1. What effect will the fact that she is a police officer have with regard to the offence of possession with intent to supply and why?

_____

2. Will the fact that PC CLOUGH possessed the drugs with intent to supply them to an undercover officer have an impact on the case?
Yes / No

3. Of the seven items seized during the search, which would be relevant evidence to show that PC CLOUGH is an active drug dealer generally and which could be used to prove a charge of possession with intent to supply?

Active Drug Dealer	Proof of the Charge

EXPLANATION 8.6.1

Possession with Intent to Supply Scenarios

1. The fact that the defendant is a police officer has no effect as the lawfulness of possession is irrelevant; what matters is the lawfulness of the intended supply.

2. No. Possession with intent to supply a controlled drug to a person who is in fact an undercover police officer amounts to an offence.

3. Your completed table should have looked like this:

Active Drug Dealer	Proof of the Charge
The clingfilm	£15,000 in cash
The scales	Bank account details of the £50,000
The book containing drug deal details	
The tin foil	
The 'Rizla' papers	

Drug dealing paraphernalia will not prove an intention to supply.
See *Investigators' Manual*, para. 2.2.5

8.7 Supplying a Controlled Drug

8.7.1 Exercise—Three Ways to Commit the Offence

This offence can be committed in three ways. What are they?

1. _____

2. _____

3. _____

EXPLANATION 8.7.1

Three Ways to Commit the Offence

The ways in which the offence can be committed are as follows:

- To supply or offer to supply a controlled drug.
- To be concerned in the supplying of such a drug.
- To be concerned in the making to another of an offer to supply.

'To be concerned' means to provide some kind of identifiable assistance such as telephoning a contact or similar helpful act.

8.7.2 Exercise—Consider 'Supply' Only

In this exercise you are only required to consider the 'supply' element of the offence. Examine the scenarios and decide whether there has been a supply.

1. KENDRICK is a registered drug addict who legally possesses a controlled drug. He is on a walking holiday with his fiancée when he decides he needs to administer the drug. He takes enough of the drug for his usual dose and leaves the remainder of the drug with his fiancée while he administers his dose out of sight behind some bushes. Does KENDRICK supply his fiancée with a controlled drug?

Yes / No

Why / Why not?

---

2. MOSSON is a drug dealer who carries out his business outside a pub called 'The Anchor'. MOSSON is drinking in 'The Anchor' when he receives a call on his mobile from SWAIN requesting a supply of heroin. MOSSON does not trust SWAIN and asks WILLIAMS (who is also drinking in the pub) to look after the bulk of his heroin until he comes back from the deal with SWAIN. WILLIAMS is aware that MOSSON deals in drugs and will sell the heroin on its return but agrees and holds onto the drugs. Thirty minutes later, MOSSON returns and WILLIAMS hands back the drugs. When WILLIAMS hands the drugs back to MOSSON, does he supply?

Yes / No

Why / Why not?

---

3. What would the situation be if, instead of asking WILLIAMS to look after the drugs, MOSSON produced a gun and said, *'I'll blow your head off if you don't look after this for me!'* and when MOSSON returned to the pub, WILLIAMS handed the drugs to him?

EXPLANATION 8.7.2

Consider 'Supply' Only

The term 'supply' (for the purposes of this Act) means to furnish a drug to another so that the other can use it for his/her own purposes and thereby gain a benefit. It is not merely the physical transfer of the drug from one person to another.

1. KENDRICK is not supplying. It does not matter that his possession of the drug is legal, what is important is what his fiancée is getting by receiving the drug from him in the first place and in this situation she is getting nothing whatsoever, i.e. she receives no benefit from the activity. If KENDRICK had given her the drug for her own use, she *would* be benefiting and consequently KENDRICK would supply to his fiancée.

2. WILLIAMS does supply. This is because handing the drugs back to MOSSON enables MOSSON to sell the drugs to his customers. This is a benefit to MOSSON and, therefore, WILLIAMS supplies.

3. WILLIAMS would still supply, as MOSSON would receive exactly the same benefit as at point 2 (see *R v Panton* [2001] EWCA Crim 611).

This can be a little confusing; see if the diagram helps you.

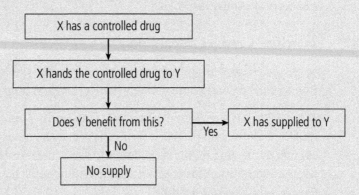

Please remember that when an *offer* is made to supply a controlled drug, the offence is complete *at that point*.

- It does not matter whether the defendant has actually got any drugs.
- It does not matter if the defendant intends to carry out the offer or not.
- It does not matter who the offer is made to.
- *The only thing that does matter is that the offer was made.*

See *Investigators' Manual*, paras 2.2.4 to 2.2.4.2

8.8 Defences

8.8.1 Exercise—Section 5 Defence to Unlawful Possession

Section 5 of the Misuse of Drugs Act 1971 creates a defence to unlawful possession. Examine the following scenarios and decide whether the defence exists or not and justify your answer.

1. LOOMES is a teacher and, while he is making his way to a class, he finds a pupil smoking a cannabis joint. LOOMES confiscates the cannabis joint in order to prevent the pupil from continuing to commit an offence with it. LOOMES places the cannabis joint in a locked drawer in his office.

If the drug were to be found in LOOMES's desk drawer, would he have a defence under s. 5?

Yes / No

Why / Why not?

_____

2. MAYBURY finds what she suspects to be LSD in her daughter's bedroom. To prevent her daughter committing an offence, she takes the item and decides to ask one of her work colleagues for his opinion as to whether the item is LSD. The following day she takes it into her workplace for that purpose. MAYBURY decides that if her colleague thinks the item is LSD then she will destroy it. On her way to work, the police stop MAYBURY and the LSD is found in her possession.

Does MAYBURY have a defence under s. 5 in these circumstances?

Yes / No

Why / Why not?

_____

3. RAINES is a youth worker. He finds several hypodermic needles containing what he suspects to be heroin in a street. He picks them up and decides that he will take them to his local police station as soon as possible.

If RAINES were found in possession would he be able to use a defence under s. 5?

Yes / No

Why / Why not?

_____

EXPLANATION 8.8.1

Section 5 Defence to Unlawful Possession

Only RAINES would be able to use the defence available under s. 5 of the Act.

1. LOOMES has confiscated the drug to prevent an offence taking place or continuing to take place and that would satisfy the first part of the defence under s. 5(4)(a). However *as soon as possible* after taking possession of the drug he must either destroy it or deliver it to the custody of someone lawfully entitled to possess it and this has not been done.

2. MAYBURY has confiscated the drug for the right reason and intends to destroy it, but this is not done as soon as possible.

3. RAINES has taken possession of the drug with a view to handing it to someone entitled to possess it as soon as possible.

See *Investigators' Manual*, para. 2.2.3.8

8.8.2 Exercise—General Defence Under s. 28

The defences under s. 28 are applicable to six offences. Name four of them.

1. _____

2. _____

3. _____

4. _____

EXPLANATION 8.8.2

General Defence Under s. 28

Three of the offences that are covered by the defence have been dealt with in this section, i.e. unlawful possession, possession with intent to supply and unlawful supply. The other offences covered are unlawful production, unlawful cultivation of cannabis and offences connected with opium.

   Section 28 of the Misuse of Drugs Act 1971 provides a general defence to certain drugs offences. Remember this as the 'Star Wars Defence'—it can only be used if you 'SUPPLY C3PO'.

SUPPLY
Cultivate cannabis
3P (production, possession, possession with intent to supply)
Opium offences

Section 28 *is not* available to a charge of conspiracy to commit the *'SUPPLY C3PO'* offences as conspiracy *is not* an offence under the Misuse of Drugs Act 1971 (it would be an offence under s. 1 of the Criminal Law Act 1977). Now that you have identified the offences that the defence is relevant to, you need to understand how to apply its provisions.

8.8.3   Exercise—Defence Under s. 28?

In the following scenarios, state whether s. 28 would provide the named person with a defence and explain your decision.

1. JAMES shares a flat with RAFFERTY and the two men often share each other's clothing. One evening, JAMES decides to go out and get a takeaway meal and puts on RAFFERTY's coat. The police stop JAMES on his way to the takeaway and find several Ecstasy tablets in the coat pocket. JAMES thought the coat was empty and has no knowledge of their presence.
Would a defence be open to JAMES?
Yes / No
Why / Why not?

---

2. In scenario 5 of Exercise 8.4.1, you examined circumstances surrounding LARTER as follows:
LARTER has been suffering from headaches in the afternoon. He picks up several aspirins from a flatmate's bedside table and goes to work. The tablets are in fact Ecstasy tablets.
Would a defence be open to LARTER?
Yes / No
Why / Why not?

---

3. PEACOCK approaches his dealer and buys £50 of heroin from him. PEACOCK is stopped by the police and the drug is found in his possession. Analysis of the drug shows that it is not heroin, it is in fact 'speed' (amphetamine).

Would a defence be open to PEACOCK?

Yes / No

Why / Why not?

EXPLANATION 8.8.3

Defence Under s. 28?

There are three defences under s. 28. Broadly speaking, they are:

- lack of knowledge (by the defendant) of some fact alleged by the prosecution;

- a general lack of knowledge about the drug in question; and

- a conditional belief about the drug in question.

1. JAMES would have a defence. He could use the defence under s. 28(2) because he neither knew nor suspected nor had reason to suspect a fact alleged by the prosecution. The fact would be possession. The 'reason to suspect' is an objective one. If the reason you did not know, suspect or had reason to suspect a fact was because you were drunk, the defence will not apply.

2. LARTER would have a defence if he proved that he neither believed nor suspected nor had reason to suspect that the substance or product was a controlled drug.

3. PEACOCK would not have a defence. Proving that the drug in question was a different controlled drug to the one he thought it was will not lead to acquittal.

There is a good example of the remaining defence in your *Investigators' Manual*.

Remember that the Misuse of Drugs Regulations 2001 provide for certain people to be exempt from committing offences of possession and supply.

See *Investigators' Manual*, paras 2.2.9 to 2.2.9.3

8.9 Occupiers

Section 8 of the Misuse of Drugs Act 1971 sets out the offence of being the occupier or manager of premises permitting drug misuse. The central elements of the offence are summarised below:

A person commits an offence if,			
being the occupier or concerned in the management of any premises,			
he *knowingly permits* or *suffers* any of the following to take place on the premises			
↓	↓	↓	↓
PRODUCE/ATTEMPT TO PRODUCE A CONTROLLED DRUG	SUPPLY/ATTEMPT TO SUPPLY A CONTROLLED DRUG	PREPARE OPIUM FOR SMOKING	*SMOKE* CANNABIS, CANNABIS RESIN OR PREPARED OPIUM

'Occupier'?

A person is an 'occupier' if, whatever their legal status, they exercised *control*, or had the authority of another, to *exclude persons* from the premises or *prohibit* any activities in s. 8.

Concerned in the Management?

A person is 'concerned in the management' of any premises if they *run* them, *organise* them or *plan* the running of them.

Premises

Not defined by the Act.

Knowingly

The defendant must knowingly permit (wilful blindness may be sufficient, *but not* mere suspicion).

Points to Note

- The smoking cannabis etc. *must have actually taken place*. Merely giving someone permission to smoke cannabis in your house (for example) *would not* qualify.
- An occupier who *permits the growing of cannabis plants* commits the offence.

See *Investigators' Manual*, para. 2.2.11

8.10 Travel Restriction Orders

If a person is *convicted* of a *drug trafficking offence*, then the court has a *duty* to consider whether a Travel Restriction Order (TRO) should be imposed.

Drug Trafficking Offence

For example, production, supplying and importing/exporting a controlled drug. It also includes the incitement of these offences along with aiding, abetting, counselling and procuring the offences.

Points to Note

- Only applicable if the person has been sentenced to *four years or more* in relation to the *drug trafficking offence*.
- The sentence of four years or more must be a single sentence over four years (*not an aggregate*).
- Minimum period for the order is *two years*—there is *no maximum*.
- Prohibits the *offender from* leaving the *United Kingdom*.
- Offender *may be* required to *surrender* their passport as part of the order.
- Begins on *release from custody* (other than on bail or temporary release for a fixed period).

An offender can apply to the *court that made the TRO* to have it revoked or suspended.

Contravening a TRO

This offence is dealt with by s. 36 of the Criminal Justice and Police Act 2001 and is summarised below:

A person who	
Leaves the UK at a time when he/she is prohibited from leaving it by a TRO	who *is not in* the UK at the end of the period during which a prohibition imposed on him/her by a TRO has been suspended
is guilty of an offence	

Points to Note

- *No state of mind is required* to commit the offence.
- There is *no need* for the person to leave the United Kingdom voluntarily. I could kidnap you in Dover, stuff you in the boot of my car and drive to Calais (France) and you would commit this offence!
- The TRO would not stop you being legally deported.

See *Investigators' Manual*, para. 2.2.16

8.11 Police Powers

Section 23 of the Misuse of Drugs Act 1971 sets out a variety of powers available to the police. The full details can be found in your *Investigators' Manual* but a useful summary of the powers in chart format can assist your knowledge and understanding of this area of law.

Note that s. 23 powers are given to a **CONSTABLE = NO UNIFORM REQUIRED!**

Business Premises

A constable (or other person authorised to)
has the power to enter the premises of any person
carrying on business as a
producer or *supplier*
of controlled drugs and
demand the *production of/inspect*
any *books* or *documents* relating to dealings in any such drugs and
inspect any stocks of any such drugs

Searching

If a constable has reasonable grounds for *suspecting*	
that *any* person	
is in *possession* of a controlled drug	
in contravention of this Act or any regulations or orders made under it,	
the constable may	
↓	↓
detain and *search* the *person*	*Stop, detain* and *search* any *vehicle* or *vessel* (includes a hovercraft) in which the constable suspects the drug will be found
↓	↓
and *seize* and *detain anything* found in the course of the search	
which appears to the constable to be *evidence of an offence* under this Act	

Points to Note

- In contravention of the Act etc.—so if possession is *lawful* then the constable *could not* search the person/vehicle.
- The power can be exercised *anywhere*.

Warrants

If a justice of the peace is satisfied by information on oath	
that there is reasonable grounds for *suspecting*	
↓	↓
that *any controlled drugs* are, in contravention of this Act or regulations/orders, in the *possession of a person on any premises*	that *any document* connected to an *offence under this Act in the UK* or corresponding *law outside the UK*, is in the possession of any person on the premises
↓	↓
he/she may grant a warrant authorising any constable	
at any time or times within **ONE MONTH** from the date of the warrant	
to enter, by force if necessary and search the premises/person found therein	
and if there is reasonable grounds for *suspecting* that an offence under the Act has been committed	
seize the drugs and/or document	

Points to Note

- Duration of the warrant is *one month* from the date of issue.
- A 'premises only' warrant *does not* allow the search of persons.
- If a warrant allows the search of persons, it is reasonable to restrict their movement to allow the search to be conducted properly.

See *Investigators' Manual*, para. 2.2.17.1

8.12 Obstruction

The offence of obstruction under s. 23(4) of the Misuse of Drugs Act 1971 is summarised below:

A person commits an offence if he/she		
s. 23(4)(a)	s. 23(4)(b)	s. 23(4)(c)
INTENTIONALLY OBSTRUCTS A PERSON EXERCISING S. 23 POWERS	CONCEALS BOOKS, DOCUMENTS, STOCKS, DRUGS (BUSINESS PREMISES)	FAILS TO PRODUCE BOOKS OR DOCUMENTS WITHOUT REASONABLE EXCUSE (proof of which shall lie on him/her)

Points to Note

- The offence under s. 23(4)(a) can only be committed *intentionally*.
- The offence under s. 23(4)(b) relates to concealing books etc. when a constable is using his/her powers to search *business premises* (see above).
- The offence under s. 23(4)(c) relates to concealing books etc. when a constable is using his/her powers to search *business premises* and also when a *warrant* is executed (see above).

See *Investigators' Manual*, para. 2.2.17.2

8.13 Conclusion

There are a large number of offences and regulations contained within the Misuse of Drugs section in your *Investigators' Manual* and it has not been possible to cover them all in detail in this section of the Workbook. You should remember that this material is, potentially, equally testable as anything you have dealt with. That said, you should now be in a position to answer questions on some of the more common offences and defences and you should have a good understanding of the concept of 'possession'. This knowledge should assist you in your further study of drug-related material.

8.14 Recall Questions

Try and answer the following questions.

- Name three Class A drugs.
- What is cannabis?
- Explain what is required to show 'possession'.

- What groups of people might be exempt from drug offences under the Misuse of Drugs Regulations 2001?
- What are the two defences available under s. 5 of the Misuse of Drugs Act 1971?
- What are the defences available under s. 28 of the Misuse of Drugs Act 1971?
- What offences does s. 28 of the Misuse of Drugs Act 1971 relate to?
- What are the maximum prison sentences for possession of a controlled drug (Classes A, B and C)?
- How could you use evidence recovered in a search of a drug dealer's house to assist you in proving a charge of possession with intent to supply?
- Define the offence of supplying a controlled drug.
- What powers do the police possess under s. 23 of the Misuse of Drugs Act 1971?

8.15 Drug Offence Scenarios

In order to provide you with an opportunity to test your knowledge relating to this material, some scenarios have been produced for you to consider. The scenarios deal with some of the offences and defences you have studied in this section, along with other legislation covered in the *Investigators' Manual*. You should consider each scenario and write down your answer on a piece of paper. The solutions to these scenarios are in the 'Answers Section' at the end of the Workbook.

Scenario Question 1

Mrs GRUNDY suffers from acute arthritic pain. She has heard that using cannabis is a good method for relieving this pain and carries out some research via the internet into the drug. She discovers that she can buy seeds online from a shop and this will enable her to grow cannabis plants at her home. She orders these seeds and when they arrive she keeps them at her home where she is the sole occupant. She knows that cannabis is a controlled drug and that possession of it is illegal.

What offence(s), if any, would Mrs GRUNDY commit and why? (Include any knowledge you have in relation to what cannabis is in your answer.)

Scenario Question 2

After receiving the seeds, Mrs GRUNDY decides to plant them in plant pots. She regularly waters and feeds the plants until they mature into large plants that contain the leaves and flowering tops of the cannabis plant.

What offence(s), if any, would you now consider and why?

Scenario Question 3

Mrs GRUNDY is a non-smoker. She decides that she will make a cake containing the dried leaves from the cannabis plant because she believes that the drug will still work if digested. Again, she is aware that cannabis is a controlled drug. A lifelong friend of hers, Mrs SWAIN, visits Mrs GRUNDY and during her visit Mrs GRUNDY offers her a slice of the cake. Mrs GRUNDY does this because she knows that Mrs SWAIN also suffers from arthritic pain. Mrs SWAIN is unaware of the contents of the cake.

What offence(s), if any, are committed by this activity and why?

Scenario Question 4

COLT lives alone in a flat. A search warrant (under s. 23 of the Misuse of Drugs Act 1971) is executed at his flat just as he is consuming drugs. The police find COLT with a syringe in his hand; the syringe contains Amphetamine Sulphate (a controlled drug). This substance had been prepared for injection.

There is no question about possession, but what class of substance is COLT in possession of?

Scenario Question 5

COLT's flat is searched and a pack of tablets are found. There should be 32 tablets in the pack but five are missing. These tablets are labelled 'MST 50 mg' (Morphine Sulphate Tablets 50 mg in strength and consequently a controlled drug). They are issued against a prescription to Mrs SUSAN COLT, who is COLT's mother. The date the tablets were dispensed is 20 days prior to the search.

What offence(s), if any, does COLT commit and why?

Scenario Question 6

Had COLT taken the tablets directly to his mother after collecting them, would he have a defence to possession of the tablets?

Scenario Question 7

Imagine that you had cause to deal with COLT as he left the chemists with the prescribed morphine tablets for his mother. You carried out a lawful search of his person and discovered the tablets. What authority would you have to enter the chemists and demand that the pharmacist show you records relating to the supply of those drugs to COLT?

Scenario Question 8

You receive specific information that a known drug dealer in your police area is in possession of a pill-making machine that he intends to use to convert amphetamine powder into amphetamine pills. He has only just acquired this machine and has made some enquiries about obtaining the necessary amphetamine powder. You decide to make an application for a search warrant under s. 23 of the Misuse of Drugs Act 1971 to search for and recover the machine.

Would a warrant be granted?

8.16　Multiple-Choice Questions

Answers to these questions can be found in the 'Answers Section' at the end of the book. All explanations also include a reference back to the *Investigators' Manual 2022*.

1. RUSH is at a party being held in the house of a well-known drug dealer. He is speaking to some friends when BALLARD slips several Ecstasy tablets into RUSH's jacket pocket without RUSH's knowledge. A short while later, RUSH leaves the party but, as he walks out of the front door, the police raid the premises and RUSH is detained by PC YOUNG. PC YOUNG searches RUSH under the powers granted by s. 23(2) of the Misuse of Drugs Act 1971 and finds the Ecstasy tablets in RUSH's outer jacket pocket. RUSH says, *'That's not mine, I've never seen those pills before!'*

Considering the concept of 'possession' alone, which of the following statements is correct?

A You do not have to show anything other than the fact that RUSH had the drugs in his physical control.

B To prove possession, you need to show that RUSH had the Ecstasy in his custody or control and that he knew of its presence.

C Custody or control is not required to prove possession, but knowledge of the drug's presence is.

D You would need to show that RUSH had physical control of the drug, along with the facts that he knew of its presence and that it was a controlled drug.

Answer _____

2. DC WALLIS (an undercover police officer) has arranged to meet GARWOOD outside a pub to buy £500 worth of cocaine from him. GARWOOD drives in to the pub car park and as he gets out of his car he is arrested by DC WALLIS for an offence of possession of a controlled drug with intent to supply. GARWOOD is searched and a large amount of drugs paraphernalia is found in his possession (clingfilm, paper, scales and contact details). In GARWOOD's pocket is £6,000 in cash and a large amount of cocaine. Later investigation of GARWOOD's financial status reveals a large amount of unexplained wealth in his bank account.

In relation to the offence of possession with intent to supply (contrary to s. 5(3) of the Misuse of Drugs Act 1971), which of the following statements is correct?

A Possession with intent to supply a controlled drug to an undercover police officer would not amount to an offence under this section.

B Possession of the drugs paraphernalia (clingfilm, paper, scales and contact details) can be used to prove the offence of possession with intent to supply.

C In proving an offence of possession with intent to supply, the prosecution can adduce evidence of GARWOOD's unexplained wealth.

D The presence of large sums of money with the seized drugs cannot be used to prove an intention to supply a controlled drug.

Answer _____

3. DAWSON is convicted of an offence of supplying a controlled drug (contrary to s. 4(3) of the Misuse of Drugs Act 1971).

Which of the following comments is correct with regard to the imposition of a Travel Restriction Order on DAWSON under the Criminal Justice and Police Act 2001?

A If an order is made, it will last for a minimum period of three years.

B DAWSON could not be subject to such an order as he has not committed an offence involving the importation/exportation of a controlled drug.

C An order can be made but only if DAWSON is sentenced to more than four years' imprisonment.

D If an order is made against DAWSON, it cannot be suspended in any circumstances.

Answer _____

4. MALLINGTHORPE has been arrested for an offence of possession with intent to supply a controlled drug (contrary to s. 5(3) of the Misuse of Drugs Act 1971). The drug MALLINGTHORPE was arrested in connection with is cocaine. MALLINGTHORPE is interviewed regarding the offence by DC ROMLEY and TI OWEN. During the interview, MALLINGTHORPE informs the officers that he was not intending to supply the cocaine but had found it in the street and had every intention of handing it over to a police officer as soon as he could but was arrested before he could do so. MALLINGTHORPE states that if he is charged with the offence of possession with intent to supply the drug, he will be relying on the defence afforded to him under s. 5(4) of the Misuse of Drugs Act 1971.

Which of the following comments is correct?

A MALLINGTHORPE would be unable to utilise the defence as it is only available to an individual charged with an offence where the drug involved is cannabis or cannabis resin.

B MALLINGTHORPE would be unable to utilise the defence as s. 5(4) only provides a defence to an offence of production of a controlled drug.

C MALLINGTHORPE would be unable to utilise the defence as he has been arrested for an offence involving a Class A drug and the defence can only be used when the charge relates to a Class C or B drug.

D MALLINGTHORPE would be unable to utilise the defence as s. 5(4) only provides a defence to an offence of unlawful possession of a controlled drug.

Answer _____

9 Firearms and Gun Crime

9.1 Introduction

At this stage of your study, you should have read the 'Firearms' section of your Manual and you will be aware that this contains some lengthy and complicated lists of what constitutes a certain type of firearm. One approach to simplifying matters (although this is not guaranteed to be successful all of the time) is to examine the exceptions rather than the rule and you will see this approach adopted in part of this section of the Workbook. The section concentrates on the criminal use of firearms as this is a particularly relevant area of law for the NIE.

9.2 Aim

The aim of this section is to supply you with an overview of offences relating to the criminal use of firearms.

9.3 Objectives

At the end of this section you should be able to:

1. Explain what a firearm is under s. 57 of the Firearms Act 1968.
2. Identify when an offence under s. 16 of the Firearms Act 1968 (possession with intent to endanger life) has been committed.
3. Point out relevant issues in an offence under s. 16A of the Firearms Act 1968 (possession with intent to cause fear of violence).
4. Outline the offence under s. 17(1) of the Firearms Act 1968 (using a firearm to resist arrest).
5. Point out relevant issues in an offence under s. 17(2) of the Firearms Act 1968 (possessing a firearm while committing or being arrested for a Schedule 1 offence).
6. Outline the offence under s. 18(1) of the Firearms Act 1968 (having a firearm with intent to commit an indictable offence or resist arrest).
7. Define the offence of having a firearm in a public place contrary to s. 19 of the Firearms Act 1968.
8. Identify when a convicted person can possess a firearm.
9. State the police powers under s. 47 of the Firearms Act 1968.
10. Apply your knowledge to multiple-choice questions.

9.4   Firearm

In order to understand offences relating to the criminal use of firearms, you must be able to understand what a firearm actually is. The definition of a firearm is provided by s. 57 of the Firearms Act 1968.

9.4.1   Exercise—What is a Firearm?

Write down what you can remember about the definition of the word 'firearm'.

Use the information you have just written down to help you decide whether the following items would, could or would not be classed as a 'firearm' for the purposes of s. 57 of the Firearms Act 1968. Place a mark in the box you consider to be appropriate.

Description	Would	Could	Would Not
A telescopic sight			
An imitation revolver			
A signalling pistol			
A silencer			
A flash eliminator			
A prohibited weapon			

EXPLANATION 9.4.1

What is a Firearm?

Let's begin with the definition of the word 'firearm' under s. 57(1) of the Firearms Act 1968. A 'firearm' can be any of the following four things:

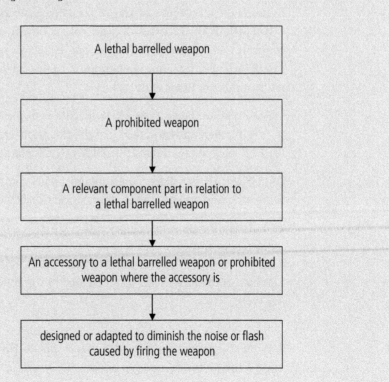

A lethal barrelled weapon

↓

A prohibited weapon

↓

A relevant component part in relation to a lethal barrelled weapon

↓

An accessory to a lethal barrelled weapon or prohibited weapon where the accessory is

↓

designed or adapted to diminish the noise or flash caused by firing the weapon

Description	Would	Could	Would Not
A telescopic sight			×
An imitation revolver*		×	
A signalling pistol*		×	
A silencer		×	
A flash eliminator		×	
A prohibited weapon	×		

You probably mentioned the fact that a firearm is a 'lethal barrelled weapon', but did you know the other parts of the definition? Depending on how much you remembered, it would obviously affect your decisions in the table. Your finished table should have looked as that shown previously.

The items marked with an asterisk (*) have all been held to be lethal barrelled weapons but this will not always be the case. This is one of those areas of the law where it is better to make a presumption in favour of the item being a 'firearm'. Rather than trying to remember what a firearm *is*, it might be easier to remember what a firearm *is not*. A firearm is not:

- a telescopic sight; or

- a silencer or flash eliminator *on its own*.

You should examine your *Investigators' Manual* to develop your knowledge of the terms 'lethal barrelled', 'component parts' and 'accessories'.
See *Investigators' Manual*, para. 2.3.2.1

9.5 Possession with Intent to Endanger Life

9.5.1 Exercise—HALLORAHAN Scenario

Examine the following scenario and provide answers where requested.

HALLORAHAN discovers that his wife is having an affair with COURT and decides to confront COURT to sort the matter out. He places several items into his car and drives to COURT's house, intending to kill him if COURT does not finish the affair. HALLORAHAN has a number of items with him:

i. an imitation firearm (an AK-47 machine gun) in the boot of his car;
ii. a 9 mm Beretta pistol, held in a shoulder holster worn by HALLORAHAN; and
iii. a 12-gauge shotgun that HALLORAHAN has placed on the front passenger seat of his car.

HALLORAHAN has placed the shotgun in his car, intending to get his friend, JAGO, to come with him and use the shotgun to kill COURT.

1. Which of the three items does HALLORAHAN have in his 'possession'?

2. Which of the three items could be used to commit an offence under s. 16 of the Firearms Act 1968?

3. What is your opinion of the fact that HALLORAHAN has brought the shotgun, intending to get a friend he has not even approached yet to use it to kill COURT?

4. HALLORAHAN is obviously not going to kill COURT if he finishes the affair with HALLORAHAN's wife. How would this affect the offence?

HALLORAHAN gets to JAGO's house but he is not in. He drives to COURT's house but as he pulls onto COURT's drive, COURT sees him and runs away before HALLORAHAN even gets out of his car.

5. COURT has not been injured. Does this make a difference to whether the offence has been committed or not?

Yes / No

HALLORAHAN decides he has had enough and takes out the Beretta pistol, intending to kill himself with the firearm.

6. What does the law say with regard to the life endangered being that of the defendant?

---

7. At what point of this scenario, if at all, does HALLORAHAN first commit the offence under s. 16 of the Act?

EXPLANATION 9.5.1

HALLORAHAN Scenario

1. The term 'possession' does not require HALLORAHAN to have actual physical possession of the items. Therefore, HALLORAHAN has possession of all three items. Possession does not even require the knowledge of the existence of the firearm and as long as the defendant knows that they have *something* then that is enough. However, in order to commit an offence under s. 16, the firearm *must be* the means by which life is endangered and you can hardly endanger life with something that you do not know exists.

2. The Beretta pistol and the shotgun. You cannot commit this offence with an imitation firearm because life *cannot be* endangered with a *fake* firearm. An imitation firearm for the purposes of the criminal use of firearms offences (ss. 16, 16A, 17(1), 17(2) and 18(1)) is anything that has the appearance of a firearm (but not fingers!).

3. The offence is complete if a person has a firearm in his/her possession with intent to enable another to endanger life. It does not matter that JAGO has not been approached and it would not matter if he was and he refused. *This is an offence of intent.*

4. This would be a conditional threat, but that would not alter the fact that the offence has been committed (*R v Bentham* [1973] QB 357). *This is an offence of intent.*

5. It does not. *This is an offence of intent.*

6. The life endangered must be the life of another and not the defendant's.

7. At the beginning of the scenario, when he has the guns (the Beretta and the shotgun) in his possession with intent to kill COURT.

See *Investigators' Manual*, para. 2.3.11.1

9.6 Possession with Intent to Cause Fear of Violence

9.6.1 Exercise—GILBERT Scenario

Consider the offence of possession with intent to cause fear of violence as you read the following scenario. When you have finished reading, complete the tasks that follow the scenario.

HANSON is continually having parties in his garden and this is disturbing GILBERT (HANSON's neighbour), who finds the noise unbearable. One night, GILBERT decides he is going to do something about the problem. He knows that HANSON is a violent individual and he will need to protect himself in some way before confronting him, so he puts an imitation firearm, which has the appearance of a Walther PPK pistol, in his jacket pocket. GILBERT goes round to HANSON's house and knocks on the door. Moments later the door is answered by HANSON's girlfriend, KILNER. As it is KILNER and not HANSON who has answered the door, GILBERT does not produce the imitation firearm. Instead, and intending to make KILNER fear that violence will be used against HANSON, he says to KILNER, *'Turn the music down or I'll break your boyfriend's arm!'* KILNER does not believe GILBERT and tells him to go away before slamming the door in his face.

1. Think of the offence under s. 16A only. You should be able to identify four issues from this scenario that will affect your decision in deciding whether or not an offence has been committed. What are they?

i. _____

_____

ii. _____

_____

iii. _____

_____

iv. _____

_____

2. Take each issue that you have identified in turn and state what effect it has regarding the offence.

i. _____

_____

ii. _____

_____

iii. _____

_____

iv. _____

_____

3. What is your conclusion regarding the scenario?

_____

EXPLANATION 9.6.1

GILBERT Scenario

1. You should have identified the following issues from the scenario:

i. GILBERT has possession of an imitation firearm. Does this offence apply to imitation firearms?

ii. The threat of violence is delivered to KILNER. Can the intention to cause fear of violence be delivered to a third party who would not be subject to violence if the threat were carried out?

iii. The imitation firearm was not produced or used to make the threat. Would this have any effect regarding this offence?

iv. KILNER did not believe GILBERT's threat. Does the fact that the person who receives the threat does not believe it make any difference?

2. Dealing with each issue in turn, you should have arrived at similar answers to those which follow:

i. The offence can be committed, as it applies to imitation firearms as well as firearms.

ii. The partial intention of the defendant must be to cause *any* person to believe that unlawful violence will be used against them *or another person*. The threat against HANSON can be delivered to KILNER.

iii. While the firearm need not be produced or shown to anyone, the firearm or imitation must be the means for the threat. Possession of a firearm while making a general threat to someone who does not know of its presence (KILNER) is unlikely to fall within this section.

iv. This is an offence of intention. Whether KILNER believes GILBERT is immaterial.

3. This information should lead you to the conclusion that GILBERT has not committed the offence under s. 16A of the Act.

See *Investigators' Manual*, para. 2.3.11.2

9.7 Using a Firearm to Resist Arrest

9.7.1 Exercise—Using a Firearm to Resist Arrest True or False?

Look at the following statements and decide whether they are true or false.

1. Using an imitation firearm as a means to resist arrest would constitute an offence under this section.
True / False

2. This offence requires proof of 'possession' of the firearm.
True / False

3. This offence requires proof that the defendant made some actual use of a firearm to resist arrest.
True / False

4. DC SMITH is in the process of arresting NAYLOR for an offence of theft when his friend, BARKER, approaches the officer and points a silencer at him. She tells DC SMITH to let NAYLOR go. BARKER commits the offence under s. 17(1).
True / False

EXPLANATION 9.7.1

Using a Firearm to Resist Arrest True or False?

1. True. However, the imitation firearm *must* be complete. Using imitation component parts to resist arrest would not constitute an offence.

2. False.

3. True. Proof of possession is not required, but proof of some use of a firearm or imitation firearm to resist arrest is.

4. False. Remember that a silencer *on its own* is not a firearm.

See *Investigators' Manual*, para. 2.3.11.3

9.8 Possessing a Firearm While Committing or Being Arrested for a Schedule 1 Offence

This offence sometimes causes difficulty because of the problems associated with identifying what a Schedule 1 offence is. The ACTOR mnemonic in your *Investigators' Manual* might help you remember what is included.

9.8.1 Exercise—CAPE Scenario

Consider the following circumstances. Identify and deal with the key issues as they occur in the scenario.

NORWOOD owes £2,000 to CAPE but has refused to pay back the money he owes on several occasions. CAPE has lost patience with NORWOOD and drives to NORWOOD's house to get the money. CAPE has an imitation Browning pistol in the glove box of his car which he considers using to threaten NORWOOD with, but then decides he does not need to and leaves it in his car which he parks outside NORWOOD's house. He knocks at the door, which is opened by NORWOOD's wife moments later. As soon as the door is opened, CAPE says, *'Give me some cash or you'll get a beating!'* NORWOOD's wife has no idea who CAPE is or that her husband owes him money and, thinking she is being robbed, she hands over £500 from her purse. CAPE, who believes that he has a right in law to the money and thinks he is doing nothing wrong, gets back into his car and drives off, but not before NORWOOD's wife writes down his registration number. Mrs NORWOOD reports the incident as a robbery.

1. Think of the offence under s. 17(2) only. You should be able to identify four issues from this scenario that will affect your decision in deciding whether or not an offence has been committed. What are they?

i. _____

ii. _____

iii. _____

iv. _____

2. Take each issue that you have identified in turn and state what effect it has regarding the offence.

i. _____

ii. _____

iii. _____

iv. _____

3. What is your conclusion regarding the scenario so far?

_____

Police enquiries trace CAPE through the registration number of his car. The police attend CAPE's house and arrest him for the offence of robbery. CAPE's house is searched and the imitation Browning pistol is found in CAPE's bedroom.

4. Think of this part of the scenario in isolation. Has CAPE committed the offence under s. 17(2)? Yes / No

CAPE is charged with robbery and possession of a firearm whilst being arrested for a Schedule 1 offence and pleads not guilty to both offences. At his trial, he is found not guilty of the robbery because there was no theft (belief in a right in law, s. 2(1)(a) of the Theft Act 1968).

5. What effect will the finding of 'not guilty' have with regard to the charge of possessing a firearm while committing a Schedule 1 offence?

EXPLANATION 9.8.1

CAPE Scenario

1. You should have identified the following issues from the scenario:

    i. CAPE has an imitation firearm. Can the offence be committed with an imitation firearm?

    ii. CAPE leaves the imitation firearm in the glove box of his car. Does this qualify as 'possession'?

    iii. The offence that Mrs NORWOOD believes has been committed is one of robbery. Is robbery a Schedule 1 offence?

    iv. CAPE believes he has a legal right to the money and has done nothing wrong. Is this a robbery?

2. Dealing with each issue in turn, you should have arrived at similar answers to those which follow:

    i. This offence can be committed with an imitation firearm (imitation in the general sense).

    ii. Remember that possession is wide and that you do not have to prove that CAPE actually had the imitation firearm with him. In his car a short distance away would constitute possession.

    iii. Robbery is a Schedule 1 offence (coming under the T of ACTOR as 'Abduction, Criminal Damage, Theft, Offences Against the Person, Rape and other sexual offences).

    iv. This is an important point. CAPE has not committed a robbery because there is no theft.

3. If there is no dishonesty, there is no theft. If there is no theft, there is no robbery. If a robbery has not been committed, CAPE cannot commit the offence under s. 17(2). He needs to have a firearm/imitation firearm in his possession at the time of committing a Schedule 1 offence and he clearly has not committed a Schedule 1 offence.

4. The imitation firearm is in CAPE's possession and he has been arrested for a Schedule 1 offence; therefore, he commits the offence under s. 17(2). You might be confused as to how this can be if he has not actually committed the robbery and that is understandable. If it helps, think of the 'arrest' as a neutral part of the proceedings and ask 'Has CAPE been arrested for a Schedule 1 offence?' The answer is 'Yes'. Whereas the answer to 'Has CAPE actually committed a Schedule 1 offence?' is 'No'.

5. In light of the explanation at 4, you should realise that the finding of 'not guilty' will not affect the charge under s. 17(2).

See *Investigators' Manual*, para. 2.3.11.5

9.9 Having a Firearm with Intent to Commit an Indictable Offence or Resist Arrest

9.9.1 Exercise—SALISBURY Scenario

Read the following scenario and answer the questions based on its circumstances.

SALISBURY is planning to rob a Post Office in a small village. He drives into the village and parks a short distance from the Post Office. SALISBURY has a 9 mm Beretta pistol hidden underneath the front driver's seat of his car but he does not intend to use it during the course of the robbery as his primary reason for having the pistol is to protect himself. SALISBURY begins walking towards the Post Office, but is arrested by the police who have been tipped-off about his plan.

Has SALISBURY committed the offence under s. 18(1)?

Yes / No

Why / Why not?

EXPLANATION 9.9.1

SALISBURY Scenario

SALISBURY commits the offence. The fact that he has a firearm (or imitation firearm) with him when intending to commit an indictable offence is all that is required. There does not have to be a connection between the firearm and the indictable offence the defendant is intending to commit.

The second part of the offence deals with the defendant resisting arrest or preventing the arrest of another.

Examine the following scenario then attempt Exercise 9.9.2 (AIDEY Scenario).

PC LEY approaches AIDEY, who is trespassing on private land with a loaded shotgun in his possession. PC LEY arrests AIDEY for the offence of trespassing on land with a firearm under s. 20(2) of the Act, but AIDEY points the shotgun at the officer and says, *'You're not arresting me, mate.'*

9.9.2 Exercise—AIDEY Scenario

Consider the circumstances regarding PC LEY and AIDEY.

Would AIDEY commit an offence under s. 18?

Yes / No

Why / Why not?

EXPLANATION 9.9.2

AIDEY Scenario

AIDEY would commit this offence. AIDEY has actually made use of the firearm but, as has already been mentioned, this is not necessary. All that is required is that he has the firearm with him.

See *Investigators' Manual*, para. 2.3.11.4

The offences under ss. 16, 16A, 17(1), 17(2) and 18 are summarised in the chart on the next page.

Criminal Use of Firearms—Summary Chart

SECTION	S. 16	S. 16A	S. 17(2)	S. 18(1)	S. 17(1)
OFFENCE	Possession W/I to Endanger Life	Possession W/I to Cause Fear of Violence	Possession Arrested/Committing Sch 1. Offence	Have Firearm W/I to Commit Indictable Offence/Resist Arrest	Using Firearm to Resist Arrest
ACTION?	→ Possession	→	→	→ 'Readily accessible'	→ Make or attempt to make any use
WHAT WITH?	→ Firearm/Ammunition	→ Firearm/Imitation Firearm	→	→ Firearm/Imitation Firearm	→ Firearm/Imitation Firearm (not component parts/silencer/flash eliminator)
WHY?	Intent by means thereof to endanger life/enable another to endanger life	Intent by means thereof to cause another to believe unlawful violence will be used against him or another	When committing or arrested for ACTOR	Intent to commit indictable offence or resist arrest or prevent arrest of another. Arrest/detention can be UNLAWFUL	Resist/prevent arrest or detention of himself or another. Arrest must be LAWFUL

9.10 Having a Firearm/Imitation Firearm in a Public Place

9.10.1 Exercise—Defining the Offence

Write down as much of the definition of this offence as you can.

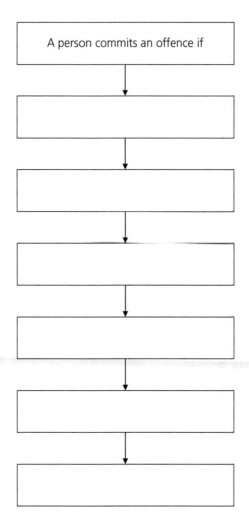

EXPLANATION 9.10.1

Defining the Offence

Your answer should have contained the following detail:

This is an 'absolute' offence and it does not matter if the person does not know that they actually have a firearm with them.

Try remembering it by using the mnemonic FAIL.

F Firearm together with ammo for it

A Air weapon

I Imitation firearm

L Loaded shotgun

Absolute failure in a public place is not allowed without lawful authority or reasonable excuse.

See *Investigators' Manual*, para. 2.3.12.1

9.11 Trespassing with Firearms

The law dealing with trespassing with a firearms in a building or on land contains similar elements—you can see these in the chart below:

Trespassing with Firearms,
ss. 20(1) and 20(2) Firearms Act 1968
A person commits an offence if,
while he has a firearm or imitation firearm with him,
he enters or is

↓   ↓

in any building or part of a building as a trespasser (s. 20(1))   on any land as a trespasser (s. 20(2))

↓   ↓

and without reasonable excuse (the proof whereof lies on him).

Points to Note

- Land includes land covered with water.
- You *do not need* to have entered as a trespasser to commit the offence. Simply *being* in the building/on the land as a trespasser with a firearm/imitation firearm is enough—that is the case even if you were not a trespasser when you originally entered or you did not have the firearm/imitation firearm with you when you originally entered the building/land (you came by it later).

EXAMPLE

You are in my house with my permission and you have an air pistol with you. We have an argument and I tell you to 'get out' as I do not want you in my house any more. That means you are a trespasser (I have removed your right to be in my house) and you have a firearm with you—you commit this offence.

9.12 Possession of Firearms by Convicted Persons

9.12.1 Exercise—How Long?

How long, if at all, would the named person be prohibited from possessing a firearm and (if there is a period of disqualification) when would it begin from?

RIPLEY was sentenced to 12 months' imprisonment for theft, but only served six months of her sentence.

Period:
Run from:
MATHER was sentenced to four months' imprisonment for assault, but was released after serving two months' imprisonment.

Period:
Run from:
GREGSON was sentenced to three years' imprisonment for robbery and served two years.

Period:
Run from:
FENNA was sentenced to 10 years' imprisonment for a s. 18 wounding. He served his full sentence.

Period:

Run from:

DOLAN was sentenced to five years' imprisonment for fraud and served three years.

Period:

Run from:

EXPLANATION 9.12.1

How Long?

Look at the following list and see if this assists you.

three years or more = banned for life

three months up to three years = banned for five years

Whatever the period of disqualification is, it begins on the day of release

$3 \times 3 = 5$

See *Investigators' Manual*, para. 2.3.14

9.13 Police Powers (s. 47)

9.13.1 Exercise—Considering Police Powers

Consider the following scenarios and decide what course of action is open to the named police officer under s. 47 of the Firearms Act 1968.

1. PC TRENT is on uniform patrol in a public place when she sees LINGUARD walking towards her carrying a shotgun. The shotgun is loaded.
Can PC TRENT require LINGUARD to hand over the shotgun for examination?
Yes / No

2. PC TRENT is on uniform patrol in a public place when she sees LINGUARD walking towards her carrying a shotgun. The shotgun is not loaded.
Can PC TRENT require LINGUARD to hand over the shotgun for examination?
Yes / No

3. PC TRENT is on uniform patrol in a public place when she sees LINGUARD walking towards her carrying a shotgun.
Can PC TRENT detain and search LINGUARD in the exercise of her powers under s. 47 of the Act?
Yes / No

4. PC TRENT is on uniform patrol in a public place when she sees LINGUARD walking towards her carrying a shotgun. LINGUARD gets into a Ford Escort car that begins to drive towards the officer.
Can PC TRENT stop and search the vehicle under s. 47 of the Act?
Yes / No

5. PC TRENT is on uniform patrol when she is called to a private school's playing fields where LINGUARD is shooting rabbits with a shotgun. LINGUARD is a trespasser.
Can PC TRENT require LINGUARD to hand over the shotgun?
Yes / No

6. PC TRENT is on uniform patrol when she is called to a house where there has been a report of a suspicious person in a private garden. When she arrives, she sees LINGUARD cleaning his shotgun in the garden, which turns out to be his property. The call was made in good faith but was incorrect.

Can PC TRENT require LINGUARD to hand over the shotgun?

Yes / No

7. DC PARKER (dressed in plain clothes) is taking a witness statement from JONES when he sees KITSON walking down the street outside JONES's house with a shotgun. The shotgun is not loaded.

Can DC PARKER require KITSON to hand over the shotgun?

Yes / No

What will happen if KITSON says 'No'?

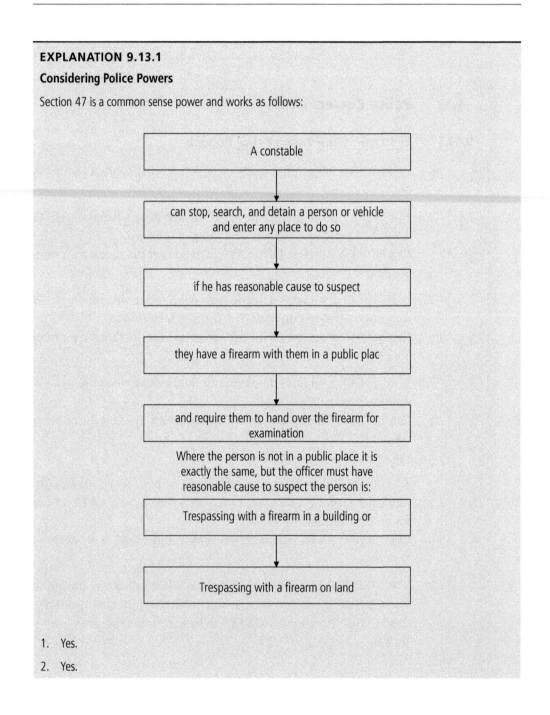

EXPLANATION 9.13.1

Considering Police Powers

Section 47 is a common sense power and works as follows:

A constable

↓

can stop, search, and detain a person or vehicle and enter any place to do so

↓

if he has reasonable cause to suspect

↓

they have a firearm with them in a public plac

↓

and require them to hand over the firearm for examination

Where the person is not in a public place it is exactly the same, but the officer must have reasonable cause to suspect the person is:

Trespassing with a firearm in a building or

↓

Trespassing with a firearm on land

1. Yes.

2. Yes.

3. Yes.

4. Yes.

5. Yes.

6. No.

7. Yes. If KITSON says 'No' a summary offence is committed.

See *Investigators' Manual*, para. 2.3.13

9.14 Conclusion

This part of the Workbook has sought to provide you with an understanding of offences relating to the criminal use of firearms, as well as some associated subjects. You should be aware that there are a number of firearms issues that can only be addressed by reading the appropriate section in your *Investigators' Manual*.

9.15 Recall Questions

Try and answer the following questions.

- What is NOT a firearm?
- Explain when a silencer could be classed as a firearm.
- What is an imitation firearm?
- What is the only offence that you have studied in this section where the offence cannot be committed with an imitation firearm?
- Can fingers be an imitation firearm?
- What does the term 'possession' mean?
- What are the two offences that deal with firearms and resisting arrest?
- What differences are there between the two offences?
- Outline the offence of possession of a firearm with intent to endanger life.
- What does the mnemonic ACTOR stand for?
- What does the mnemonic FAIL stand for?
- What does 3 × 3 equal and why?
- What are your powers under s. 47 of the Firearms Act 1968?

9.16 Multiple-Choice Questions

Answers to these questions can be found in the 'Answers Section' at the end of the book. All explanations also include a reference back to the *Investigators' Manual 2022*.

1. ROBE is a drug dealer and he is becoming concerned that KNIGHT, a rival dealer, is taking over his area. ROBE drives around looking for KNIGHT in order to warn him off. He sees KNIGHT dealing drugs on a street corner and loses his temper because KNIGHT is dealing in his area again. ROBE drives his car towards KNIGHT, intending to kill him by running him over. KNIGHT manages to jump out of the way and is uninjured, but ROBE loses control of his car and it crashes into a wall. When the police arrive, they find ROBE

unconscious in his car. They search his car and find a revolver hidden in the glove box of the car.

Does ROBE commit the offence of possession of a firearm with intent to endanger life (contrary to s. 16 of the Firearms Act 1968)?

A No, the firearm was not the means by which KNIGHT's life was endangered.

B Yes, he had possession of a firearm at the time of endangering KNIGHT's life.

C No, because KNIGHT was uninjured as a result of the attack.

D Yes, as there is no need for the firearm to be produced or shown to KNIGHT.

Answer _____

2. MOSELEY is visiting his friend CHAMBERS. CHAMBERS asks MOSELEY if, on his way home, he will be passing 'The Swan' pub. When MOSELEY states that he will be, CHAMBERS asks MOSELEY to drop a package containing several fishing rods off to the licensee of 'The Swan', KILBURN. MOSELEY agrees and takes the package, which actually contains an unloaded shotgun. On his way to the pub, MOSELEY is stopped by PC FRENCH and the contents of the package are discovered.

Considering the offence under s. 19 of the Firearms Act only (having a firearm/imitation firearm in a public place), which of the following comments is correct?

A This offence is 'absolute' and MOSELEY's possession of the unloaded shotgun is all that is required.

B MOSELEY would not commit the offence because the shotgun is unloaded.

C An offence under s. 19 cannot be committed by being in possession of a shotgun, loaded or unloaded.

D The offence is not committed because MOSELEY had no knowledge that the package actually contained a firearm.

Answer _____

3. FOULGER is planning to burgle an office on an industrial estate and as part of his plan he drives to the road where the office is situated, parks his car and walks toward the office to make a note of the security arrangements that are in place. FOULGER always carries a Magnum 44 firearm when he is out of his house and this occasion is no exception. The gun is tucked into his trousers with FOULGER's T-shirt pulled over the top of the firearm. The gun is not loaded. FOULGER walks around the office on the pavement making notes as he does so, but a member of staff at the office becomes suspicious of FOULGER's behaviour and calls the police. PC NASH attends the scene and stops FOULGER in the street. The officer notices the shape of the firearm underneath FOULGER's clothing.

Considering PC NASH's powers under s. 47 of the Firearms Act 1968, which of the following comments is correct?

A If PC NASH has reasonable cause to suspect that FOULGER has a firearm with him in a public place, he may require him to hand over the firearm.

B PC NASH can only use his powers under s. 47 of the Act if he reasonably believes that FOULGER has a firearm in a public place.

C PC NASH can only require the firearm to be handed over if he reasonably suspects it is loaded or reasonably suspects FOULGER has ammunition for the firearm in his possession.

D PC NASH cannot request that the firearm be handed over unless he reasonably suspects that FOULGER is committing or about to commit a relevant offence for the purposes of this section.

Answer _____

4. NORTH and ZULFIKAR are neighbours who do not like each other. They have had several arguments about the noise NORTH makes when playing music. One afternoon NORTH is sitting on his front lawn with the doors and windows of his house wide open so that he can hear his music. ZULFIKAR arrives home from work and, on seeing NORTH and hearing the music, he decides that he has had enough. He grabs hold of a leather case for an air rifle that he has in his car (the case has nothing in it as the air rifle is in ZULFIKAR's house but it looks as if an air rifle is contained inside it and the words 'Air Rifle' are printed on the case) and approaches NORTH. Intending to make NORTH fear that violence will be used against him, he holds the empty case out and says *'You know what is in here. If you don't turn that music off, I'll use this air rifle on you!'* NORTH laughs at ZULFIKAR as he does not believe that ZULFIKAR will do anything to him.

Considering the offence under s. 16A of the Firearms Act 1968 only, which of the following comments is correct?

A The offence is not committed because NORTH does not believe that ZULFIKAR will use violence against him.

B ZULFIKAR commits the offence in these circumstances.

C The offence is not committed because there is nothing in the leather case that ZULFIKAR has in his possession.

D The offence is not committed as although the empty case is an imitation firearm, this offence can only be committed using a firearm.

Answer _____

10 Racially and Religiously Aggravated Offences

10.1 Introduction

The law in relation to racially and religiously aggravated offences can be the subject of questions in its own right but perhaps more importantly it can form part of multiple-choice questions based on the offences that can be racially or religiously aggravated.

10.2 Aim

The aim of this section is to provide you with an understanding of the legislation in relation to racially and religiously aggravated offences.

10.3 Objectives

At the end of this section you should be able to:

1. List the offences that can become racially or religiously aggravated under ss. 28 to 32 of the Crime and Disorder Act 1998.
2. Identify the central elements of a racially aggravated offence.
3. Identify who is covered by s. 28 of the Crime and Disorder Act 1998.
4. Apply your knowledge to multiple-choice questions.

10.4 Racially and Religiously Aggravated Offences

For the purposes of your examination, there are three questions to ask when deciding whether an offence is racially or religiously aggravated.

10.4.1 Question 1

Is the offence capable of being racially or religiously aggravated?

One of the most common errors that students make when considering what a racially or religiously aggravated offence is, is to confuse the definition of what makes an offence racially or religiously aggravated (under s. 28 of the Crime and Disorder Act 1998) with the definition of a *racist incident* (as per the Stephen Lawrence enquiry). A *racist incident* is 'any incident which is perceived to be racist by the victim or any other person'. This definition can be applied to any offence or, indeed, any incident and is entirely unrelated to that under s. 28 of the Act.

The purpose of this legislation is to provide the court with the ability to sentence offenders to a lengthier term of imprisonment thus reflecting the serious nature of the racially or religiously aggravating factors of the offence.

10.4.2   Exercise—Offences That Are Covered

There are four broad categories of offence that can be racially or religiously aggravated under the Crime and Disorder Act 1998. What are they?

1. _____

2. _____

3. _____

4. _____

EXPLANATION 10.4.2

Offences That Are Covered

Your answer may have looked something like this:

1. Assaults.

2. Criminal damage.

3. Public order offences.

4. Harassment.

One way to remember this is with the mnemonic CHAP.

C	Criminal damage
H	Harassment
A	Assaults
P	Public order offences

You now need to identify what *particular* offences within those headings are subject to the legislation.

10.4.3   Exercise—Be More Precise

What particular offences are capable of being racially or religiously aggravated under the Crime and Disorder Act?

Criminal damage

1. _____

Harassment

1. _____

2. _____

3. _____

4. _____

Assault

1. _____

2. _____

3. _____

Public order offences

1. _____

2. _____

3. _____

Remember that you cannot get longer than 'life' so aggravated criminal damage (s. 1(2) of the Criminal Damage Act 1971) and s. 18 wounding (Offences Against the Person Act 1861) will never be racially or religiously aggravated in terms of increasing the sentence available.

EXPLANATION 10.4.3

Be More Precise

Your answer should have looked like this:

Criminal damage

1. 'Simple' criminal damage (s. 1(1) of the Criminal Damage Act 1971).

Harassment

1. Harassment (s. 2 of the Protection from Harassment Act 1997).

2. Putting people in fear of violence (s. 4 of the Protection from Harassment Act 1997).

3. Stalking (s. 2A of the Protection from Harassment Act 1997).

4. Stalking involving fear of violence or serious alarm or distress (s. 4A of the Protection from Harassment Act 1997).

Assaults

1. Common assault (s. 39 of the Criminal Justice Act 1988).

2. Actual bodily harm (s. 47 of the Offences Against the Person Act 1861).

3. Wounding or grievous bodily harm (s. 20 of the Offences Against the Person Act 1861).

Public order offences (note that these three offences *are not on your syllabus* but are correctly mentioned in the Manual when discussing this topic)

1. Causing fear or provocation of violence (s. 4 of the Public Order Act 1986).

2. Intentional harassment, alarm or distress (s. 4A of the Public Order Act 1986).

3. Causing harassment, alarm or distress (s. 5 of the Public Order Act 1986).

Another way of comprehending the offences that are covered and the connection to the CHAP mnemonic would be to use the chart below:

C	'Simple' Criminal Damage (s. 1(1) of the Criminal Damage Act 1971)			
H	Harassment (s. 2 of the Protection from Harassment Act 1997)	Stalking (s. 2A of the Protection from Harassment Act 1997)	Putting people in fear of violence (s. 4 of the Protection from Harassment Act 1997)	Stalking involving fear of violence or serious alarm or distress (s. 4A of the Protection from Harassment Act 1997)
A	Common Assault (s. 39 of the Criminal Justice Act 1988)	ABH (s. 47 of the Offences Against the Person Act 1861)	Wounding/GBH (s. 20 of the Offences Against the Person Act 1861)	
P	Causing fear or provocation of violence (s. 4 of the Public Order Act 1986)	Intentional harassment, alarm or distress (s. 4A of the Public Order Act 1986)	Causing harassment, alarm or distress (s. 5 of the Public Order Act 1986)	

10.4.4 Question 2

Let us say that the offence you are being questioned on is one of the offences that is capable of being racially or religiously aggravated.

Are all of the elements of the offence present?

You do not need to concern yourself with the public order offences as they are not on your syllabus but all the other offences are. You must consider if all of the relevant elements of the offence are present. For example, in a criminal damage matter, is the property concerned 'property' for the purposes of the Criminal Damage Act 1971? If the defendant has not committed the basic offence, then it does not matter what he/she has said or done; the offence *cannot be* racially or religiously aggravated.

10.4.5 Question 3

Let us presume that the offence is one capable of being racially or religiously aggravated and the defendant has no defences and is guilty of the basic offence. You should now ask:

Is the offence racially or religiously aggravated?

This final question involves an understanding of s. 28 of the Crime and Disorder Act 1998.

10.4.6 Exercise—When and How?

Answer the following questions on s. 28.

There are two ways the offence can become racially or religiously aggravated; what are they?

1. _____

2. _____

When considering a 'demonstration of hostility' what time periods are relevant?

_____

EXPLANATION 10.4.6

When and How?

The offence can become racially or religiously aggravated if either:

1. the offender *demonstrates* hostility towards the victim; or

2. the offence is *motivated* by such racial or religious hostility.

The demonstration or motivation must be based on the victim's membership or presumed membership of a racial or religious group.

   The time period is:

immediately before, during or after.

There is no statutory definition of what these terms actually mean so you should approach them from a common-sense angle. However, in the 'Criminal Damage' section of your Manual, the case of *DPP* v *Parry* [2004] EWHC 3112 (Admin) states that comments made 20 minutes after the defendant had caused damage *would not* qualify as 'immediately after' when considering a 'demonstration' of hostility.

10.4.7 The Two Arms of Racially/Religiously Aggravated Offences

This involves looking at the definition of a racially or religiously aggravated offence under s. 28(1) of the Crime and Disorder Act 1998.

An offence is racially or religiously aggravated if	
DEMONSTRATION (s. 28(1)(a))	MOTIVATION (s. 28(1)(b))
↓	↓
immediately before, during or immediately after the offence is committed the offender **DEMONSTRATES** hostility towards the victim of the offence based on the victim's membership (or presumed membership) of a racial or religious group	the offence is **MOTIVATED** (in whole or in part) by hostility towards members of a racial or religious group based on their membership of that group

Points to Note

- Demonstrates—ANY type of demonstration (words, banners, placards etc.).
- The victim does not have to be present when the hostility is demonstrated.

EXAMPLE

TAYLOR and GOLDBERG are involved in a dispute in a supermarket car park. GOLDBERG walks off and into the supermarket. TAYLOR presumes GOLDBERG to be Jewish (because of his clothing) and causes criminal damage to GOLDBERG's car shouting *'Fuckin' Jewish bastard—we should gas them all!'*

• Based on the Victim's Membership

To be a member of a racial or religious group, you have to be a person. Therefore, companies and corporations cannot be subject to the s. 28(1)(a) (demonstration) version of this offence.

• Or Presumed Membership?

When you presume something, you might not be right. If I approach an Asian male, punch him in the face (a s. 47 ABH) and at the time shout 'Muslim pig!', the aggravated offence would be committed even if the person I attacked was a Hindu—I presumed the person I attacked was a Muslim.

• Motivation

The reason this thing (assault, damage etc.) was done was because of hostility towards members of a racial or religious group. So the 'victim' could be anybody or anything (this is where companies and corporations come in).

EXAMPLE

I go to Birmingham Symphony Hall (premises owned by Birmingham City Council) where a musician of Indian origin is performing. Using a can of spray-paint, I spray the words *'Indian Whore! Leave the Country Now!'* on the side of the building. Criminal damage has been caused to the building but it cannot be aggravated under s. 28(1)(a) as the 'victim' of the criminal damage is Birmingham City Council and the council cannot have a racial or religious characteristic. But if the reason I did it was because of my hostility towards Indian people, then the offence would be committed under s. 28(1)(b)—my motivation.

• In Whole or in Part

The hostility might be the reason or one of them (there may be other reasons for the offence being committed).

10.4.8 Exercise—Groups That Are/Are Not Covered

Decide whether or not the following groups of people would or would not be covered by s. 28 of the Act based on the fact that they are from a particular race, religion or group alone.

Group	Would	Would Not
Sikhs		
The English		
Traditional Gypsies		
Catholics		
The French		
Rastafarians		
Travellers		
Muslims		
Atheists		

EXPLANATION 10.4.8

Groups That Are/Are Not Covered

This exercise may cause you some concern as, after all, you are a police officer not an anthropologist! The relevant sections in your Manual describe racial and religious groups in some detail and it is easy to become confused by seemingly complex explanations as to who is what and why. Rather than try to remember who is covered, choose the easier alternative and remember *who is not covered*. Your Manual makes one exception stating that:

'Traditional "gypsies" (*as opposed to travellers*) are capable of being a racial group.'

In other words, everybody BUT TRAVELLERS would be covered by the legislation. So unless the victim is a traveller the offence can be racially or religiously aggravated (if all the other elements are satisfied). Note that this does not mean a traveller cannot be the victim of such an offence if the hostility is aimed at a racial and/or religious element covered by the Act—it is just that being a 'traveller' is not covered. So if hostility was directed at a black traveller because of their race or a Catholic traveller because of their religion, then the offence would be committed in relation to the race/religion (black/Catholic) element but NOT the traveller element. So your list from Exercise 10.4.8 would look like this:

Group	Would	Would Not
Sikhs	×	
The English	×	
Traditional Gypsies	×	
Catholics	×	
The French	×	
Rastafarians	×	
Travellers		×
Muslims	×	
Atheists	×	

Remember that police officers are entitled to the protection this legislation offers.

See *Investigators' Manual*, paras 2.6 to 2.6.12

10.5 Conclusion

Now that you have finished this section of the Workbook, you should have a greater awareness of what makes an offence racially or religiously aggravated. Remember that questions on this subject often come in two parts so make sure you apply the law in relation to both to get the question correct.

10.6 Recall Questions

Try and answer the following questions.

- What does the mnemonic CHAP stand for?
- What specific offences can be racially and religiously aggravated under ss. 28 to 32 of the Crime and Disorder Act 1998?

- When (time period) can an offence relating to a demonstration of hostility be racially or religiously aggravated?
- What are the two ways in which a defendant might illustrate racial or religious hostility?
- Who IS NOT covered by this legislation?

10.7   Multiple-Choice Questions

Answers to these questions can be found in the 'Answers Section' at the end of the book. All explanations also include a reference back to the *Investigators' Manual 2022*.

1. TI MADGE is investigating a number of incidents and is unsure as to whether they are racially aggravated (under s. 28 of the Crime and Disorder Act 1998).

Which of the incidents the officer is investigating could be racially aggravated?

A A s. 20 wounding (grievous bodily harm, Offences Against the Person Act 1861).

B An affray (contrary to s. 3 of the Public Order Act 1986).

C An aggravated criminal damage (contrary to s. 1(2) of the Criminal Damage Act 1971).

D A robbery (contrary to s. 8 of the Theft Act 1968).

Answer _____

2. When considering racially and religiously aggravated offences (under the Crime and Disorder Act 1998), a 'demonstration' of hostility must take place within a certain time frame.

What is that time frame?

A The time frame is limited to a demonstration of hostility immediately before an offence takes place.

B The time frame is limited to a demonstration of hostility immediately before an offence takes place or during the commission of the offence.

C The time frame is limited to a demonstration of hostility immediately before, during or after an offence takes place.

D The time frame is limited to a demonstration of hostility during the commission of an offence or immediately after it has taken place.

Answer _____

11 Non-fatal Offences Against the Person

11.1 Introduction

Offences covered in this chapter are regularly tested in the NIE. Therefore, it is necessary that you are familiar with the law surrounding these offences. Concentrating on and understanding the basic terminology of the offence of assault will achieve this. As you will discover, the language you feel familiar and secure with is not all it appears to be.

11.2 Aim

The aim of this section is to amplify your current knowledge surrounding offences of assault.

11.3 Objectives

At the end of this section you should be able to:

1. Define the term 'assault'.
2. Explain the terms within the definition of assault.
3. Identify when the defences of 'consent' and 'lawful chastisement' may be used.
4. Define the offences under ss. 47, 20 and 18 of the Offences Against the Person Act 1861.
5. Give examples of the injuries that will amount to 'actual bodily harm' and 'grievous bodily harm'.
6. Interpret the terminology of the Offences Against the Person Act 1861.
7. Apply your knowledge to multiple-choice questions.

11.4 Assault

The term 'assault' is not defined in statute but in common law. Nevertheless, you will probably have a good idea of what the term means.

11.4.1 Exercise—Elements of Assault

Write down the essential elements of an 'assault' (you have been provided with pointers to assist you).

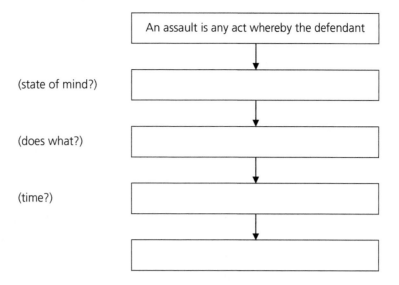

An assault is any act whereby the defendant

(state of mind?)

(does what?)

(time?)

EXPLANATION 11.4.1

Elements of Assault

This interpretation of the term 'assault' came from the case of *Fagan* v *Metropolitan Police Commissioner* [1969] 1 QB 439. You will have come across this case when you read the chapter on 'Criminal Conduct'. The brief facts are that a constable told Fagan to park his car near to a kerb. Fagan did so but unintentionally parked on the constable's foot. The constable is reported to have said, *'Get off, you are on my foot,'* to which Fagan replied, *'Fuck you, you can wait,'* and switched off the car ignition. Fagan was convicted of assaulting the constable and appealed. His appeal was dismissed in the speech of James J, who said:

An assault is any act which intentionally—or recklessly—causes another person to apprehend immediate and unlawful violence.

11.4.2   Exercise—States of Mind

The *mens rea* for the offence of assault is intention or recklessness. Answer the following questions with regard to these terms.

1. What do you think 'intention' means?

_____

2. Recklessness in assaults must be 'subjective'. In your own words, explain what subjective recklessness means to you.

_____

EXPLANATION 11.4.2

States of Mind

1. There are a number of issues with regard to 'intent' that are discussed at greater length in the section on '*Mens Rea* (State of Mind) and *Actus Reus* (Criminal Conduct)'. For the purposes of this question, we will keep the answer simple: intent means that you *meant something to happen*.

2. Recklessness is also discussed in the '*Mens Rea* (State of Mind) and *Actus Reus* (Criminal Conduct)' section. Subjective recklessness is all about *what the defendant thinks*. In assaults, the defendant will be

subjectively reckless if he/she saw a risk that someone would be harmed, but went on to take that risk nevertheless.

See *Investigators' Manual*, paras 2.7.2 to 2.7.2.4

11.4.3   Exercise—Cause to Apprehend

Look at the following scenario and answer the associated questions.

1. EARL and ASH used to be business partners but fell out when the company they had formed went into liquidation and closed. EARL blames ASH for the situation and wants to make ASH pay for the trouble he has caused. EARL buys an imitation revolver and waits outside ASH's house. ASH leaves his house and EARL approaches him. He points the imitation revolver at ASH and says, *'It's all your fault and now you're gonna pay for it by getting kneecapped!'* It is EARL's intention to make ASH believe that he is going to be assaulted. Based on these circumstances alone, do you have enough information to decide whether there has been an assault?
Yes / No
Why / Why not?

_____

2. ASH looks at the imitation revolver, immediately realises that it is a fake and, believing that he is in no danger whatsoever, says to EARL, *'You always were a dick, weren't you? I know that's not real so piss off and leave me alone!'* and walks away.
How, if at all, will this affect the situation?

_____

3. Let's change the circumstances slightly. When ASH sees the imitation revolver, he believes that it is real and thinks that he is going to be kneecapped by EARL there and then. Does this change the situation?
Yes / No
Why / Why not?

_____

Does the fact that the revolver is an imitation and can never actually harm ASH make any difference?
Yes / No

EXPLANATION 11.4.3

Cause to Apprehend

1. You do not. This is because you need to know the state of mind of ASH as well as the state of mind of EARL. The victim must apprehend (believe) that they are going to be subjected to immediate and unlawful violence.

2. You now possess information on the state of mind of the victim but this will not be an assault. ASH does not fear immediate and unlawful violence.

3. This does change the situation because you have the victim's belief that they are about to be subjected to unlawful violence. The fact that the gun cannot fire bullets does not matter as EARL's desired intentions have come to fruition.

    See *Investigators' Manual*, paras 2.7.2 to 2.7.2.4

11.4.4   Exercise—Immediate

This word always causes doubt in the minds of those examining the law surrounding assaults. What does 'immediate' actually mean?

Answer the following questions relating to the concept of 'immediacy'. You can presume that in all the scenarios the required state of mind for offender and victim is present.

1. CARP is sitting in her house watching the television when she sees GARNET looking at her through her lounge window—CARP apprehends violence from GARNET.
This would satisfy the requirements of the term 'immediacy'.
True / False

2. AMBROSE is working in his back garden, which backs on to a railway line. A train passes en route to a station two miles away from AMBROSE's house and JELPH (a passenger on the train) leans out of a window and shouts to AMBROSE, *'I'm coming for you!'*
This would satisfy the requirements for 'immediacy'.
True / False

3. FOULTON and MERTON are on separate sides of a deep and raging river. There is no way to cross the river. FOULTON shouts to MERTON, *'I'm going to kick your head in!'*
This would not satisfy the requirements of the term 'immediacy'.
True / False

4. CREW is standing outside HODSON's house. CREW phones HODSON using his mobile phone. When HODSON answers the phone, CREW says, *'I'll be round to your house in a minute or two to kick your head in!'* HODSON believes the threat.
This would not satisfy the requirements for 'immediacy'.
True / False

EXPLANATION 11.4.4

Immediate

1. True (*Smith* v *Chief Superintendent, Woking Police Station* (1983) 76 Cr App R 234).

2. False.

3. True.

4. False (*R* v *Ireland* [1997] 4 All ER 225).

Immediacy has been described as meaning 'imminent' (in *R* v *Ireland*) but not 'instantaneous' (*Horseferry Road Magistrates, ex parte Siadatan* [1991] 1 All ER 324). Hence, the 'minute or two' time frame might be enough (as stated in *Ireland*). This is the only precise time frame referred to in your *Investigators' Manual* regarding assaults. Remember that the victim must fear *violence* immediately. In the circumstances at 2 and 3, violence *cannot be* feared immediately because of the circumstances.
See *Investigators' Manual*, para. 2.7.2.2

11.4.5   Exercise—Words, Gestures and Conditional Threats

Consider the use of words when completing the following exercises.

1. Write down an example of the use of words alone to commit an assault.

---

2. Provide an example of the use of a gesture alone to commit an assault.

_____

3. An assault cannot be committed by the use of silence.
True / False

4. You cannot commit an assault by sending someone a letter containing a threat of immediate unlawful violence.
True / False

5. Explain what a 'conditional threat' is.

_____

6. PARK is leaving his house for a weekend business trip. As he kisses his wife, he says, _'If I hear one word about you sleeping around while I'm away, I'll beat you black and blue.'_
PARK does not commit an assault as this is a conditional threat.
True / False

7. BRISTOW is having an argument with his wife. BRISTOW puts a knife to his wife's throat and says, _'Shut it or I'll cut your throat!'_
BRISTOW does not commit an assault as this is a conditional threat.
True / False

EXPLANATION 11.4.5

Words, Gestures and Conditional Threats

1. Words alone can constitute an assault and there is no requirement that they be offensive. _'I am going to kick your head in'_ will suffice.

2. The same applies for gestures. Dragging a finger across the throat or shaking a fist will be enough.

3. False (_R_ v _Ireland_ (see previously)). The defendant made a large number of phone calls to three women—on one occasion, 14 to one of them within an hour—and remained silent when the phone was answered.

4. False (_R_ v _Constanza_ [1997] 2 Cr App R 492). The victim, who had for some time been harassed by the defendant, received two letters from him, one on 4 June and one on 12 June, which she interpreted as clear threats. It was held that they amounted to an assault occasioning actual bodily harm.

5. You should have stated that a conditional threat negates an assault. For example, _'I'd beat you up if the police officer wasn't here'_ actually means, _'Because the police officer is here I am_ not _going to beat you up.'_

6. True, this is a good example of a conditional threat.

7. False. This might seem like a conditional threat that negates an assault, but it is not as it is an immediate threat that will be carried out if the demand is not met. If the wife does not shut up, she will have her throat cut there and then—do this _now_ or else this will happen _now_.

See _Investigators' Manual_, paras 2.7.2.3, 2.7.2.4

11.5   **Battery**

Like the offence of assault, 'battery' is an offence under common law. It is often associated with the offence of assault because where there is a battery there will often be an assault, although this is not an automatic result in all cases.

11.5.1   Exercise—Elements of Battery

Answer the following questions with regard to the offence of 'battery'.

1. What is a battery?

_____

_____

2. What degree of violence will constitute a battery?

_____

_____

3. Force can be applied directly but can it be applied indirectly?
Yes / No

4. If you replied 'Yes', then give an example of the indirect application of force constituting a battery. If you replied 'No', then justify your answer.

_____

_____

EXPLANATION 11.5.1
Elements of Battery

1. A battery consists of the *actual* infliction (intentionally or recklessly) of unlawful physical violence (*R v Rolfe* (1952) 36 Cr App R 4).

2. The slightest degree of contact will be enough as the merest touching without consent is a criminal offence (although there is an implied consent to touching that takes place in the course of everyday life).

3. Force *can* be applied *indirectly*.

4. Your Manual provides an example of a defendant punching a woman, causing her to drop and injure a child she was holding.

See *Investigators' Manual*, para. 2.7.3

11.6   Unlawful

In certain circumstances, an assault/battery will not be committed because the action will be lawful. Your Manual concentrates on two significant defences to these offences: consent and lawful chastisement.

11.6.1   Exercise—Consent?

Answer the following questions in relation to the defence of consent.

1. The courts are prepared to accept consent to injury as a defence in certain circumstances. Provide three examples.

  i. _____

  ii. _____

  iii. _____

2. In what circumstances might the courts limit the defence of consent? (Think about the degree of harm.)

_____

3. Based on your answers and your knowledge of the subject, state whether consent would provide a potential defence in the following circumstances:

 i. KHAN injures LOWE during a properly conducted wrestling match.

Defence / No defence

 ii. GABLE scores a goal in a football match. Three minutes later, DABNER deliberately jumps on and breaks GABLE's leg as revenge for scoring the goal. Neither of the men were near the ball when this occurred.

Defence / No defence

iii. Rather than having her husband's initials tattooed on her buttocks, FARR's wife asks her husband to brand his initials on her buttocks with a hot knife (an act designed to show that she loves her husband).

Defence / No defence

iv. CEDER and BLASE are members of a sado-masochistic group who cause serious injuries to each other (at each other's request) for their own sexual gratification.

Defence / No defence

4. HOLROYD (a male doctor) has served his local community as a GP for a number of years. BAKEWELL (a female patient) has just been examined by HOLROYD after discovering a lump in her breast. HOLROYD was suspended two weeks ago by the General Medical Council for neglect of a patient and has not informed anyone.
Has an offence been committed against BAKEWELL?
Yes / No
Why / Why not?

5. CARD falsifies a set of formal dental qualifications and obtains a job as a dentist. He carries out a dental operation on PHILLIPS before his deception is discovered. Has an offence been committed against PHILLIPS?
Yes / No
Why / Why not?

EXPLANATION 11.6.1

Consent?

1. There are a number of examples of where consent may be allowed. These include injuries received during the course of a properly conducted sporting event, injuries received when receiving a tattoo and injuries received as a consequence of a medical operation.

2. This was mentioned in *R v Brown* [1994] 1 AC 212. The courts stated that all assaults resulting in more than transient harm will be unlawful unless there is a good reason for allowing the plea of 'consent'.

3. The answers are as follows:

    i. Defence available—this is a properly conducted sporting event.

    ii. No defence as the activity falls outside the parameters of a properly conducted sporting event (*R v Barnes* [2004] EWCA Crim 3246).

iii. Defence available—see *R* v *Wilson* [1997] QB 47.

iv. No defence—see *R* v *Brown* [1994] 1 AC 212.

4. An offence has not been committed. This is because BAKEWELL has not been deceived as to the nature and quality of the act, nor the *identity* of HOLROYD (the fact that HOLROYD concealed his suspension does not affect his identity).

5. An offence has been committed as CARD has no formal qualifications at all and so the quality of the act has been misrepresented.

11.6.2   Exercise—Lawful Chastisement?

Examine the following scenario and consider the defence of lawful chastisement when answering the questions.

WILLIAMSON is in favour of physical discipline as part of his Christian beliefs. He sends his son, ADAM, to a local secondary school and tells the headmaster that he can impose corporal punishment on his son should he merit it.

1. The European Convention on Human Rights requires a State to have regard to the religious and philosophical convictions of parents. As a result, the headmaster could use corporal punishment on ADAM.
True / False

2. Corporal punishment has been outlawed in all British schools by the Education Act 1996.

True / False

3. The headmaster of the school would be acting *in loco parentis* of ADAM and may use corporal punishment if necessary.
True / False

4. There are no circumstances where a teacher can use reasonable force to control the behaviour of a child.
True / False

EXPLANATION 11.6.2

Lawful Chastisement?

1. False. Although this is a consideration it does not provide a licence to use corporal punishment.

2. True.

3. False. Corporal punishment has been outlawed.

4. False. Staff may use reasonable force in restraining violent and disruptive pupils (Education Act 1996).

See *Investigators' Manual*, paras 2.7.9

11.7   Section 47 Assault

You have examined 'assault' and 'battery' and these activities may well constitute an offence contrary to s. 39 of the Criminal Justice Act 1988. However, the nature of the injury received by the victim may make the offence committed by the defendant a more serious one. A s. 47 assault is an assault causing actual bodily harm. While the section does not provide a definition as such, 'bodily harm' has been held to be *any hurt or injury calculated to interfere with the health and comfort of the victim* (*R* v *Donovan* [1934] 2 KB 498). As the *mens rea* for this offence is exactly the same as for the offence of assault, the central issue is to decide whether the injury qualifies as ABH. CPS charging standards state that ABH should generally be charged where the injuries and overall circumstances indicate that the offence:

• merits clearly more than six months' imprisonment; and
• where the prosecution intends to represent that the case is not suitable for summary trial.

Examples may include cases where there is a need for a number of stitches (but not superficial application of steri-strips) or a hospital procedure under anaesthetic.

Injuries that have been classed as ABH include:

• a kick leading to a momentary loss of consciousness;
• cutting a person's hair against their will.

See *Investigators' Manual*, para. 2.7.13

11.8 Section 20 Wounding

The next level of assault is catered for under s. 20 of the Offences Against the Person Act 1861. This legislation is probably the oldest you will come across in your study. The actual age of the legislation is not a problem on its own; the true problem lies in interpreting legislation that is over 150 years old.

11.8.1 Exercise—Updating the Definition

The definition of this offence has been supplied for you. Your task is to substitute the words and phrases with their accepted legal meaning. If you cannot do this, then substitute the words or phrases with a modern equivalent.

	Whosoever shall
s. 20 OAPA 1861 =	Unlawfully and maliciously
Your translation =	
s. 20 OAPA 1861 =	wound
Your translation =	
s. 20 OAPA 1861 =	or inflict
Your translation =	
s. 20 OAPA 1861 =	any grievous bodily harm upon any person
Your translation =	
s. 20 OAPA 1861 =	either with or without any weapon or instrument
Your translation =	
	shall be guilty of an offence

EXPLANATION 11.8.1

Updating the Definition

Maliciously does not mean some kind of evil intention or malice, it means 'subjective recklessness' as discussed earlier in this section. This is the state of mind required to commit the offence.

Wound means to break the continuity of the whole skin (seven layers).

Inflict means 'cause'.

Grievous bodily harm means serious or really serious harm. Examples of this are:

- permanent disability or visible disfigurement;

- broken or displaced limbs or bones;

- injuries requiring blood transfusion or lengthy treatment; or

- infection of another with HIV/genital herpes

either with or without any weapon or instrument. So therefore:

- This offence can be committed with a weapon.

- This offence can be committed with an instrument.

- But you can also commit it without either of these.

In other words, you can commit this offence by any means, so *why bother with this line of the definition?* A simple and modern version of this offence should read:

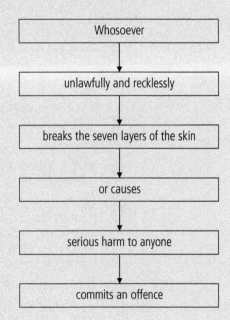

See *Investigators' Manual*, para. 2.7.14

Essentially, this offence is a reckless assault resulting in serious injury.

11.9 Section 18 Wounding

What would you say if you were told that the word 'recklessly' forms part of the definition of the offence under s. 18?

Most people think of this offence as one where serious injury (as per the GBH in s. 20) is caused to the victim, but the significant difference is that the defendant *intended* to cause that injury. There is nothing wrong with this approach and it is a simple but effective way of understanding *part* of the offence.

The offence is committed as follows:

> Whosoever shall unlawfully and maliciously by any means whatsoever wound or cause any grievous bodily harm to any person with intent to do some grievous bodily harm to any person, or with intent to resist or prevent the lawful apprehension or detainer of any person, shall be guilty of a felony.

There are *two* basic forms of the offence here.

The first offence is committed when the offender wounds or causes GBH intending to do so—note that the intention is to cause GBH to ANY person with the result that GBH is caused to ANY person. This is the s. 18 offence you will be familiar with.

Now think about the translation of the s. 20 offence and apply those principles to the other side of the offence.

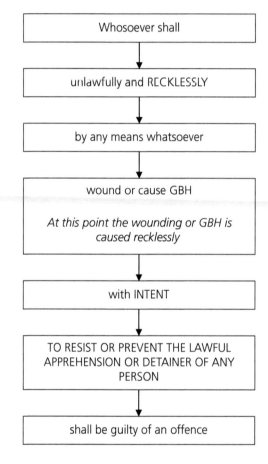

The intention here is to resist arrest or prevent arrest, *NOT* to wound or cause GBH. For example, a police officer is chasing a suspect who picks up a wooden box and throws it at the officer intending to stop the officer from arresting him. The offender realises that if the box strikes the officer it will hurt him, but he throws it anyway. The box hits the officer and breaks her arm. The s. 18 offence is committed.

See *Investigators' Manual*, para. 2.7.15

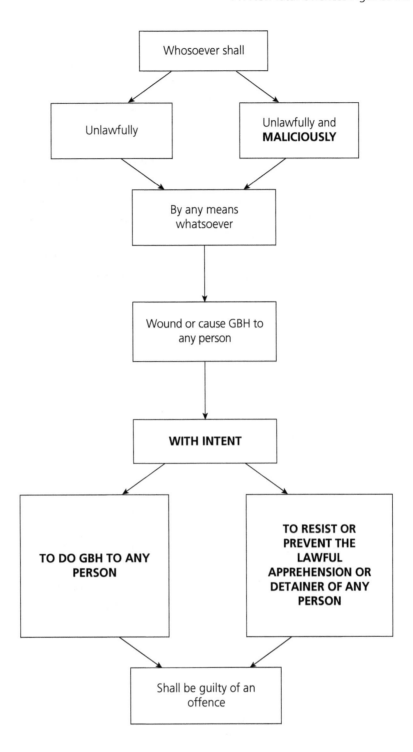

11.10 Conclusion

Now that you have finished this section of the Workbook, your viewpoint in relation to assault-related offences should have changed. You will realise that the basic offence forms the foundation for any understanding of the more serious offences associated with it. These offences require deciphering from their Victorian origins into the language of the twenty-first century.

11.11   Recall Questions

Try and answer the following questions.

- What is the definition of an assault according to *R v Fagan*?
- What is a battery?
- What does the term 'immediate' mean?
- Explain what is meant by a 'conditional threat'.
- When would consent be a valid defence to a charge of assault.
- Provide some examples of injuries that would constitute a s. 47 assault?
- What are the two points that will assist the CPS to decide whether an offence should be dealt with as a s. 47 assault?
- Provide a modern definition of the offence of s. 20 wounding.
- Give four examples of injuries (consider CPS Charging Standards) that would constitute a s. 18 offence.

11.12   Multiple-Choice Questions

Answers to these questions can be found in the 'Answers Section' at the end of the book. All explanations also include a reference back to the *Investigators' Manual 2022*.

1. ABBOTT and KENNA are next-door neighbours, but do not get on as they share a driveway and are always in dispute about car parking. One afternoon, ABBOTT parks his car, leaving a small part of it on KENNA's side of the driveway. KENNA comes out of his house and begins a heated argument with ABBOTT about his parking. Another neighbour calls the police and PC RAYSON arrives to sort the incident out. While the officer is dealing with the two men, they calm down. The neighbour who called the police attracts the attention of PC RAYSON and, while the officer speaks to the neighbour, ABBOTT whispers in KENNA's ear, *'I've had enough of you, you tosser. You're lucky this copper's here because if he wasn't I'd chin you.'*

Does ABBOTT commit an assault in these circumstances?

A No, an assault has not been committed because the words used by ABBOTT make this a hypothetical threat.

B Yes, this would be an assault as the words used imply that as soon as PC RAYSON has left the scene, KENNA will be assaulted.

C No, an assault has not been committed, as you cannot assault someone by the use of words alone.

D Yes, ABBOTT has committed an assault as he has intentionally caused KENNA to apprehend unlawful violence.

Answer _____

2. MATONI is walking along the street holding her three-month-old child in her arms when she is approached by THEAKSTON who was, up until two weeks ago, living with MATONI. An argument develops between the two resulting in MATONI walking away from and past THEAKSTON. As MATONI passes THEAKSTON and has her back to him, THEAKSTON punches MATONI in the back of her head causing minor bruising and some swelling to MATONI's head (whilst this causes injury to MATONI, the injuries would only ever be considered to be minor). However, the force of the blow causes MATONI to drop her three-month-old child. The child falls to the pavement and receives minor bruising to

the left leg as a direct consequence of the fall (again, this injury would only ever be considered minor).

What is THEAKSTON's liability in this matter?

A THEAKSTON is liable for a common battery (contrary to s. 39 of the Criminal Justice Act 1988) against MATONI but there is no liability for the injury caused to the child.

B THEAKSTON is liable for a common battery against MATONI and a common battery against the child (both contrary to s. 39 of the Criminal Justice Act 1988).

C THEAKSTON is liable for a common assault against MATONI (contrary to s. 39 of the Criminal Justice Act 1988) and a s. 47 assault (contrary to the Offences Against the Person Act 1861) against the child.

D THEAKSTON is liable for a s. 47 assault (contrary to the Offences Against the Person Act 1861) against MATONI and the child.

Answer _____

3. TI HOVE is dealing with a public order incident where several people were arrested for affray. DUBLIN, one of the people arrested for affray, assaulted the police officer who arrested him in an effort to resist the arrest. RUNCORN, a member of the public, saw what was happening and attempted to assist the police officer who was restraining DUBLIN. As RUNCORN tried to help the officer, DUBLIN assaulted him as well.

Considering the offence of assault with intent to resist arrest (contrary to s. 38 of the Offences Against the Person Act 1861), which of the following statements is correct?

A DUBLIN has committed the offence but only in respect of the police officer who arrested him for affray.

B DUBLIN has committed the offence in respect of both the police officer and also RUNCORN.

C DUBLIN would have a defence to the offence if he could show that he was innocent of the offence of affray.

D The offence has not been committed as DUBLIN was trying to resist his arrest and not trying to prevent the arrest of some other person.

Answer _____

4. WEST has an argument with SARTIN and CRAIG. During the argument, SARTIN and CRAIG provoke WEST about the fact that he lost an arm in a car crash. WEST becomes very angry and shouts, *'You pair are the biggest idiots I've ever met and you don't deserve to live. In fact, I'll sort that problem out. I've got a shotgun and I'll visit you both tomorrow and kill you, one arm or not!'* WEST does not intend either SARTIN or CRAIG to believe the threat, he just wants to shut them up. SARTIN laughs at WEST as he does not believe the threat but CRAIG runs away as he does believe that WEST will kill him the following morning.

Considering the offence of threats to kill (contrary to s. 16 of the Offences Against the Person Act 1861), which of the following statements is correct?

A WEST has not committed the offence in this situation.

B WEST has committed the offence but only in respect of CRAIG.

C WEST has committed the offence in respect of both SARTIN and CRAIG.

D WEST has committed the offence but would be able to use the defence of loss of control.

Answer _____

12 | Child Protection

12.1 Introduction

This section of the Workbook concentrates on offences associated with child abduction. Offences relating to child abduction are covered in just over two pages of your *Investigators' Manual*. Nevertheless, these offences can easily be made the subject of questions within your examination. As such, you will require an understanding of who can commit these offences and how, along with their related defences.

12.2 Aim

The aim of this section is to help you understand the law relating to child abduction.

12.3 Objectives

At the end of this section you should be able to:

1. Outline the offence of child abduction (contrary to s. 1 of the Child Abduction Act 1984).
2. Outline the offence of child abduction (contrary to s. 2 of the Child Abduction Act 1984).
3. Identify when a defence to an offence under ss. 1 and 2 of the Child Abduction Act 1984 may be available.
4. Apply your knowledge to multiple-choice questions.

12.4 Child Abduction (s. 1—Person Connected with the Child)

12.4.1 Exercise—Five Points to Prove

There are five points to prove in relation to this offence. You have been given the first but what are the rest? (Do not worry about the order of the points to prove.)

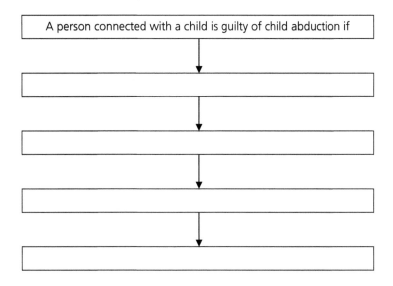

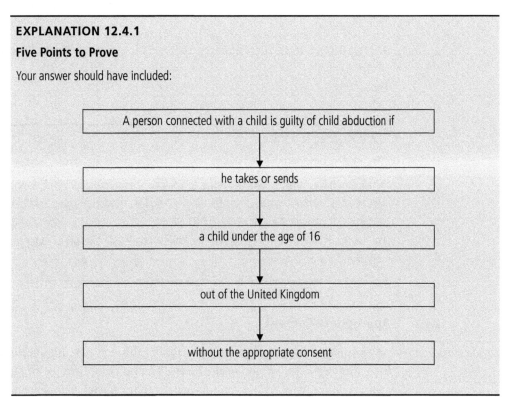

EXPLANATION 12.4.1

Five Points to Prove

Your answer should have included:

12.4.2 'Connected' with a Child

It is important to note that the only person capable of committing this offence is someone 'connected' with the child. Section 1(2) of the Act details those persons who fall into this category. Rather than attempt to remember this section, think about the potential offender and ask, 'Does this person have a biological (e.g. a parent) or legal (e.g. a guardian) connection with the child?' If the answer is 'no', then they are not 'connected' to the child and cannot commit this offence.

12.4.3   Age

A common requirement of the offences under ss. 1 and 2 of the Act is that the child victim of the offences *must be under 16*.

12.4.4   Exercise—The United Kingdom

MILTON and his 12-year-old daughter live in London. MILTON decides to take his daughter on a two-week holiday without the appropriate consent. Consider the following statements and decide whether they are true or false.

1. If MILTON took his daughter to Wales, the offence would be complete.
True / False

2. If MILTON took his daughter to Scotland, the offence would be complete.
True / False

3. If MILTON took his daughter to Northern Ireland, he would not commit the offence.
True / False

4. If MILTON took his daughter to Eire (Southern Ireland), the offence would be complete.
True / False

EXPLANATION 12.4.4

The United Kingdom

You might have considered this exercise to be more about geography than law but it matters—a mark lost by not knowing what countries the United Kingdom consists of could lead to difficulty in the examination (and think how many times the United Kingdom is mentioned in your syllabus). The United Kingdom consists of England, Wales, Scotland and Northern Ireland. On that basis, comments 3 and 4 are true and comments 1 and 2 are false.

12.4.5   Appropriate Consent

Appropriate consent is covered by s. 1(3) of the Act. Ask the question, 'Who has a biological or legal connection with the child?' and compile a list of answers; think of this as a school register. Whoever appears on that register *must have* a 'tick' next to their name in a column entitled 'consent given'. If the 'consent given' column is not full, then an offence has been committed as the consent of *each and every one* in that column is required.
See *Investigators' Manual*, para. 2.9.2.1

12.4.6   Exercise—Defences to an Offence Under s. 1 of the Child Abduction Act 1984

Consider the following statements and decide whether the named person would have a defence to a charge under s. 1 of the Act. Give a short explanation for your answer.

1. SMITH is a person named in a child arrangements order as a person with whom his eight-year-old child REBECCA is to live. He takes REBECCA to Germany for six weeks without the consent of REBECCA's mother.
Defence available?
Why / Why not?

2. EMMS takes his six-year-old child to France for two weeks without the consent of the child's mother. EMMS mistakenly believes the child's mother has consented to the trip.
Defence available?
Why / Why not?

3. PRATT takes his two-year-old child to Spain for a week. This is against the wishes of the child's mother who has unreasonably refused to consent to the trip.
Defence available?
Why / Why not?

EXPLANATION 12.4.6

Defences to an Offence Under s. 1 of the Child Abduction Act 1984

In the first scenario, no defence is available. SMITH is a person named in a child arrangements order as a person with whom his child will live and this satisfies the first part of the defence under s. 1(4)(a). However, he has taken the child out of the United Kingdom for more than a month and, therefore, does not satisfy the requirement under the second part of this defence. If he had taken the child to Germany for less than one month, the defence would be available. The *only* occasion where the time period of *one month* is relevant to this offence is when this defence is raised.

In the second scenario, a defence is available under s. 1(5)(a). This is because EMMS has taken his child out of the United Kingdom in the belief that the child's mother consented to the trip.

In the third scenario, a defence is available under s. 1(5)(c) as, although PRATT has taken his child out of the United Kingdom without the appropriate consent, the mother of the child has unreasonably refused to consent to the trip. There are several other occasions where a defence may be available. You should refer to the *Investigators' Manual* to ensure you have a full understanding of these defences.

See *Investigators' Manual*, para. 2.9.2.2

12.5 Child Abduction (s. 2—Person Not Connected with the Child)

12.5.1 Exercise—Six Points to Prove

There are six points to prove in relation to this offence. You have been given the first but what are the rest? (Do not worry about the order of the points to prove.)

A person not connected with a child is guilty of child abduction if

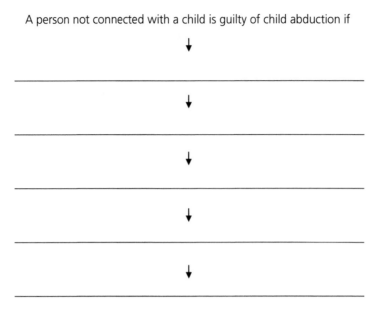

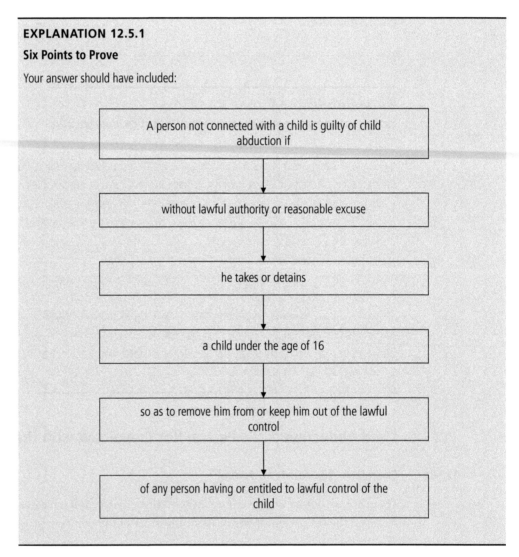

EXPLANATION 12.5.1

Six Points to Prove

Your answer should have included:

```
┌──────────────────────────────────────────────┐
│ A person not connected with a child is guilty │
│              of child abduction if             │
└──────────────────────────────────────────────┘
                        ↓
┌──────────────────────────────────────────────┐
│      without lawful authority or reasonable    │
│                    excuse                      │
└──────────────────────────────────────────────┘
                        ↓
┌──────────────────────────────────────────────┐
│                 he takes or detains            │
└──────────────────────────────────────────────┘
                        ↓
┌──────────────────────────────────────────────┐
│            a child under the age of 16         │
└──────────────────────────────────────────────┘
                        ↓
┌──────────────────────────────────────────────┐
│   so as to remove him from or keep him out of  │
│              the lawful control                │
└──────────────────────────────────────────────┘
                        ↓
┌──────────────────────────────────────────────┐
│   of any person having or entitled to lawful   │
│              control of the child              │
└──────────────────────────────────────────────┘
```

12.5.2   Exercise—Developing the Offence Under s. 2

Read the following circumstances and then answer the following questions. Give reasons for your answers where appropriate.

OAKES (a 30-year-old male) enters a child's play area in a park where he sees VATER (an eight-year-old child) playing on some swings. VATER's mother is talking to some friends nearby. OAKES approaches VATER and asks VATER to come and play on a roundabout 20 feet away. VATER consents and walks with OAKES towards the roundabout. VATER's mother sees OAKES walking with her child and asks him what he is doing. OAKES tells the mother to shut up or he will hit her. The mother fears for herself and her child and does nothing. OAKES has no criminal intentions with regard to VATER and talks with her for a few minutes before leaving the play area.

1. OAKES is not 'connected' to VATER.
Why?

2. Does the fact that VATER's mother is nearby make any difference?
Why / Why not?

3. VATER consented to walk to the roundabout with OAKES. Does this have any effect when considering an offence under s. 2?
Why / Why not?

4. Does the fact that OAKES has no ulterior criminal intention with regard to VATER make any difference?
Why / Why not?

5. OAKES has not used any form of physical violence or a fraud to get VATER to accompany him to the roundabout. Does this prevent him committing an offence under s. 2?
Why / Why not?

EXPLANATION 12.5.2

Developing the Offence Under s. 2

1. OAKES is not 'connected' to VATER because he has no *biological or legal connection* to the child. This offence is the 'stranger' abduction and can only be committed by a person to whom s. 1 of the Act *does not apply*, i.e. a person other than a parent, a guardian, a person having custody of the child etc.

2. It does not matter where VATER's mother is. What matters is that her lawful control of the child has been substituted by OAKES's control.

3. The consent of the victim is irrelevant; it is the consent of the person with lawful control that matters. In *R v A (Child Abduction)* [2000] Cr App R 418, the Court of Appeal held that the offence of taking a child may be committed notwithstanding that the child consents to the taking, the test being whether the accused caused the child to accompany him/her.

4. OAKES's lack of an ulterior criminal intent does not preclude an offence under this legislation (although you would have to consider whether he had lawful authority or a reasonable excuse). In *R v Mousir* [1987] Crim LR 561, it was said that the phrase 'so as to' in s. 2(1)(a) of the Act is concerned with the objective consequences of the taking or detaining, and not with the accused's subjective motives.

5. Force or fraud of any kind does not form part of this offence and a lack of one or both of these factors will not prevent OAKES from committing the offence.

12.5.3 Removal of Control/Keep Out of Control

When you consider this part of the offence, you should bear in mind the Court of Appeal's comments in *R v Leather* [1994] Cr App R 179.

- The court held that the concept of 'control' does not have any 'spatial' element, and it followed that the phrase 'so as to remove from the lawful control' did not impose a geographical element to the offence (*in other words, the child does not have to be physically moved by the actions of the defendant for the offence to be committed*).
- The test to be applied is whether the child has been deflected by the action of the accused from doing that which he/she would have been doing with the consent of the person having lawful control of the child (*in other words, the authority of the person in 'lawful control' has been substituted by that of the offender and the child is now under his/her control*).

See *Investigators' Manual*, para. 2.9.2.3

12.5.4 Exercise—Defences to an Offence Under s. 2 of the Child Abduction Act 1984

There are three defences to an offence under s. 2 of the Act. What are they? (You have been provided with the first part of this section.)

It shall be a defence for the defendant to prove (where the father and the mother of the child in question were not married to each other at the time of his birth):

1. _____

2. _____

or

3. _____

EXPLANATION 12.5.4

Defences to an Offence Under s. 2 of the Child Abduction Act 1984

Research these defences by referring to your *Investigators' Manual*.
See *Investigators' Manual*, para. 2.9.2.4

12.6 Conclusion

You will have realised that these offences are not straightforward and demand concentration to understand, particularly when you have to consider the various defences available. This section should have assisted you in that task.

12.7 Recall Questions

Try and answer the following questions.

- What is the relevant age of a child for offences under ss. 1 and 2 of the Child Abduction Act 1984?
- What countries make up the United Kingdom?
- You are explaining 'appropriate consent' to a colleague; what will you say?
- When is the time period of one month relevant?
- What are the defences to a charge under s. 1 of the Child Abduction Act 1984?
- Who can commit an offence under s. 2 of the Child Abduction Act 1984?
- What are the defences to a charge under s. 2 of the Child Abduction Act 1984?
- What does the phrase 'so as to remove from lawful control' actually mean?

12.8 Multiple-Choice Questions

Answers to these questions can be found in the 'Answers Section' at the end of the book. All explanations also include a reference back to the *Investigators' Manual 2022*.

1. COLETO has been divorced from his wife for several years. He is the father of three children by the relationship with his wife: ANTHONY (aged 16 years), PHILLIPPA (aged 14 years) and MARK (aged 12 years). His ex-wife has lawful custody of all three children. COLETO takes all three children on a trip to Italy for six weeks even though he knows his ex-wife does not consent to the trip.

Considering the offence under s. 1 of the Child Abduction Act 1984 only, which of the following statements is correct?

A COLETO commits an offence with regard to all three children.

B COLETO commits an offence with regard to PHILLIPPA and MARK.

C COLETO commits an offence with regard to MARK only.

D COLETO does not commit an offence because he is the father of the children.

Answer _____

2. LEE (who is 12 years old) is playing in a park with a group of friends (his parents are not present in the park). CURTIS (who is 18 years old) approaches LEE and asks him to help him search for his lost wallet (this is a lie as CURTIS's real motive is to sexually assault LEE). LEE agrees and looks behind several bushes in another part of the park along with CURTIS. LEE becomes bored and tells CURTIS he is going back to continue playing with his friends. CURTIS tries to persuade LEE to stay with him but LEE pays no attention and walks off.

Has CURTIS committed an offence of child abduction under s. 2 of the Child Abduction Act 1984 (person not connected with a child)?

A Yes, because CURTIS has removed LEE from his parents' lawful control.

B No, CURTIS has not used force or tried to physically restrain LEE.

C Yes, but only because CURTIS has an ulterior motive in mind.

D No, because LEE consented to accompany CURTIS.

Answer _____

3. Fifteen months ago, PELL had a sexual relationship with DAY but then the two split up. Some time later, PELL discovers that DAY has a six-month-old daughter and, because PELL knows that DAY is a loner and very rarely has any relationships, he believes that the child is his. PELL is mistaken in this belief. Although PELL asks, DAY repeatedly refuses to let PELL near her child. One afternoon when DAY is pushing the child in a pram, PELL approaches mother and child and grabs hold of the child. PELL holds on to the child for several minutes before giving her back to DAY.

Considering the offence under s. 2 of the Child Abduction Act 1984 only, which of the following statements is correct?

A In these circumstances, PELL commits the offence as he is not the father of the child.

B PELL commits an offence but would have a defence if he believes, on reasonable grounds, that he is the father of the child.

C The only defence is that at the time of the offence the defendant believes the child has attained the age of 16.

D PELL does not commit the offence because he did not remove the child from DAY's lawful control.

Answer _____

Flowchart for ss. 1 and 2 of the Child Abduction Act 1984

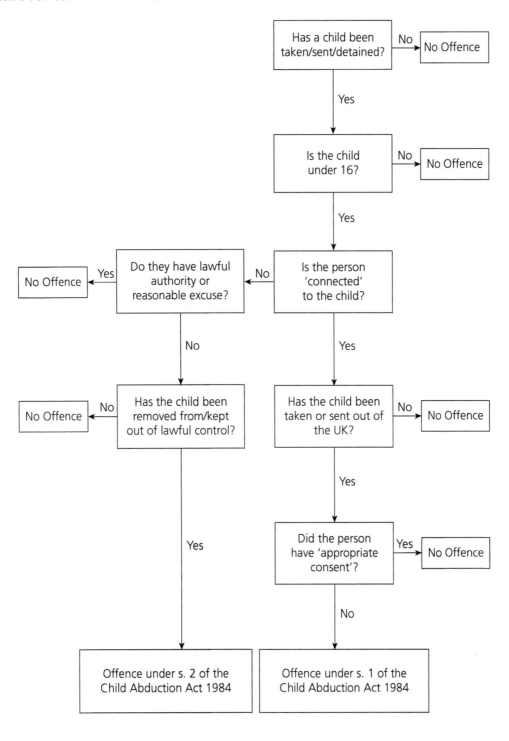

13 | Offences Involving the Deprivation of Liberty

13.1 Introduction

This chapter concentrates on the closely related offences of false imprisonment and kidnapping. This close relationship may cause you difficulty in your examination if you do not understand the individual offences and their differences. This section is designed to provide you with that knowledge.

13.2 Aim

The aim of this section is for you to be able to explain and distinguish between the offences of kidnapping and false imprisonment.

13.3 Objectives

At the end of this section you should be able to:

1. Outline the offence of kidnapping.
2. Outline the offence of false imprisonment.
3. Distinguish between the offences of kidnapping and false imprisonment.
4. Apply your knowledge to multiple-choice questions.

13.4 False Imprisonment (Common Law)

13.4.1 Exercise—False Imprisonment?

Examine the following comments and decide whether they are 'true' or 'false'.

1. False imprisonment can only be committed intentionally.
True / False

2. An offence of false imprisonment is complete when the victim's freedom of movement is restrained.
True / False

3. The offence of false imprisonment is complete even though the restraint may be momentary only.
True / False

4. A physical assault is a necessary ingredient of the offence of false imprisonment.
True / False

5. An offence of false imprisonment may take place anywhere so long as the victim is prevented from moving from a particular place.
True / False

EXPLANATION 13.4.1

False Imprisonment?

There is nothing complicated about this offence.

False imprisonment is committed by unlawfully restraining the freedom of the victim and may be committed either intentionally or recklessly. As soon as the freedom of the victim is restrained, the offence is committed and this restraint need only be momentary. There is no requirement for a physical assault to take place and the offence can be committed anywhere.

Therefore, comments 1 and 4 are false and comments 2, 3 and 5 are true.

See *Investigators' Manual*, para. 2.10.1

13.5   Kidnapping (Common Law)

13.5.1   Exercise—Four Points to Prove

There are four points to prove when considering the offence of kidnapping. What are they? (Do not worry about the order of the points to prove.)

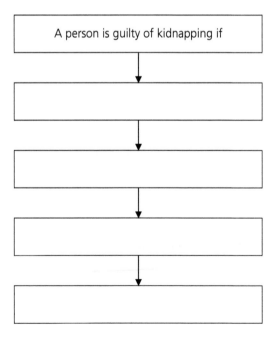

EXPLANATION 13.5.1

Four Points to Prove

Your answer should have included:

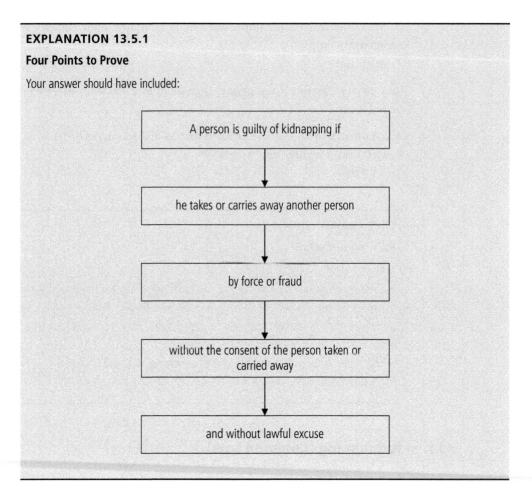

A person is guilty of kidnapping if

↓

he takes or carries away another person

↓

by force or fraud

↓

without the consent of the person taken or carried away

↓

and without lawful excuse

Kidnapping is an aggravated form of false imprisonment. It can be committed by any person against any person, i.e. there are no exceptions; a husband can kidnap his wife, a father can kidnap his child.

For the offence of kidnapping, think of all the elements of false imprisonment but also think of the offender causing some form of *movement of the victim* by taking or carrying them away (whether this movement is achieved by force or fraud is immaterial). Do not concern yourself about the distance that the victim has been moved (in *R v Wellard* (1978) 67 Cr App R 364, a distance of 100 yards was held to be 'ample evidence' of such movement), as any distance will suffice. Once movement occurs, the offence is committed.

It is important to remember that the offence can be committed by the use of fraud. This is well illustrated by the case of *R v Metcalfe* ((1983) 10 CCC (3d) 114). The victim entered the vehicle of the accused, a former acquaintance, in which a friend of the accused was also sitting. The victim was driven to a garage in the belief that he was either going to talk about 'old times' or alternatively was going to be given drugs. In fact, the accused and his friend were planning to lure the victim to the garage where he was to be confined and held to ransom. In refusing the appeal, Nemets CJBC said: *'In my opinion the offence of kidnapping was complete on the victim's entry into the car. His agreement to go with the abductors was no consent in law. It was obtained by a fraudulent stratagem. Fraud was used as a substitute for force.'*

Therefore, *as soon* as the victim is moved from one point to another (by force *or* by fraud) the offence is committed.

Remember that consent can be removed at any time. If a victim willingly accompanies the offender (no force or fraud is used by the offender at this stage) and a point is reached where the victim removes that consent, any further movement of the victim by the offender (by force or fraud) will constitute an offence.

A final point to note (which would make for a great examination question) relates to *R v Hendy-Freegard* [2007] EWCA Crim 1236. Effectively, the principle is that kidnap can only occur when the kidnapper accompanies the victim—not a 'remote' movement as in this case.

See *Investigators' Manual*, para. 2.10.2

13.6 Red Light or Green Light?

You might like to think about the two offences and the relationship between them as two of the colours at a set of traffic lights.

FALSE IMPRISONMENT

Common Law Offence

It is an offence to

unlawfully and intentionally/recklessly

restrain a person's freedom of movement

Imprison = No Movement (<u>Red Light</u> Offence)

EXAMPLES	
Locking someone in a car.	
Keeping someone in a particular place.	**RED LIGHT**
Unlawfully arresting someone.	

KIDNAPPING

Common Law Offence

It is an offence to

unlawfully/recklessly

take or carry away another person

(by force/threat of force or by fraud)

without the consent of that person or without lawful excuse

Kidnap = Movement (<u>Green Light</u> Offence)

EXAMPLES	
Dragging someone (**FORCE**) 10 feet along a road and against their will.	
Lying to someone (**FRAUD**) to get them to accompany you while you walk along a street.	**GREEN LIGHT**

13.7 Conclusion

Although the offences of kidnapping and false imprisonment are relatively uncommon and only briefly mentioned in the *Investigators' Manual*, you would be ill-advised to exclude them from your study and revision. This short section should have assisted you in understanding and differentiating between the two offences.

13.8   Recall Questions

Try and answer the following questions.

- What are the points to prove for an offence of kidnapping?
- What is the sentence for an offence of kidnapping?
- What are the points to prove for an offence of false imprisonment?
- What type of 'recklessness' is required for an offence of false imprisonment?
- What are the differences between an offence of kidnapping and an offence of false imprisonment?

13.9   Multiple-Choice Questions

Answers to these questions can be found in the 'Answers Section' at the end of the book. All explanations also include a reference back to the *Investigators' Manual 2022*.

1. NICKLIN is going through a difficult divorce after his wife left him and moved in with POYNER. NICKLIN intends to force his wife to come back to him and drives to POYNER's address, where he speaks to his wife at the front door of the house. NICKLIN asks his wife to sit with him in his car on the false pretext of trying to sort out some of their differences. NICKLIN's wife agrees and walks to the car with him. After several minutes, the two begin to argue and NICKLIN's wife attempts to get out of the car. NICKLIN grabs hold of her and locks the car doors. He then drives the car 200 metres along the road, before unlocking the doors and letting his wife out.

At what stage, if at all, does NICKLIN first commit the offence of kidnapping?

A When his wife agrees and walks with him to his car.

B When he grabs hold of his wife and locks the car doors.

C When he drives her 200 metres along the road.

D NICKLIN does not commit the offence, as a husband cannot kidnap his wife.

Answer _____

2. UDALL is walking through a park looking for someone to sexually assault. He plans to take his victim back to his house to carry out the assault. He sees YOUNG and ACTON (boyfriend and girlfriend) taking some drugs near a tree and approaches them. UDALL falsely states that he is a plain-clothes police officer searching for drugs. He tells YOUNG that he has been cautioned and his punishment is to stay in the same spot for 30 minutes, but tells ACTON that she will have to come with him to the police station. YOUNG remains next to the tree while ACTON, who believes UDALL is a police officer, walks several metres with him. As ACTON and UDALL are walking together, ACTON asks to see UDALL's warrant card. UDALL panics and runs away.

Which of the following statements is correct?

A UDALL has kidnapped ACTON and falsely imprisoned YOUNG.

B UDALL has kidnapped ACTON but has not falsely imprisoned YOUNG because no force was used.

C UDALL has attempted to kidnap ACTON and falsely imprisoned YOUNG.

D UDALL has not kidnapped ACTON as she was not taken to UDALL's house, but has falsely imprisoned YOUNG.

Answer _____

3. TURNER comes home to her 10th floor flat and sees that the front door to the flat is slightly open. There have been a spate of burglaries in the block of flats and as TURNER looks through her front door she can see FELLOWES in her lounge dismantling her hi-fi system and placing it into a bag. TURNER genuinely believes that FELLOWES is a burglar and locks her front door to prevent FELLOWES from escaping. There is no other route out of the flat as it is on the 10th floor. TURNER calls the police but when they arrive five minutes later it transpires that TURNER's partner had let FELLOWES in to install a new hi-fi system as a surprise for TURNER.

Which of the following comments is correct in respect of TURNER?

A TURNER has committed the offence of false imprisonment in these circumstances and has no defence to the charge.

B TURNER has not committed the offence as the period of imprisonment was too short.

C TURNER has committed the offence of false imprisonment but would have a defence in that she genuinely believed FELLOWES to be a burglar.

D TURNER has not committed the offence as she has not used any form of physical force against FELLOWES in order to imprison him.

Answer _____

PART 3

Property Offences

14 | Theft

14.1 Introduction

Brushing up on your knowledge of the offence of theft is a crucial part of your study and revision. The offence can be the subject of questions in its own right, but you must not forget that theft has major links to a number of other offences such as robbery and burglary. Before you study any offence where theft forms part of the definition, you must ensure that you have a good understanding of the basic material; this is what this section of the Workbook sets out to achieve.

14.2 Aim

The aim of this section is to provide you with an understanding of the offence of theft.

14.3 Objectives

At the end of this section you should be able to:

1. Define the offence of theft contrary to s. 1 of the Theft Act 1968.
2. Identify the different sections of the offence of theft.
3. Explain what is meant by the term 'dishonesty'.
4. Describe the implications of case law on dishonesty.
5. State the meaning of ss. 3, 4, 5 and 6 of the Theft Act 1968.
6. Demonstrate your knowledge by completing the exercises in this section.
7. Apply your knowledge to multiple-choice questions.

14.4 Theft

Theft is probably one of the first criminal law definitions any officer learns 'off by heart'. You *must be* able to define the offence before progressing any further.

14.4.1 Exercise—Definition of Theft?

What is the definition of the offence of theft contrary to s. 1 of the Theft Act 1968?

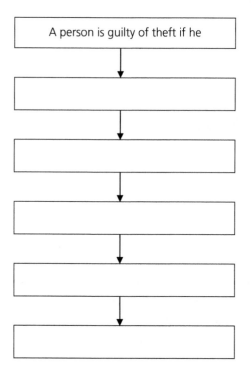

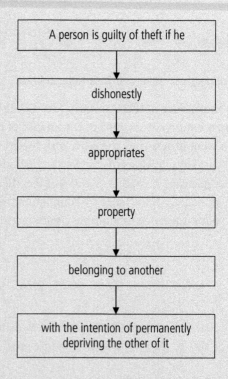

EXPLANATION 14.4.1

Definition of Theft?

Your answer should look something like this:

Do not forget that there is more to this definition! The above exercise allows you to provide what is considered to be the 'traditional' definition of theft but if you look at s. 1(1) there is more. The final element of the definition is 'and "thief" and "steal" shall be construed accordingly'.

See *Investigators' Manual*, para. 3.1.1

14.4.2   Exercise—Identifying the Sections of the Offence of Theft

Defining the offence of theft should be relatively straightforward. However, it is not uncommon for questions to be posed that ask about the details of the specific sections of the offence. These questions may ask you about a *section* of the Theft Act 1968 rather than tell you *what* the section is. As a consequence, you need to be able to identify the different sections of the offence.

Answer the following questions and write your answer in the space provided.

What does s. 4 of the Theft Act 1968 relate to?

_____

What does s. 6 of the Theft Act 1968 relate to?

_____

EXPLANATION 14.4.2

Identifying the Sections of the Offence of Theft

When a question is phrased in this fashion it becomes harder to answer, but you should be able to do so nevertheless. If you can remember the definition of theft, then remembering what a section relates to should cause you little difficulty. This is because the way in which candidates often learn to remember definitions is to break them down into lines (as we have done previously). Once you break the offence into lines, then the sections of the offence simply follow in the same order as the lines.

Section 1 of the Theft Act 1968 is the whole definition. You then simply place numbers 2, 3 and so on next to each line of your definition, as demonstrated in the following.

A person is guilty of theft if he	Section
Dishonestly	2
Appropriates	3
Property	4
Belonging to another	5
With the intention of permanently depriving the other of it	6

You should now be able to identify what each relevant section relates to.

14.5   Dishonesty

14.5.1   Exercise—Dishonesty True or False?

Examine the following comments and decide whether they are 'true' or 'false'.

1. If a person cannot be shown to have acted 'dishonestly', he/she is not guilty of theft.
True / False

2. The decision as to whether or not a defendant was in fact dishonest is one for the jury or magistrates.
True / False

3. There is a statutory definition of 'dishonesty'.
True / False

EXPLANATION 14.5.1

Dishonesty True or False?

Comments 1 and 2 are true; comment 3 is false.

Without 'dishonesty' there can be no theft. Although this part of the offence is important, there is no actual definition of what dishonesty is; rather, there is a 'negative' definition set out in s. 2(1) of the Act telling you when a defendant will not be dishonest.

See *Investigators' Manual*, para. 3.1.3

14.5.2   **Exercise—Dishonest or Not? You Decide**

In the following examples state whether the defendant is dishonest or not and give a short reason for your answer.

1. ORPWOOD is owed £100 by his employer. Without the permission of his employer but honestly believing he has a legal right to do so, ORPWOOD takes £100 from his employer's petty cash box.
Is ORPWOOD dishonest?

_____

Why / Why not?

_____

2. GAFFNEY is a cinema manager who needs £30 to repair his car. He takes £30 as an advance on his salary from the cinema till. He knows that he does not have a legal right to do so, but believes that the cinema owner would consent if he knew about the taking and the circumstances.
Is GAFFNEY dishonest?

_____

Why / Why not?

_____

3. ROBERTS finds a football season ticket with HUBER's details printed in it. ROBERTS keeps and uses the season ticket even though he knows he could easily find HUBER by taking reasonable steps.
Is ROBERTS dishonest?

_____

Why / Why not?

_____

4. BRUNTON finds a football season ticket with TAYLOR's details printed in it. Although BRUNTON realises that he could easily find TAYLOR and return the ticket to him, he keeps it because he honestly believes that he has a legal right to do so.
Is BRUNTON dishonest?

_____

Why / Why not?

_____

5. ALLEN is a shoplifter who is arrested for theft. He has £20 in his pocket and states that he is willing to pay for the goods he has taken.

Is ALLEN dishonest?

_____

Why / Why not?

_____

EXPLANATION 14.5.2

Dishonest or Not? You Decide

If you have read the *Investigators' Manual* you may have decided that Examples 1, 2 and 4 will not be dishonest. This is because of the effect of s. 2 of the Theft Act 1968, i.e. the defendant honestly believed they could act in a certain way.

Remember that a defendant will not be dishonest if he/she honestly believes in the LAW:

L   Legal right

A   Appropriated with consent

W   Will not find owner

Example 3 will be dishonest because ROBERTS can easily find HUBER. Example 5 may be dishonest under s. 2(2).

14.5.3   How Case Law Impacts on Dishonesty

Sometimes, s. 2 of the Theft Act 1968 will not be applicable or helpful and consequently the jury or magistrates will have to consider dishonesty in light of case law decisions. The case law in question is that of *Barlow Clowes International (in liq)* v *Eurotrust International Ltd* [2006] 1 All ER 333.

When dishonesty is in question, the magistrates/jury will first have to ascertain the actual state of the individual's knowledge or belief as to the facts (this does not have to be a reasonable belief—the question is whether the belief is genuinely held). Once his/her actual state of mind as to knowledge or belief is established, the question of whether his/her conduct had been honest or dishonest is to be determined by the magistrates/jury by applying the (objective) standards of ordinary decent people. There is no requirement that the defendant had to appreciate that what he/she had done was, by those standards, dishonest.

Taking this approach means that to prove dishonesty a prosecutor need only place before a court facts of what the defendant did and thought and then invite the court to hold that he/she was dishonest according to the standards of ordinary decent people.

See *Investigators' Manual*, para. 3.1.4

14.6   Appropriation

14.6.1   Exercise—Describe 'Appropriation'

Using only one sentence, describe what the term 'appropriation' means to you.

_____

EXPLANATION 14.6.1

Describe 'Appropriation'

You may have said something like 'an assumption by a person of the rights of an owner' and this would follow the spirit of s. 3 of the Theft Act 1968. However, the meaning of the term has been modified by a number of case law decisions. In order to test your knowledge, attempt the following exercises regarding appropriation.

14.6.2 Exercise—Developing the Term 'Appropriation'

In each of the following examples, state whether there has been an 'appropriation' and give your reason(s) for your decision.

1. REINER is a tourist who gives his wallet (full of unfamiliar English currency) to a taxi driver to remove the correct fare. The taxi driver helps himself to more than the amount owed. Is this an appropriation by the taxi driver?

_____

Does it matter that REINER handed the wallet over with consent?
Why / Why not?

_____

2. VALE swaps a number of price labels on goods displayed for sale in a shop. Is this an appropriation by VALE?

_____

Would it matter that VALE has no intention actually to steal the goods?
Why / Why not?

_____

3. HUNT is given an absolute gift of a valuable picture by KELSO, who retains no proprietary interest in the picture.
Is this an appropriation by HUNT?

_____

Could this become a criminal matter?
Why / Why not?

_____

4. CHAPPLE buys a bike from HEATH for £100. The bike is actually stolen but CHAPPLE does not know this.
Is this an appropriation by CHAPPLE?

_____

Would CHAPPLE be liable for theft at this stage?
Why / Why not?

_____

CHAPPLE finds out that the bike is stolen but refuses to give it back to the original owner.
Would CHAPPLE be liable for theft at this stage?
Why / Why not?

_____

EXPLANATION 14.6.2

Developing the Term 'Appropriation'

For Examples 1, 2 and 3, case law has illustrated that:

Consent is irrelevant to the issue of appropriation, whether or not the owner consented to that appropriation (Example 1). In this case, there has been an appropriation by the taxi driver (see *Lawrence* v *Metropolitan Police Commissioner* [1972] AC 626).

Swapping price labels amounts to appropriation (Example 2). This is so regardless of any future intention (see *DPP* v *Gomez* [1993] AC 442).

Providing an absolute gift in which no proprietary interest is held can amount to appropriation (Example 3). Whether this becomes a criminal matter would depend on the circumstances of the case (see *R* v *Hinks* [2000] 3 WLR 1590).

In Example 4, s. 3(2) of the Theft Act 1968 provides that although an appropriation has taken place, CHAPPLE will not, without more evidence, attract liability for an offence of theft.

See *Investigators' Manual*, para. 3.1.5

14.7 Property

14.7.1 Exercise—Property, True/False

Examine the following statements and decide whether they are true or false.

1. There are no circumstances under which land can be stolen.
True / False

2. The term 'property' does not include money.
True / False

3. Intangible property cannot be stolen.
True / False

4. The term 'property' includes human bodies.
True / False

5. Electricity is not property for the purposes of the Theft Act 1968.
True / False

EXPLANATION 14.7.1

Property, True/False

If you examine the *Investigators' Manual*, you will see that comments 1, 2, 3 and 4 are all false. Comment 5 is true.

See *Investigators' Manual*, para. 3.1.6

The definition of the term 'property' is somewhat lengthy. Rather than trying to remember what property is, try to remember what property is not.

Broadly speaking. property is not:

W Wild plants (unless the whole plant is taken for sale or reward (s. 4(3))) or wild animals (unless the animal has been or is in the process of being reduced into captivity (s. 4(4))).

H Human corpse (note that products of the body, such as urine, can be stolen and bodies/body parts can be stolen if some skill has been exercised on them).

> I Information (*Oxford* v *Moss* (1979) 68 Cr App R 183).
>
> L Land (although land can be stolen by (a) trustees etc., (b) someone not in possession of the land can appropriate anything severed from the land, and (c) a tenant can appropriate any fixture (s. 4(2)).
>
> E Electricity (*Low* v *Blease* (1975) 119 SJ 695).

14.8   Belonging to Another

14.8.1   Exercise—Developing a Scenario

Consider the following scenario and decide who the property is appropriated from, giving your reason(s).

CARROW owns a plant-hire business, hiring various tools to customers from a small industrial unit.

1. LINT enters the unit and takes a chainsaw from a display.
Who does LINT appropriate from and why?

_____

2. CARROW hires a wallpaper stripper to BRENT, who takes it to his home. LINT takes the wallpaper stripper from BRENT.
Who does LINT appropriate from and why?

_____

3. CARROW hires a cement mixer to FAY. FAY takes the cement mixer to PARK's house. PARK is using the cement mixer and leaves it unattended for several minutes. During this time, LINT takes the cement mixer.
Who does LINT appropriate from and why?

_____

4. CARROW hires a generator to RICE. RICE takes the generator home and leaves it outside his house. CARROW passes RICE's house and, seeing the generator, he decides to take it to compel RICE to pay for it. RICE tells CARROW that the generator has gone and CARROW demands a replacement generator from RICE.
Does CARROW appropriate property belonging to another?
Why / Why not?

_____

> **EXPLANATION 14.8.1**
>
> **Developing a Scenario**
>
> Under s. 5 of the Theft Act 1968, property will 'belong to another' if that person has possession or control of it or has a proprietary right or interest in it.
>
> At point 1, LINT appropriates from CARROW who is the owner of the property.
>
> At point 2, LINT appropriates from both CARROW and BRENT. CARROW hires the wallpaper stripper to BRENT and therefore retains ownership of it; however, BRENT has possession of it.
>
> At point 3, LINT appropriates from CARROW, FAY and PARK. CARROW remains the owner of the cement mixer, FAY has control of it and PARK has possession of it.

At point 4, CARROW appropriates property from RICE (even though he is the actual owner of the generator). This is because you can steal your own property in some circumstances (see *R v Turner* [1971] 1 WLR 901).

See *Investigators' Manual*, para. 3.1.8

14.9 Intention of Permanently Depriving

14.9.1 Exercise—Meaning of the Words

Write down what the intention to permanently deprive means to you.

EXPLANATION 14.9.1

Meaning of the Words

This part of the definition is often expressed using terms like, 'an intention to treat property as if it is your own' or 'ignoring others' rights regarding their own property', and terms similar to these are contained in the section.

Remember that there is no need to prove that the victim *is* actually permanently deprived of the property in question for the offence to be complete, but it must be shown that this was the *intention* of the defendant at the time he/she took the property. In many circumstances this intention will be plain, but s. 6 of the Theft Act 1968 gives you further direction as to when this intention can be inferred from the conduct of the defendant.

14.9.2 Exercise—Permanently Deprive? You Decide

Consider the following scenarios and explain if there is an intention to permanently deprive, giving your reason(s) why or why not.

1. BLACK takes a valuable painting belonging to DUFF. BLACK asks for £500 to be paid to a charity and then he will return the painting.
Is there an intention here?
Why / Why not?

---

2. COTTON borrows HILL's rugby season ticket for one game but then retains it, causing HILL to miss the remaining four games of the season.
Is there an intention here?
Why / Why not?

---

3. HURD is unemployed and pawns his mother's engagement ring for £1,000 in order to obtain money for cigarettes and beer.
Is there an intention here?
Why / Why not?

EXPLANATION 14.9.2

Permanently Deprive? You Decide

In all of the scenarios there is an intention to permanently deprive by virtue of s. 6 of the Theft Act 1968.

Holding property 'to ransom' qualifies as an intention to treat the property as one's own to dispose of, regardless of the other's rights (scenario 1). The same can be said for scenario 2, as the borrowing becomes the equivalent of an outright taking. Both are covered under s. 6(1) of the Act.

Scenario 3 would also illustrate an intention to permanently deprive but under s. 6(2) of the Act. Here, there is a likelihood that HURD will be unable to meet the conditions under which he parted with the property, i.e. there is little chance that HURD will ever have the money to obtain the ring from the pawnbrokers. See *Investigators' Manual*, para. 3.1.11

14.10 Conclusion

You should now have a good understanding of the offence of theft and its constituent parts. If you do not understand theft, then you will find it difficult to understand other offences where theft is a component part, and consequently you may answer a question incorrectly.

14.11 Recall Questions

Try and answer the following questions.

- What is the full definition of theft (s. 1 of the Theft Act 1968)?
- What are the three circumstances (under s. 2 of the Act) when a defendant *will not* be dishonest?
- What *is not* property?
- What does s. 5 of the Act relate to?
- What does case law tell us to do when s. 2 of the Theft Act 1968 is of no assistance?
- When can someone steal 'land or things forming part of the land and severed from it by him/her'?
- What does the term 'belonging to another' mean?

14.12 Multiple-Choice Questions

Answers to these questions can be found in the 'Answers Section' at the end of the book. All explanations also include a reference back to the *Investigators' Manual 2022*.

1. The Theft Act 1968 sets out a number of circumstances where a person will not be treated as dishonest and one circumstance where a person may be dishonest.

In which of the following circumstances may the person have acted 'dishonestly' for the purposes of theft?

A ATKINSON takes £50 from GIBSON's wallet in the honest belief that he has the right in law to do so in settlement of a debt.

B KEYTE finds a diamond ring worth £1,000 and decides to keep it as he honestly believes he could never find the owner even though the owner could, as it turns out, have been traced by making some simple enquiries.

C HILL urgently needs £100 to pay for repairs to his car and takes this amount from his employer's petty cash honestly believing that his employer would consent if he knew of the appropriation and its circumstances.

D RAND is selling computer games at a car boot sale. STOWE offers him £10 for a computer game which RAND refuses. STOWE throws down a £10 note and takes the computer game.

Answer _____

2. SMITH buys a second-hand car from LAUDER for £25,000. This is a reasonable price for the car at current market value and SMITH has every reason to trust LAUDER as LAUDER was recommended to SMITH by several of his close friends as a reliable car dealer. SMITH is later stopped by the police who discover that the car is stolen and originally belonged to GOODALL. When SMITH is informed, she refuses to hand the car back to GOODALL.

Would SMITH attract liability for theft?

A Yes, SMITH assumes the rights of the owner even though she has come by the property innocently.

B No, SMITH has purchased the car in good faith and for a reasonable price.

C Yes, when SMITH is informed of the circumstances and does not return the car she commits theft.

D No, SMITH was not the original thief and the same property cannot be appropriated on more than one occasion.

Answer _____

3. DELACY is a solicitor dealing primarily with mortgages. He is provided with £180,000 by BOOTH to buy a house. DELACY's business is in financial difficulties and so DELACY transfers BOOTH's mortgage money to his company account rather than holding the funds for the mortgage. DELACY knows that his actions are, at least, unethical.

Taking account of s. 5 of the Theft Act 1968, which of the following statements is correct?

A DELACY is under a legal obligation to deal with the money in a particular way. He has breached this obligation and has therefore committed theft.

B Ownership of the money has been transferred to DELACY's firm. Therefore, if DELACY has possession/control of the money, he cannot commit theft.

C When BOOTH transfers the money to DELACY, he revokes any proprietary interest in the money. This would be a contractual issue between BOOTH and DELACY.

D The property belongs to both parties. BOOTH would have to prove that DELACY did not intend to repay the money to prove theft.

Answer _____

15 Robbery and Blackmail

15.1 Introduction

Robbery and blackmail are closely related offences. As you work through this section you will see that there are distinct similarities between the two offences and it is important that you are able to identify which offence you are dealing with.

15.2 Aim

The aim of this section is for you to be able to identify when offences of robbery and blackmail may have been committed.

15.3 Objectives

At the end of this section you should be able to:

1. Define the offence of robbery contrary to s. 8 of the Theft Act 1968.
2. Explain the law with regard to the use of force in a robbery offence.
3. Identify who can be the subject of force in a robbery offence.
4. Identify when a robbery can be committed.
5. Define the offence of blackmail contrary to s. 21 of the Theft Act 1968.
6. Explain the meaning of the term 'gain and loss'.
7. Distinguish between the offence of robbery and the offence of blackmail.
8. Apply your knowledge to multiple-choice questions.

15.4 Robbery

As with so many other offences, you must know the definition of robbery before you move on to examine the offence in detail.

15.4.1 Exercise—Define the Offence of Robbery

What is the full definition of the offence of robbery contrary to s. 8 of the Theft Act 1968?

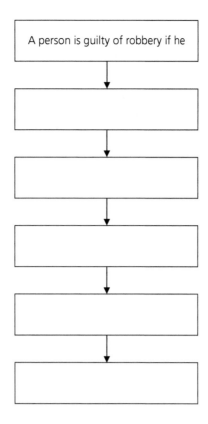

EXPLANATION 15.4.1

Define the Offence of Robbery

Your answer should have included:

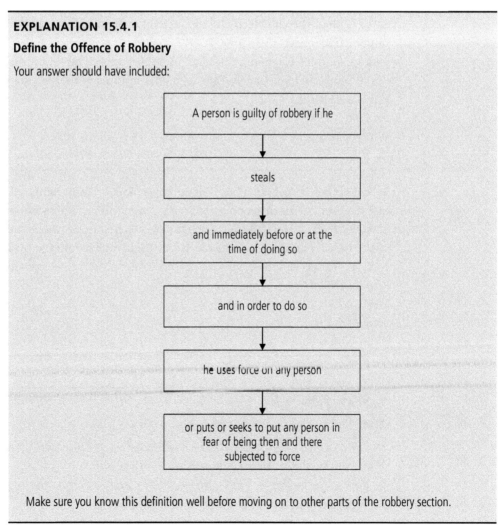

Make sure you know this definition well before moving on to other parts of the robbery section.

15.4.2 Steals

If you have followed the Workbook in content order you will have completed the 'Theft' section at this stage. If you have not, then you should complete 'Theft' before you go any further. This is because the word 'steal' in the definition of robbery means 'theft' and therefore if there is no theft then there can be no robbery.

As a consequence, if you do not understand theft then you cannot understand robbery. When you are considering whether or not there has been a robbery, you must first ask, 'Was there a theft?' You *must* consider *every* section of the theft definition when you ask that question.

15.4.3 Exercise—Think Theft!

Answer the following scenarios and give a short reason for your answer. Remember to think theft!

1. BARKER believes his employer owes him £20 for petrol expenses. BARKER's employer refuses to give him the money so BARKER puts a knife to his employer's throat and demands the money. The employer hands over £20. BARKER honestly believes he has a right in law to the money and the demand is a proper way of reinforcing it.
Is this a robbery?
Yes / No
Why / Why not?

_____

2. SCOTT has wired his electricity supply to his neighbour's house. His neighbour discovers this and disconnects the wiring. SCOTT goes to his neighbour's house and, once inside, he puts a gun to his neighbour's head and tells him he will be shot if the electricity supply is not reconnected immediately. The neighbour reconnects the electricity supply.
Is this a robbery?
Yes / No
Why / Why not?

_____

3. NORTH is driving his car but is stationary at a set of traffic lights. HUGHES has been to a nightclub and needs to get home but has no money for a taxi, so he opens the driver's door of NORTH's car and tells NORTH to hand over the car or he will be stabbed. Fearing for his safety, NORTH jumps out of the car. HUGHES drives five miles to his home and abandons NORTH's car (as he only wanted to use the car for a short time as transport to his home).
Is this a robbery?
Yes / No
Why / Why not?

_____

EXPLANATION 15.4.3

Think Theft!

If you were thinking 'theft', then you should have worked out that none of the previous incidents would be classed as a robbery. This is because in each case there is no theft.

1. There is no dishonesty on BAKER's part because he honestly believes he has a right in law to deprive his employer of the £20 (see s. 2(1)(a) of the Theft Act 1968).

2. There is no theft because electricity is not property for the purposes of the offence of robbery ('and thief and steal shall be construed accordingly' means that the 'steal' element in robbery links to the offence of theft and s. 4 of the Theft Act 1968. Just as you cannot 'steal' electricity, you cannot 'steal' it in a robbery).

3. There is no intention to permanently deprive and therefore no theft (see s. 6 of the Theft Act 1968).

See *Investigators' Manual*, paras 3.1.1 to 3.1.11, 3.2.1

15.4.4 Exercise—Immediately Before or at the Time of Doing So

Think about this term and ask whether the following scenarios would fit it.

1. LIMM approaches DOWD in a street and says, *'I've been following you and I know where you live. Give me your watch or I'll be waiting for you outside your house to beat you up when you get home.'*
Is this a robbery?
Yes / No

2. BURNS is in a shop and sees a cashier place a bag of coins near her till. BURNS grabs the bag of coins and runs out of the shop. The cashier chases BURNS into the street and shouts for help. PC HULL is in the street near to the shop and tries to stop BURNS who punches PC HULL in the face.
Is this a robbery?
Yes / No

EXPLANATION 15.4.4

Immediately Before or at the Time of Doing So

Neither scenario would be a robbery.
1. This is a threat to use force *at a time in the future* and *at a place other than the scene*.

2. Violence has been used but this is *after* the theft has taken place.

15.4.5 Exercise—In Order to Do So

Consider this term when you examine the following scenario.

1. MASON is drinking at a pub with his girlfriend. FIRTH approaches MASON's girlfriend and asks her what she is doing hanging around with a loser like MASON. MASON punches FIRTH in the face and FIRTH falls to the floor. MASON kicks FIRTH a number of times while he is on the floor and FIRTH's wallet falls out of his jacket. MASON decides to steal the wallet.
Is this a robbery?
Yes / No

2. KING is a pickpocket. On a busy train, he steals a wallet from inside PALIN's jacket. As KING is stealing the wallet, he accidentally catches PALIN on the chin with the wallet.
Is this a robbery?
Yes / No

3. BREWIN sees ELLIOT steal £50 from the till of a pub. ELLIOT approaches BREWIN and says, *'If you tell anyone about what you just saw, I'll beat you to a pulp.'*
Is this a robbery?
Yes / No

EXPLANATION 15.4.5

In Order to Do So

None of the previous scenarios would constitute a robbery.

1. This is not a robbery because the force was used for a reason *other than* to commit the theft. The whole point of the use or threatened use of force is to enable a theft to take place and nothing else.

2. The *accidental* application of force during a theft would not turn a theft into a robbery.

3. Once again, the threat of force is used for some other purpose than to commit theft, i.e. deterring a witness from revealing the theft.

15.4.6 Exercise—He Uses Force on Any Person

Examine the following statements and decide whether they are true or false.

1. RHONE was walking along a street holding a sports bag. WORLEY ran up behind him and pulled the bag from his hand using considerable force on the bag and dragging RHONE's hand downwards in the process. WORLEY ran off. This is a robbery.
True / False

2. When force is used or threatened, it must be towards the person from whom the theft is committed.
True / False

3. WRIGHT is working behind the counter of a jeweller's shop. LIGHTFOOT walks into the shop and stands several feet away from WRIGHT, next to an expensive cut glass decanter. LIGHTFOOT shouts over to WRIGHT and says, *'Give me £100 or I'll smash the decanter. This is a robbery.'*
True / False

EXPLANATION 15.4.6

He Uses Force on Any Person

Comment 1 is true; comments 2 and 3 are false.

1. In *R v Clouden* [1987] Crim LR 56, it was held that force applied to a person's property is force applied to the person. 'Force' is not defined, so whether a particular action amounts to force will be a question for the jury but see *P v DPP* [2012] EWHC 1657 (Admin) for the 'minimum' use of force on property.

2. Force can be used or threatened on *any* person and not necessarily the person who is the subject of the theft. For example, think about a security van (carrying cash belonging to a bank) being subject to a robbery offence. The van is stopped and an offender points a shotgun towards the head of the driver of the van. He shouts to a second security guard inside the 'vault' of the van to pass out the cash they are carrying or he will shoot the driver. The cash belongs to a bank but this does not matter. The guard inside the 'vault' is not being subjected to force or a threat of force, but the driver is and he is *any person*. This would be a robbery.

3. The force used must be on a person and not against property. This might seem contrary to point 1, but there is a difference between scenarios 1 and 3. In scenario 1, there is a direct physical connection between the sports bag and RHONE; this is not the case with WRIGHT.

15.4.7   Exercise—Puts or Seeks to Put Any Person in Fear of Being Then and There Subjected to Force

Consider this term and decide whether there has been a robbery in the following scenarios, giving a short reason for your answer.

1. TELFER is walking along a street having just left a karate class. TELFER is a fitness instructor and is highly qualified in martial arts. KOLADE approaches TELFER and points a knife at his chest, demanding his wallet. TELFER is not frightened at all and believes he could easily disarm KOLADE, but hands his wallet over to KOLADE as it has nothing of value in it.

Is this a robbery?

Yes / No

Why / Why not?

---

2. JOYNER is in a pub when FIDDICK approaches her. FIDDICK says, *'My friend is behind you with a knife. Don't turn around or you'll be stabbed. Just hand over your bag and everything will be alright.'* JOYNER believes the threat and hands her bag to FIDDICK. FIDDICK was lying to JOYNER, as there was no 'friend' standing behind her.

Is this a robbery?

Yes / No

Why / Why not?

---

3. Does it matter what TELFER or JOYNER think or believe?

Yes / No

Why / Why not?

EXPLANATION 15.4.7

Puts or Seeks to Put Any Person in Fear of Being Then and There Subjected to Force

There has been a robbery in both scenarios. This is because whether or not the victim is frightened or whether or not the threats made are capable of being carried out, *does not matter*. What is important here is the *intention* of the *offender*. If the offender actually puts or seeks to put the victim in fear of being then and there subjected to force, this part of the offence is complete.

See *Investigators' Manual*, para. 3.2.1

15.5   Blackmail

As you work through this section dealing with blackmail, you may well see where the connections to the offence of robbery exist. For the moment, we will concentrate on the offence of blackmail alone.

Complete Exercises 15.5.1, 15.5.2 and 15.5.3 before referring to the joint explanation which follows.

15.5.1   Exercise—Blackmail?

Begin this part of the section by writing down what you know about the offence of blackmail.

15.5.2   Exercise—Blackmail True or False?

Using the information you have written down, consider the following statements and decide whether they are true or false.

1. The offence of blackmail is all about the person making the demand actually gaining something; it has nothing to do with loss.
True / False

2. An offence of blackmail can only be committed when the defendant makes a demand for his/her own benefit.
True / False

15.5.3   Exercise—Blackmail Scenarios

Using the information in the first exercise and your answers to the true/false statements, examine the following scenarios and state whether or not there has been an offence of blackmail. Give a short reason for your answer.

1. MUTCH is playing a gaming machine in a licensed club. He wins the jackpot of £250 that is still stored within the machine and has not yet been dispensed to him. BULL is watching this and walks up to MUTCH and tells him to walk away from the machine and not to collect the money. BULL tells MUTCH that if he does not agree then he will tell MUTCH's wife that he is having an affair with the barmaid.
MUTCH is aware that BULL knows of his illicit affair and, in fear of his wife finding out, he walks away. BULL collects the winnings.
Is an offence of blackmail committed?
Yes / No
Why / Why not?

2. DIXON buys a £1,000 television from an electrical store owned by BUTLER. DIXON agrees to pay a monthly sum to settle the debt. There is no written agreement and there are no interest charges. DIXON falls behind with his payments and BUTLER visits him at his home. BUTLER tells DIXON that unless he pays a substantial part of the money owed, he will be barred from his shop and he will take the matter to a small claims court and recover the money through bailiffs. BUTLER believes this is a reasonable demand in the circumstances and his threat is warranted.
Is an offence of blackmail committed?
Yes / No
Why / Why not?

EXPLANATIONS 15.5.1, 15.5.2 AND **15.5.3**

Blackmail?, Blackmail True or False? and Blackmail Scenarios

You will probably have remembered that the central element of the offence of blackmail is a 'demand with menaces', but there is more to the offence than that.

Let's break the offence down into two parts.

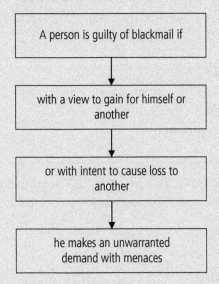

A person is guilty of blackmail if

with a view to gain for himself or another

or with intent to cause loss to another

he makes an unwarranted demand with menaces

You can see from this part of the definition that statements 1 and 2 (in the previous true/false exercise) are false. It also provides you with enough information to state that the first scenario (MUTCH) would constitute an offence of blackmail. This is because a demand with menaces has been made with a view to gain (on BULL's part) and an intention to cause loss (to MUTCH).

The next part of the offence is:

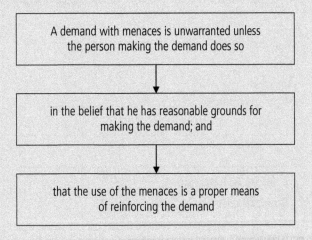

A demand with menaces is unwarranted unless the person making the demand does so

in the belief that he has reasonable grounds for making the demand; and

that the use of the menaces is a proper means of reinforcing the demand

You can see that in the second scenario (DIXON), the offence will not be made out. This is because the person making the demand does so believing he has reasonable grounds for making the demand and the menaces are a proper means of reinforcing it.

15.5.4 Exercise—Gain and Loss

Section 34(2) of the Theft Act 1968 defines 'gain' and 'loss' for the purposes of blackmail.

Examine the following scenarios and decide whether there has been a 'gain' or 'loss' for the purposes of blackmail.

1. MILLS approaches NEAL and tells her that if she does not have sexual intercourse with him he will tell her husband that the two of them have been having an affair. This is not true but NEAL is frightened of her husband and decides to have sexual intercourse with MILLS.
Gain?
Yes / No
Loss?
Yes / No
Why / Why not?

_____

2. MACDONALD approaches JUKKA and tells her that unless she allows him to use her car for a day he will tell her employer that she used to be a prostitute and get her fired.
Gain?
Yes / No
Loss?
Yes / No
Why / Why not?

_____

3. HAYWOOD has borrowed a computer from DRAYCOTT. DRAYCOTT asks for the computer to be returned but, when asked, HAYWOOD tells DRAYCOTT that unless he lets him keep the computer he will spread rumours that DRAYCOTT is a paedophile. DRAYCOTT does not want his reputation to be damaged and allows HAYWOOD to keep the computer.

Gain?
Yes / No
Loss?
Yes / No
Why / Why not?

_____

EXPLANATION 15.5.4
Gain and Loss

1. There is no gain or loss in these circumstances. This is because the gain or loss in blackmail must be one of money or other property. Sexual favours would not fall into this category.

2. There is a gain for MACDONALD and a loss for JUKKA. A gain or loss can be temporary as well as permanent.

3. There is a gain for HAYWOOD and a loss for DRAYCOTT. This is because a 'gain' includes a gain by keeping what one has (the computer) and a 'loss' includes a loss by not getting what one might get. This also applies to the MUTCH previous scenario.

See _Investigators' Manual_, paras 3.3.1 to 3.3.4

15.5.5   Exercise—Robbery, Blackmail or Both?

Go back to the beginning of the robbery part of this section and read every robbery scenario exercise, beginning at Exercise 15.4.2, that begins with a capitalised name (but do not include the SCOTT scenario at 15.4.3). Some of those scenarios will constitute offences of robbery only, some will be blackmail only, some will be both robbery and blackmail and others will be neither. Compile a list of those surnames under the appropriate heading in the following table.

Robbery	Blackmail	Robbery and Blackmail	Neither

EXPLANATION 15.5.5

Robbery, Blackmail or Both?

Your finished list of surnames should look like the following table.

Robbery	Blackmail	Robbery and Blackmail	Neither
WORLEY		FIDDICK	BARKER
	HUGHES	KOLADE	BURNS
	LIMM		MASON
	ELLIOT		KING
	LIGHTFOOT		

15.6   Conclusion

Understanding the similarities and differences between robbery and blackmail is an important part of your study and revision and can only be accomplished by having a sound knowledge of both offences. Now that you have finished this section, you should appreciate that blackmail is committed more often than you think. This is because an offence of robbery may also be an offence of blackmail, i.e. a robbery will often involve a demand with menaces. That said, it is far more likely that you would charge an offender with robbery as not only may this be a more appropriate charge but also the offence carries a life imprisonment sentence as opposed to 14 years for blackmail.

15.7   Recall Questions

Try and answer the following questions.

• What is the definition of robbery?
• What is the definition of blackmail?

- What is the defence to blackmail?
- Who can be subjected to force in a robbery?
- Can you explain the meaning of the terms 'gain' and 'loss' in blackmail?
- What is the difference between the offences of robbery and blackmail?

15.8 **Multiple-Choice Questions**

Answers to these questions can be found in the 'Answers Section' at the end of the book. All explanations also include a reference back to the *Investigators' Manual 2022*.

1. FISHER is expecting a parcel through the post. He is driving along the street where he lives when he sees the postman entering the street. FISHER stops his car, gets out and approaches the postman. FISHER asks the postman if there is a parcel for him and gives his name and address. The postman checks in his van, picks up a parcel addressed to FISHER at his address and says that there is. FISHER asks for it and the postman refuses, saying that he has to deliver it to the address stated upon it. Honestly believing he has a right in law to the parcel, FISHER demands the parcel and threatens to assault the postman, who again refuses to hand it over. FISHER then steps forward and punches the postman who drops the parcel on the pavement. FISHER picks the parcel up and walks to his car.

At what stage, if at all, does FISHER commit the offence of robbery?

A When he demands the parcel and threatens to assault the postman.

B When he punches the postman who drops the parcel to the pavement.

C When FISHER picks the parcel up and walks to his car.

D FISHER does not commit the offence in these circumstances.

Answer _____

2. LEWIN approaches RIHAN who is sitting on a bench in a park. LEWIN says, *'Give me your wallet or I'll follow you to your house and beat you up.'* RIHAN does not respond at all. LEWIN then says, *'Do you think I'm joking? Hand over your wallet or I'll beat you up right now!'* RIHAN still does not respond. LEWIN produces a knife and waves it in front of RIHAN saying, *'Last chance before you get stabbed!'* RIHAN does not respond. This is because RIHAN is deaf and blind and has not heard or seen any of LEWIN's threats.

When, if at all, does LEWIN commit an offence of attempted robbery?

A When he threatens to follow RIHAN home and beat him up.

B When he threatens to beat RIHAN up 'right now'.

C When he produces the knife and threatens to stab RIHAN.

D The offence is not committed in these circumstances.

Answer _____

3. CHUNG and O'COUGHLAN work in the same office and are both up for promotion; whoever gets that promotion will earn far more money as a result. Intending to gain money, CHUNG writes a letter to O'COUGHLAN stating that unless O'COUGHLAN pulls out of the promotion race, he will burn down O'COUGHLAN's house. CHUNG puts the letter into a postbox near his house but the letter gets lost in the post and O'COUGHLAN never sees it.

Is this an offence of blackmail (contrary to s. 21 of the Theft Act 1968)?

A No, because it is not possible to commit blackmail by sending the demand in the form of a letter.

B Yes, but the permission of the DPP would be required to prosecute CHUNG.

C No, because O'COUGHLAN never actually received the letter and does not know about CHUNG's demand.

D Yes, and CHUNG could be sentenced to a maximum of 14 years' imprisonment for committing the offence.

Answer _____

16 | Burglary and Aggravated Burglary

16.1 Introduction

There is a very strong chance that multiple-choice questions on the offences of burglary and aggravated burglary will form part of your NIE. Therefore, your understanding of this area of law is vitally important if you are to be successful.

In this section of the Workbook, you will examine these offences in some depth. This will involve breaking the offences down into their component parts in order to provide you with the necessary comprehension you require. Some of these component parts are common among all the offences relating to burglary.

16.2 Aim

The aim of this section is to provide you with knowledge of the offences of burglary and aggravated burglary.

16.3 Objectives

At the end of this section you should be able to:

1. Define the offences of burglary contrary to ss. 9(1)(a) and 9(1)(b) of the Theft Act 1968.
2. Identify when a defendant has 'entered' a building.
3. State what a 'building or part of a building' means.
4. Identify when a defendant becomes a 'trespasser'.
5. List the differences between the offences of burglary in ss. 9(1)(a) and 9(1)(b).
6. Define the offence of aggravated burglary contrary to s. 10.
7. Demonstrate your knowledge by completing the exercises in this section.
8. Apply your knowledge to multiple-choice questions.

16.4   Burglary, s. 9(1)(a)

There are hundreds of offence definitions contained within the *Investigators' Manual*. To set yourself the task of being able to memorise and recall every single one of them 'word perfect' may be difficult, to say the least. However, because the offence of burglary is a relatively common occurrence, it is highly likely that in order to answer questions on the subject correctly this is one of the offence definitions that you will need to know word for word.

16.4.1   Exercise—Define Burglary, s. 9(1)(a)

What is the full definition of the offence of burglary contrary to s. 9(1)(a) of the Theft Act 1968? (Include the offences that the defendant must intend to commit under s. 9(2) of the Act.)

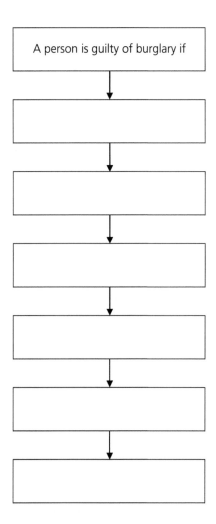

EXPLANATION 16.4.1

Define Burglary, s. 9(1)(a)

Your answer should look something like this:

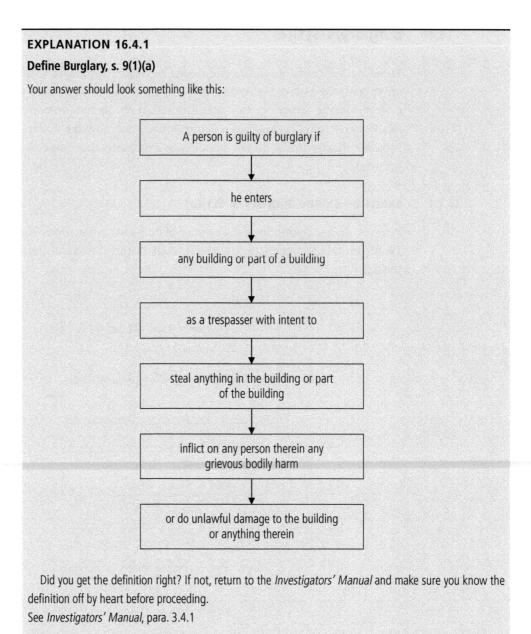

Did you get the definition right? If not, return to the *Investigators' Manual* and make sure you know the definition off by heart before proceeding.

See *Investigators' Manual*, para. 3.4.1

Now that you can define the basic definition of burglary under s. 9(1)(a), you should examine each part of the offence in turn. Questions on offences such as burglary will often concentrate on the individual elements of the offence in order to test your knowledge and understanding of the subject.

16.4.2   Exercise—Entry

Consider the following scenarios and decide whether an 'entry' (for the purposes of burglary) has been made by the defendant.

1. CRAVEN and HAMILTON are walking past a house when CRAVEN pushes HAMILTON. HAMILTON falls over and through an open door leading into the hall of the house.
Entry / No Entry

2. BURSELL intends to steal and leans through a kitchen window in order to grab hold of a purse on a kitchen work surface. BURSELL's legs remain outside the building when he leans through the window.
Entry / No Entry

3. HICKSON puts his hand through a porch letterbox and steals some letters lying on the floor of the porch.
Entry / No Entry

4. McKAY pushes a fishing rod through a window to try and hook a wallet from the pocket of a coat hanging on a coat hook.
Entry / No Entry

EXPLANATION 16.4.2

Entry

The test for whether an entry has been made is to ask if it was 'effective' (*R v Brown* [1985] Crim LR 212).

In example 1 there has been no 'entry' by HAMILTON. This is because his actions are involuntary, i.e. CRAVEN pushed him and he accidentally fell into the house. As entry is part of the *actus reus* of burglary and the *actus reus* of an offence must be voluntary, there can be no entry in these circumstances.

Examples 2 and 3, although slightly different as to the extent that the defendant's body crosses the threshold of the building, would both qualify as an 'entry'. In *R v Brown* (noted earlier), the defendant had leant through a shop window so that the upper half of his body was inside it (as with BURSELL in example 2).

The degree that a defendant's body enters may only need to be slight (as in example 3). In this example, it is only HICKSON's hand that enters the porch but this would still be an entry as it allows him to steal letters; in other words, it is 'effective'.

Example 4 also constitutes 'entry'. A defendant can use any object as an extension of themselves (such as McKAY using the fishing rod).

See *Investigators' Manual*, para. 3.4.1

16.4.3 Exercise—Building

The first question you must ask when looking at this part of the definition is, 'What is a building?'

Examine the following comments and decide whether they are 'true' or 'false'.

1. A burglary can only be committed if the building is a dwelling.
True / False

2. An unfinished house can be a building.
True / False

3. A tent can be a building.
True / False

4. An industrial freezer can be a building.
True / False

5. An inhabited houseboat is not a building.
True / False

6. An abandoned caravan is a building.
True / False

EXPLANATION 16.4.3

Building

Comments 1, 3, 5 and 6 are all false. Comments 2 and 4 are true. Your Manual details some of the cases that led to these decisions.

16.4.4   Exercise—Part of a Building

The second question you must ask is, 'What is part of a building?'

How can you tell a person has moved from one part of a building into another? (Write your answer in the following space.)

EXPLANATION 16.4.4

Part of a Building

You are probably aware that just because someone legally enters one part of a building, it does not necessarily mean that they can then legitimately access all areas/rooms of that building. As such, your answer may have said that a person would have to walk through a doorway or enter a separate room, but what if there is no significant 'physical' separation like a door or barrier? This does not mean that a person has not entered a separate part of a building.

A good example of this concept is the case of *R v Walkington* [1979] 1 WLR 1169, where it was held that a person entered an entirely separate part of a building when they moved from a shop floor to an area behind a movable three-sided counter. Think of this as 'crossing a line in the sand'. If the defendant moves over the line, for example by walking into an area marked by a warning sign that says 'Private' or 'Staff only', then by crossing the line the defendant has moved from one part of a building into another.

See *Investigators' Manual*, para. 3.4.2

16.4.5   Exercise—Trespasser

You should now consider whether or not the defendant is a 'trespasser' when he/she enters the building.

In the following examples state whether the defendant is a trespasser or not (from a burglary perspective) and give a short reason for your answer.

1. MAYNE intends to steal and approaches a house belonging to STEELE. MAYNE smashes a front window and climbs into the living room. MAYNE knows that he does not have permission to enter the house.
Is MAYNE a trespasser?

Why / Why not?

---

2. STARK is wandering around a large shop. He sees a sign on a wall indicating that an area in front of him is open to staff only. STARK thinks that he may not be allowed into the area but goes in anyway.

Is STARK a trespasser?

_____

Why / Why not?

_____

3. YALE visits his friend, JINKS. JINKS allows YALE into his house and they sit in the lounge. JINKS then leaves the room and, while he is out, YALE steals some money from a shelf above the fireplace in the lounge.
Is YALE a trespasser?

_____

Why / Why not?

_____

4. BRACE asks TALBOT to look after her house while she goes on holiday for a week. BRACE gives TALBOT the keys to her house and tells TALBOT she can use the house while she is away. TALBOT decides to steal BRACE's DVD player while she is away and enters with that intent.
Is TALBOT a trespasser?

_____

Why / Why not?

_____

EXPLANATION 16.4.5

Trespasser

The 'state of mind' required for the defendant to be a trespasser is knowledge that they do not have express or implied permission to enter, or subjective recklessness as to that fact.

This should not cause too many problems when faced with the obvious circumstances such as example 1, where MAYNE is a trespasser because he knows that he does not have permission to enter the house.

Example 2 deals with the subjective recklessness side of trespass. STARK is a trespasser because he realises that he should not go in to the area but does so anyway.

In example 3, YALE is not a trespasser (at least not when he enters the house). There are two reasons for this:

1. YALE never entered the house as a trespasser, i.e. JINKS invited him into his house, but more importantly and in addition to this fact,

2. YALE never had any of the criminal intentions required for burglary when he entered JINKS's house (see the explanation for example 4 for the difference when this intent is present).

What about example 4? Although BRACE has given TALBOT permission to enter her house, TALBOT is still a trespasser. This is because BRACE has given TALBOT a 'conditional permission' to use the house and TALBOT has exceeded that permission. Ask yourself the question, 'Would BRACE have expected TALBOT to enter her house and steal?' The answer must be 'No'. Therefore TALBOT's intention to steal makes her a trespasser from the moment she enters the house. Compare this with example 3. The subtle but important difference is the intention of the defendant when entering a building or part of a building. There have been a number of cases dealing with this issue, but perhaps the best way of remembering this information is to recall a comment made by Lord Justice Scrutton, who said, 'When you invite a person into your house to use the staircase you do not invite him to slide down the banister.' What we can say about example 3 is that at the point when YALE steals he DOES become a trespasser—JINKS did not invite him in to steal! However, he DID NOT ENTER as a trespasser so only commits theft.

See *Investigators' Manual*, para. 3.4.1

16.4.6 To Steal, to Inflict Grievous Bodily Harm and to Cause Damage

To steal (as per s. 1 of the Theft Act 1968), to commit grievous bodily harm (as per s. 18 of the Offences Against the Person Act 1861) and to commit criminal damage (as per s. 1(1) of the Criminal Damage Act 1971).

Remember that it is only an intention to commit one of these three 'trigger' offences that will constitute an offence of burglary under s. 9(1)(a).

As a consequence, you must also consider all the elements of those offences, particularly 'steal' and 'damage'. For example, if a defendant enters a building as a trespasser with the intent to steal, but believes he/she has a right in law to take the property, there will be no burglary.

This is because:

i. the defendant intends to appropriate property, but
ii. does so in the belief that he has a right in law to deprive the other person of it, therefore,
iii. there is no dishonesty and, consequently,
iv. there is no theft, and
v. if the theft (stealing) element is missing, there can be no burglary.

See *Investigators' Manual*, para. 3.4.3

16.5 Burglary, s. 9(1)(b)

16.5.1 Exercise—Define Burglary, s. 9(1)(b)

What is the full definition of the offence of burglary contrary to s. 9(1)(b) of the Theft Act 1968?

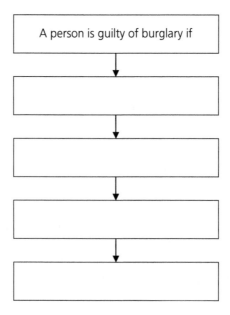

A person is guilty of burglary if

EXPLANATION 16.5.1

Define Burglary, s. 9(1)(b)

Your answer should look something like this:

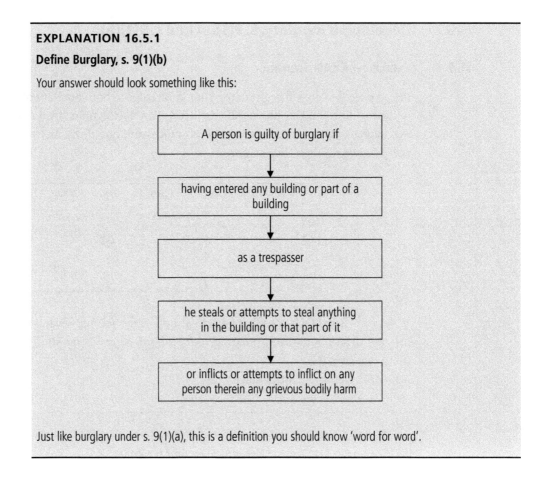

```
┌─────────────────────────────────────────────┐
│        A person is guilty of burglary if      │
└─────────────────────────────────────────────┘
                      │
                      ▼
┌─────────────────────────────────────────────┐
│     having entered any building or part of a  │
│                   building                    │
└─────────────────────────────────────────────┘
                      │
                      ▼
┌─────────────────────────────────────────────┐
│                as a trespasser                │
└─────────────────────────────────────────────┘
                      │
                      ▼
┌─────────────────────────────────────────────┐
│    he steals or attempts to steal anything    │
│       in the building or that part of it      │
└─────────────────────────────────────────────┘
                      │
                      ▼
┌─────────────────────────────────────────────┐
│       or inflicts or attempts to inflict on any│
│    person therein any grievous bodily harm    │
└─────────────────────────────────────────────┘
```

Just like burglary under s. 9(1)(a), this is a definition you should know 'word for word'.

16.6 The Difference between Burglary, s. 9(1)(a) and s. 9(1)(b)

16.6.1 Exercise—Identify the Differences

What are the differences between the offences of burglary under ss. 9(1)(a) and 9(1)(b)?

EXPLANATION 16.6.1

Identify the Differences

Your answer may have included:

1. Section 9(1)(a) relates to *enter*, whereas s. 9(1)(b) relates to *having entered*.

2. Section 9(1)(a) has *three* 'trigger' offences; s. 9(1)(b) has *two*.

3. The offence of criminal *damage* is *excluded* from the s. 9(1)(b) definition.

4. Section 9(1)(b) *includes attempts* to commit the two 'trigger' offences.

5. Section 9(1)(b) includes GBH of the s. 18 AND s. 20 variety (s. 9(1)(a) is s. 18 only).

The law relating to 'entry', 'building or part of a building' and 'trespasser' has already been discussed and the basic principles remain the same for the offence under s. 9(1)(b).

16.7 Developing Burglary, s. 9(1)(a) and s. 9(1)(b)

16.7.1 Exercise—KHAN Scenario

In this exercise you will begin to use your knowledge of both burglary offences. Look at the following diagram. Our potential defendant, KHAN, is signified by a mark ⊙. Underneath the diagram, you are given a set of circumstances and questions. Answer these questions as you progress through the exercise.

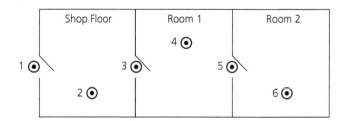

1. At point 1, KHAN is standing outside a shop. The shop has several rooms behind it but they are all part of the same building. He decides to go inside the shop and browse through the goods on display.
Is KHAN a trespasser at this stage?

_____

2. At point 2, KHAN is browsing through some books and decides to steal them. Does this decision make KHAN a trespasser? (Give your reason(s).)

_____

If it does, does he commit burglary and under which section of the Act?

_____

3. At point 2 again, KHAN *actually places* several books into his coat pocket. Does this action make KHAN a trespasser? (Give your reason(s).)

_____

If it does, does he commit burglary and under which section of the Act?

_____

4. KHAN sees a door marked 'Private—no customers allowed beyond this door'. He takes no notice of the sign and decides to go through it to have a look around out of curiosity. This takes place at point 3.
As KHAN enters the door at point 3, is he a trespasser? (Give your reason(s).)

_____

If he is, does he commit burglary and under which section of the Act?

_____

5. At point 4, KHAN is looking round the room when he sees a glass vase; KHAN smashes the vase out of spite.
Does KHAN commit burglary and, if so, under which section of the Act?

_____

6. After smashing the vase at point 4, KHAN decides to steal anything he can.
Does this intention make KHAN guilty of burglary? (Give your reason(s).)

_____

If it does, under which section of the Act is it committed?

_____

7. KHAN can see nothing of value in Room 1 and so decides he will steal anything he can find of value in Room 2. KHAN goes through the door into Room 2 (point 5).
Does KHAN commit burglary and, if so, under what section of the Act?

_____

8. At point 6, KHAN is searching for something to steal when GROVE, a shop assistant, interrupts him. KHAN pushes her to the floor and kicks her so hard that the force of the kick breaks her arm.
Does KHAN commit burglary and, if so, under what section of the Act? (Give your reason(s).)

_____

EXPLANATION 16.7.1

KHAN Scenario

1. Point 1. KHAN is not a trespasser, as he has not illegally entered any premises.

2. Point 2. KHAN has entered the shop as a legitimate customer but then decides to steal. This intention (a pure mental state) *does not* make KHAN a trespasser. Remember that a person must enter a building or part of a building as a trespasser at the point of entry or they will not commit burglary—merely thinking about stealing something would not turn KHAN into a trespasser because of his dishonest thoughts. Any subsequent criminal activity will not retrospectively change the 'entry' status of the person. At this point, KHAN is not a trespasser and commits no offence of burglary.

3. Point 2. KHAN would be considered a trespasser. Imagine the shop owner standing next to KHAN watching him steal the books. The reaction of the shop owner would be, at least, to throw KHAN out of the shop. So we can say that KHAN's theft turns him into a trespasser as it extinguishes his right to be in the shop. However, he DID NOT ENTER as a trespasser—he subsequently became a trespasser by exceeding a condition of entry (stealing). At this stage, KHAN commits theft.

4. Point 3. KHAN is now a trespasser. The door is clearly marked and he is moving from one part of a building to another. However, because he has no criminal intent at this stage, he does not commit burglary.

5. Point 4. Inside this room KHAN is a trespasser. However, once inside the room he can only become a burglar by committing one of the two 'trigger' offences under s. 9(1)(b), i.e. theft or GBH (or attempting either offence). As KHAN commits criminal damage, he is not a burglar at this stage.

6. Point 4. The only time a burglary under s. 9(1)(a) can be committed is *at the actual entry point* to a building or part of a building, *not after entry*. KHAN has not committed a burglary at this stage.

7. Point 5. At this point, KHAN becomes a burglar under s. 9(1)(a). He is entering part of a building as a trespasser with the intention to steal.

8. Point 6. KHAN commits another burglary at this point but this time under s. 9(1)(b). Having entered the room as a trespasser, he inflicts GBH on the shop assistant.

See *Investigators' Manual*, para. 3.4.5

16.8 Aggravated Burglary

Before you study the offence of aggravated burglary, make sure that you understand the basic offences of burglary. If you do not, you will find it difficult to tell when an aggravated burglary has been committed.

16.8.1 Exercise—Define Aggravated Burglary, s. 10

What is the full definition of the offence of aggravated burglary contrary to s. 10 of the Theft Act 1968?

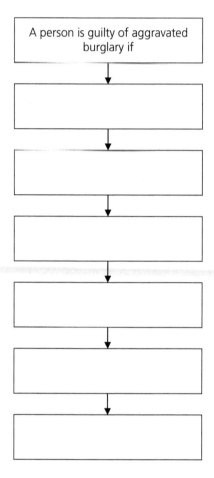

EXPLANATION 16.8.1

Define Aggravated Burglary, s. 10

Your answer should look something like this:

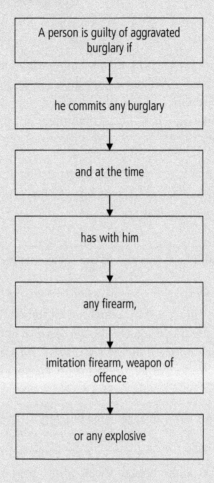

The most common way of remembering the articles needed for the burglary to become aggravated is WIFE.

W   Weapon of offence

I   Imitation firearm

F   Firearm

E   Explosive

The definitions of firearm, imitation firearm, weapon of offence and explosive are contained within your Manual.

The important parts of this definition are 'has with him' and 'at the time'. These elements will be considered in the next exercise.

See *Investigators' Manual*, para. 3.5.1

16.8.2   Exercise—Exploring s. 10 Aggravated Burglary

In this exercise, you will use your knowledge of both burglary offences and your knowledge of aggravated burglary. Look at the following diagram. Our potential defendant, HALL, is signified by a mark ⊙. Underneath the diagram you are given a set of circumstances and questions.

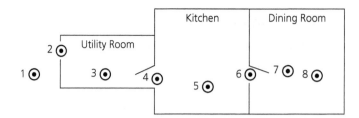

1. At point 1, HALL is standing outside a house. He intends to break in and steal from the house. HALL has a screwdriver in his possession in order to force a window into the utility room.

At this stage, has HALL committed an offence in relation to burglary and, if so, what offence?

_____

2. At point 2, HALL breaks into the house by forcing a window with the screwdriver. What type of burglary is this?

_____

Would it be aggravated in the circumstances? (Give your reason(s).)

_____

3. At point 3, HALL is searching for something to steal when he hears a noise from the kitchen. He thinks it might be the occupier and quickly picks up an iron (he does not intend to steal the iron). He decides that he will use the iron to hit anybody who disturbs him.

Is the iron a weapon of offence? (Give your reason(s).)

_____

Would this be an aggravated burglary? (Give your reason(s).)

_____

4. HALL looks through the door into the kitchen and sees that a dog is making the noise. He puts the iron down and picks up several ties from a wash basket. He intends to steal from the kitchen but wants to tie up the dog so that it does not cause him any problems during the burglary.

Are the ties a weapon of offence? (Give your reason(s).)

_____

5. At point 4, HALL enters the kitchen with these intentions.

Is this a burglary? (Give your reason(s).)

_____

If it is a burglary, is it aggravated? (Give your reason(s).)

_____

6. At point 5, HALL has tied up the dog. He is now looking for something to steal when he hears a noise from the dining room. He sees an air pistol on the kitchen work surface and grabs hold of it to hurt anyone who gets in his way (he does not intend to steal the air pistol).

Is the air pistol a firearm? (Give your reason(s).)

_____

7. At point 6, and still in possession of the air pistol, HALL enters the dining room intending to steal.

What type of burglary is this?

_____

Is it aggravated? (Give your reason(s).)

_____

8. At point 7, PRIME (the occupier of the house) disturbs HALL. HALL takes out the screwdriver he used to force the window and, pointing it at PRIME, he tells her to stay back or she will be stabbed.

Is the screwdriver a weapon of offence? (Give your reason(s).)

_____

Is this an aggravated burglary? (Give your reason(s).)

_____

9. At point 8, PRIME is backing away from HALL. Still pointing the screwdriver at PRIME, HALL grabs hold of some cash on the dining room table and then makes his escape.

What type of burglary is this?

_____

Is it aggravated? (Give your reason(s).)

_____

EXPLANATION 16.8.2

Exploring s. 10 Aggravated Burglary

1. Point 1. HALL has not committed an offence in relation to burglary at this stage (although he has the required intent for an offence of burglary under s. 9(1)(a)).

2. Point 2. This is a burglary contrary to s. 9(1)(a) but it is not aggravated. Although HALL has a screwdriver in his possession, the screwdriver is to facilitate entry and would not qualify as a weapon of offence.

3. Point 3. The iron is a weapon of offence. Although it is an innocent enough object in itself, HALL's intentions to use it to cause injury instantaneously change it from a household item into a weapon of offence. Absolutely anything at all, even the most innocuous of items, can immediately become a weapon of offence because of this intended use.

   At this point there is no aggravated burglary. This is because HALL has already entered the utility room and, once inside the room, he can only commit a burglary contrary to s. 9(1)(b). Remember that aggravated burglary requires the WIFE to be with the defendant when the burglary takes place, so unless HALL actually steals, causes GBH or attempts either, there is no offence under s. 10 of the Act.

4. Point 3. The ties are not weapons of offence. This is because HALL intends to use them to incapacitate a dog and not a *person*.

5. Point 4. This is a burglary contrary to s. 9(1)(a). HALL enters part of a building as a trespasser with the intention of stealing. It is not aggravated because the ties are not weapons of offence.

6. Point 5. The air pistol is a firearm by virtue of s. 10(1)(a) of the Act.

7. Point 6. Once again, HALL commits a burglary contrary to s. 9(1)(a). It is an aggravated burglary because *at the time of entry* he had a firearm with him.

8. Point 7. As explained previously, the screwdriver changes from an instrument to force entry into an offensive weapon the moment HALL threatens PRIME with it. However, at this stage no aggravated burglary is committed because HALL only threatens PRIME; this threat would not qualify as an attempt to cause GBH.

9. Point 8. As soon as HALL steals, he commits a burglary contrary to s. 9(1)(b). As he *has with him* a weapon of offence (the screwdriver) when he commits the offence, this becomes an aggravated burglary.

See *Investigators' Manual*, paras 3.5.1 to 3.5.2

16.9   Conclusion

Now that you have finished this section of the Workbook, you should appreciate that although burglary may seem to be a simple offence, this is not always the case. Remember that each part of the definition of the offence must be proved in order for the offence to be complete. You should supplement the knowledge gained from this section and exercises with the continued examination of the law in the *Investigators' Manual*.

16.10   Recall Questions

Try and answer the following questions.

- What two sections of the Theft Act 1968 define burglary?
- What section of the Theft Act 1968 defines aggravated burglary?
- What is the sentence for an offence of aggravated burglary?
- What is the sentence for an offence of burglary committed in a dwelling?
- What is the sentence for an offence of burglary committed in a shop?
- What are the three 'trigger' offences for the purposes of burglary under s. 9(1)(a)?
- What are the 'trigger' offences for the purposes of burglary under s. 9(1)(b)?
- State the full definition of the offence of aggravated burglary contrary to s. 10.
- What does the term 'enter' mean?
- Define the full offence of burglary contrary to s. 9(1)(b).
- What is a 'weapon of offence' for the purposes of aggravated burglary?
- Define the full offence of burglary contrary to s. 9(1)(a).
- What is a 'firearm' for the purposes of aggravated burglary?
- Give different examples of a 'building'.
- What does the term 'trespasser' mean?

16.11   Multiple-Choice Questions

Answers to these questions can be found in the 'Answers Section' at the end of the book. All explanations also include a reference back to the *Investigators' Manual 2022*.

1. REDGRAVE believes that he has been unfairly dismissed from his job as a garage mechanic. He plans to break into his ex-employer's garage and turn on all the electrical machines over the company's two-week Christmas break, thereby causing the company's electric bill to be extremely high. REDGRAVE breaks into the garage and turns on all the machines. As he is doing this, he loses his temper and smashes several car windscreens in the garage.

He then decides to hide one of the cars being repaired in the garage and drives off in a car, abandoning it 10 miles away.

At what point, if at all, does REDGRAVE first commit an offence of burglary?

A When he initially breaks into the garage.

B When he smashes the car windscreens in the garage.

C When he drives the car away from the garage.

D No offence of burglary is committed in these circumstances.

Answer _____

2. HILDRED is going on holiday for two weeks and asks her friend, BURTOFT, to look after her house while she is away. HILDRED tells BURTOFT that she is free to use the whole of her house at any time while she is away. BURTOFT goes to the house one day to do some household chores and while cleaning an upstairs bedroom she finds £100 cash. BURTOFT decides to steal the money. She then decides to look around the bedroom for anything else of value and finds and steals an antique watch. BURTOFT then sees a loft hatch in the bedroom and decides she will search the loft for anything to steal. BURTOFT enters the loft but finds nothing of value.

Which of the following statements is true?

A BURTOFT commits a burglary contrary to s. 9(1)(b) when she steals the £100 cash from the bedroom.

B BURTOFT commits a burglary contrary to s. 9(1)(b) when she steals the antique watch from the bedroom.

C BURTOFT commits a burglary contrary to s. 9(1)(a) when she enters the loft.

D BURTOFT never commits burglary because at no point is she a trespasser.

Answer _____

3. WARREN and OAK decide to break into and steal from a house owned by HOLLAND. They think HOLLAND may be inside the house when they break in so they take several lengths of rope with them to tie up HOLLAND. The two get to HOLLAND's house with WARREN carrying the rope. OAK has a screwdriver with him that he uses to force a window. OAK has sharpened the end of the screwdriver to use it against HOLLAND if the need arises; WARREN does not know of OAK's intentions regarding the screwdriver. When both men enter the house, it becomes apparent that HOLLAND is not at home.

Considering the offence of aggravated burglary (contrary to s. 10 of the Theft Act 1968) only, which of the following is true?

A Neither WARREN nor OAK commit the offence because HOLLAND is not in the house.

B WARREN and OAK commit the offence, but WARREN only commits it in relation to the rope.

C WARREN and OAK commit the offence in relation to both the rope and the sharpened screwdriver.

D WARREN and OAK commit the offence, but OAK only commits it in relation to the sharpened screwdriver.

Answer _____

4. MARKER is owed £500 by LOVELL. LOVELL tells MARKER that he has no intention whatsoever of paying the debt to him. MARKER is outraged by this and, believing he has a lawful right to the money, he visits LOVELL's house. LOVELL answers the front door to

MARKER who pushes LOVELL aside and enters the hall of LOVELL's house. LOVELL tells MARKER to get out but MARKER takes no notice of LOVELL and produces a 12-inch knife that he had hidden in his belt and waves it under LOVELL's nose. MARKER tells LOVELL that unless he produces the £500 cash immediately, he will stab him. LOVELL is terrified and gives in to MARKER's demand and gives him the cash. On his way out of the front door of the house, MARKER shouts to LOVELL, *'Here is something to remember me by!'* and, using the 12-inch knife, he slashes a painting near to the front door, causing £5,000 worth of damage to the painting.

Considering the law relating to the offences of burglary and aggravated burglary, which of the following statements is correct?

A MARKER commits a burglary contrary to s. 9(1)(a) of the Theft Act 1968 when he enters the house.

B MARKER commits an aggravated burglary contrary to s. 10 of the Theft Act 1968 when he produces the knife and threatens LOVELL with it.

C MARKER commits a burglary contrary to s. 9(1)(b) of the Theft Act 1968 when he causes criminal damage to the painting.

D MARKER does not commit an offence of burglary in these circumstances.

Answer _____

17 Handling Stolen Goods

17.1 Introduction

It has been said that without receivers there would be no thieves (*R* v *Battams* (1979) 1 Cr App R 15). The symbiotic relationship between handler and thief is one reason why the offence of handling stolen goods is deemed to be a more serious offence than theft, with the maximum sentence for handling being set at 14 years as opposed to seven years for theft.

17.2 Aim

The aim of this section is to assist in your understanding of the law surrounding the offence of handling stolen goods.

17.3 Objectives

At the end of this section you should be able to:

1. Outline the offence of handling stolen goods contrary to s. 22 of the Theft Act 1968.
2. Explain the term 'stolen goods' for the purposes of the offence of handling stolen goods.
3. Identify when guilty knowledge in cases of handling can be used in a trial under s. 27 of the Theft Act 1968.
4. Apply your knowledge to multiple-choice questions.

17.4 Handling Stolen Goods

17.4.1 Exercise—Handling Stolen Goods Scenarios

Examine the following scenario and then answer the associated questions. Give a short reason for your answer where you are asked.

1. FARRIN is a well-known handler of stolen goods. She receives a visit from one of her criminal associates, ISAACS, who has been a fruitful source of stolen goods in the past. ISAACS and FARRIN discuss the theft of a lorry load of cigarettes that ISAACS and his gang are going to steal that evening. After considerable haggling between the two, FARRIN agrees to pay ISAACS £5,000 when he delivers the cigarettes later on.

Does FARRIN commit the offence of handling stolen goods?

Yes / No

Why / Why not?

2. MILLER owes PUGH £2,000 and has refused to pay the debt. PUGH is an accomplished burglar and breaks into an office owned by MILLER and takes a computer worth about £1,000 in settlement of the debt, because he believes he has a right in law to do so. PUGH takes the computer to his handler, SHARROD, and asks him if he wants to buy it. As it is PUGH who is offering the computer to him, SHARROD automatically presumes that it has been stolen during a burglary. SHARROD offers PUGH £100 and PUGH accepts the offer. Does SHARROD commit the offence of handling stolen goods?
Yes / No
Why / Why not?

_____

3. Before you read the explanation of the previous two scenarios, what can you remember about the offence of handling stolen goods?

_____

EXPLANATION 17.4.1

Handling Stolen Goods Scenarios

Let's begin this explanation with a look at the first few words of the definition of the offence of handling stolen goods:

> A person handles stolen goods if

The first line of this definition is important. You can only handle goods that have actually been stolen. It is also a reminder that a thorough understanding of theft will assist you to comprehend other offences.

1. FARRIN does not commit the offence. There are no stolen goods to handle because the theft has yet to take place and you cannot handle goods that have yet to be stolen (although you might have a conspiracy).

2. SHARROD does not commit the offence. PUGH has taken the goods in the belief that he has a legal right to do so, meaning he is not dishonest. Therefore, the goods are not stolen. It does not matter what SHARROD believes, the first part of the definition has not been satisfied (SHARROD may be guilty of an attempt).

17.4.2 Exercise—Handling True or False?

Answer the following true or false questions.

1. A person can only be guilty of handling stolen goods where they know or believe the goods are stolen at the time they do the act that constitutes handling.
True / False

2. To be guilty of an offence of handling stolen goods, the defendant must suspect that the goods are stolen.
True / False

3. If you cannot prove that the defendant knew the goods were stolen, then it will be sufficient to prove that any reasonable person would have realised the goods were stolen.
True / False

4. The *mens rea* required to prove handling is that the defendant knew or believed goods to be stolen.

True / False

EXPLANATION 17.4.2

Handling True or False?

The whole of the definition of handling stolen goods is:

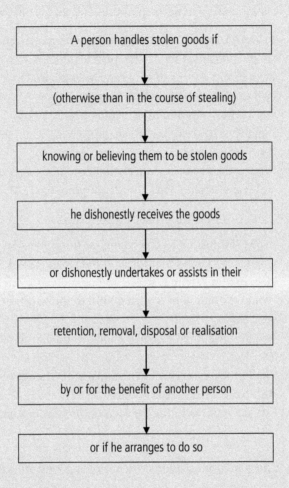

A person handles stolen goods if

↓

(otherwise than in the course of stealing)

↓

knowing or believing them to be stolen goods

↓

he dishonestly receives the goods

↓

or dishonestly undertakes or assists in their

↓

retention, removal, disposal or realisation

↓

by or for the benefit of another person

↓

or if he arranges to do so

Comment 1 is true. If a person bought property in good faith and later found out that it was in fact stolen, this would not make them guilty of handling.

Comment 2 is false. Mere suspicion, however strong, that the goods were stolen will not be enough.

Comment 3 is false. What you or I think about the circumstances in which a person obtains property does not matter. It is the mind of the defendant that is important (but there are special rules of evidence with regard to this offence).

Comment 4 is true.

See *Investigators' Manual*, paras 3.7.1 to 3.7.6

17.5   Stolen Goods

Section 24 of the Theft Act 1968 defines the term 'stolen goods' for the purpose of this offence. You have already seen the importance of ensuring that the goods are actually stolen, but now you must decide whether they fall within the terms of this part of the definition.

17.5.1   Exercise—Stolen Goods or Not?

Examine the following scenarios and decide whether the goods mentioned would be classed as stolen for the purposes of s. 24 of the Act.

1. WHITE steals a diamond necklace from a jeweller's shop in Australia. The owner of the shop reports the theft to the Australian police but WHITE manages to avoid capture for the offence and returns to his home in England. On his return to England, he takes the necklace to YEO and asks him if he wishes to buy it. YEO asks where the necklace came from and WHITE tells him how he obtained it.

Would the necklace be 'stolen goods'?

Yes / No

What is the key to deciding whether or not goods stolen in a place other than England and Wales are 'stolen goods' for the purposes of s. 24?

_____

2. LAPPER steals a laptop computer from JERRAM. LAPPER sells the laptop to his handler, GAGE, who knows that the laptop is stolen. GAGE sells the laptop to DOBSON who has no idea that the laptop is stolen and pays GAGE a fair market price for the laptop.

Would the laptop be 'stolen goods' in the hands of LAPPER?

Yes / No

Would the laptop be 'stolen goods' in the hands of GAGE?

Yes / No

Would the laptop be 'stolen goods' in the hands of DOBSON?

Yes / No

Explain your reasoning for each of the previous decisions.

_____

There are two occasions when 'stolen goods' will cease to be 'stolen'. What are they?

i. _____

ii. _____

_____

3. TI O'BYRNE has arrested COOKE for an offence of burglary. When the officer and her colleagues searched COOKE's house, several items of property were recovered that did not belong to COOKE. In interview, COOKE states that he bought them from a person he would not name, but admits that they are stolen property. TI O'BYRNE makes enquiries regarding the property and finds out the following:

i. An antique gold watch (recovered from COOKE's living room table) was stolen in the course of a robbery.

ii. A flat-screen television (recovered in COOKE's bedroom) was stolen when a local electrical store was subject to an offence of fraud by false representation.

iii. A collection of rare coins (recovered in COOKE's kitchen) was taken from the owner who was blackmailed into parting with the coins.

Deal with each item of property in turn. State whether the property would be 'stolen goods' and give a short reason why.

i. _____

_____

ii. _____

_____

iii. _____

_____

EXPLANATION 17.5.1

Stolen Goods or Not?

1. The diamond necklace is 'stolen goods'. The rule is that if the goods are stolen outside England or Wales then they will be stolen goods if the stealing amounts to an offence where and at the time the goods were stolen.

2. The laptop is 'stolen goods' in the hands of all three people. Knowing or believing that the laptop is stolen is important when considering the offence of handling, but we are looking purely and simply at whether the property is 'stolen goods' and not at the offence as a whole. The laptop will remain 'stolen goods' until one of the following occurs:

   i. the goods are restored to the person from whom they were stolen or to other lawful possession or custody (e.g. the police); or

   ii. after that person and any other person claiming through him to have otherwise ceased as regards those goods to have any right to restitution in respect of the theft.

3. Goods are 'stolen goods' when they have been obtained as a consequence of an offence of theft, an offence of fraud (i.e. the general offences of fraud under ss. 2, 3 and 4 of the Fraud Act 2006) or as a consequence of an offence of blackmail. All three items recovered from COOKE's house would fall within the definition.

This does not deal with the concept of 'stolen goods' in its entirety, as there is still the area under s. 24(2)(a) and (b) to deal with. You will remember that these sections talk about goods that directly or indirectly represent the stolen goods in the hands of the thief or the handler.

17.5.2   Exercise—A Stolen Goods Scenario

Look at the following unfolding scenario. As you examine the scenario, think about the term 'stolen goods'. A table follows the scenario and underneath the name of the person named you should state what 'stolen goods' they possess or possessed. A small section has been completed for you as an example.

1. BRAY steals a state-of-the-art computer from HART. BRAY takes the computer to TWEED who buys the computer from BRAY for £2,000, knowing that it has been stolen. Then,

2. BRAY contacts NIXON (a friend of his who is selling a Ford Fiesta car). BRAY boasts to NIXON about how he obtained the £2,000 and then offers NIXON the money in exchange for the Ford Fiesta he is selling. NIXON agrees. Then,

3. TWEED dismantles the computer. He sells half of the parts to RENSHAW for £500 and the other half to PRICE for £500. Neither RENSHAW nor PRICE knows or believes that the parts they have bought are stolen. Then,

4. NIXON uses the £2,000 paid for the car to buy a fitted kitchen for his house. Then,

5. TWEED uses the £1,000 he made from selling the computer parts to RENSHAW and PRICE to buy a Land Rover 4 × 4 car. Then,

6. RENSHAW sells the computer parts he purchased from TWEED to POWELL for £600.

BRAY	TWEED	NIXON	RENSHAW	PRICE	POWELL
The computer The £2K from TWEED	The computer				

EXPLANATION 17.5.2

A Stolen Goods Scenario

Your table should have looked something like this:

BRAY	TWEED	NIXON	RENSHAW	PRICE	POWELL
The computer	The computer	The £2K from BRAY	The computer parts bought from TWEED	The computer parts bought from TWEED	The computer parts bought from RENSHAW
The £2K from TWEED	The £500 from RENSHAW	The fitted kitchen in his house			
The Ford Fiesta bought from NIXON	The £500 from PRICE				
	The Land Rover 4 ×4				

1. The computer stolen from HART by BRAY is 'stolen goods' and remains so throughout the scenario, no matter who has possession of it or its parts and regardless of whether they knew or believed that it was stolen. This is because once goods become stolen, they cannot be anything other than that unless they are returned to the owner etc. (as per s. 24(3) of the Act). Remember that just because someone has possession of stolen goods will not mean that they are a handler; the person must know or believe that the goods are stolen when they come into their possession. BRAY is paid £2K for the computer and this is 'stolen goods' because it represents the computer in the hands of the thief (BRAY).

2. BRAY then buys a car with the £2K. Now the car represents the computer in the hands of the thief (BRAY). The £2K paid to NIXON is 'stolen goods' because NIXON knows the origin of the money that now represents the stolen goods in the hands of the handler (NIXON).

3. As stated previously, the computer always remains stolen goods and that is the case for parts of the computer when it is dismantled. Thus, the parts sold to RENSHAW and PRICE are 'stolen goods'. The £500 paid to TWEED by RENSHAW and the £500 paid to TWEED by PRICE are both 'stolen goods'. Both of these cash payments represent the stolen goods in the hands of the handler.

4. The fitted kitchen is 'stolen goods'; it represents the stolen goods in the hands of the handler (NIXON).

5. The Land Rover is 'stolen goods'; it represents the stolen goods in the hands of the handler.

6. The computer parts sold to POWELL are 'stolen goods' as at 1. The £600 paid to RENSHAW by POWELL is not 'stolen goods'. Although the £600 represents the stolen goods, it is not in the hands of the thief or the handler.

Point to Note

- Section 24A(8) of the Theft Act states:

References to stolen goods include money which is dishonestly withdrawn from an account to which a wrongful credit has been made, but only *to the extent that the money derives from the credit.*

EXAMPLE

If a wrongful credit of £500 is made to your bank account which already has £200 in it and you (being aware that the wrongful credit had been made) then withdraw £600, the 'stolen goods' would be £500 of that £600—£500 was the extent of the credit.

See *Investigators' Manual*, paras 3.7.2 to 3.7.3

17.6 Guilty Knowledge in Cases of Handling

Section 27 of the Theft Act 1968 allows the prosecution to admit evidence of the defendant's previous behaviour in support of the current charge.

17.6.1 Exercise—Section 27 Scenarios

In the following examples, state whether or not evidence of the defendant's previous behaviour would be admitted. ALL of the offences charged were committed in October 2021.

1. OPPITZ is charged with offences of theft and handling stolen goods. OPPITZ was convicted of handling in June 2018. Can OPPITZ's previous conviction for handling be admitted?
Yes / No
Why / Why not?

2. MATHAM is charged with handling stolen goods. In February 2021, he innocently bought a leather jacket that had been stolen in January 2021 and, although he was charged with handling the jacket, he was later acquitted of that offence. Can the fact that MATHAM had a stolen jacket in his possession in February 2021 be admitted?
Yes / No
Why / Why not?

3. GREATREX is charged with handling stolen goods. GREATREX was convicted of handling stolen goods in September 2015. Can this previous conviction be admitted?

Yes / No

Why / Why not?

EXPLANATION 17.6.1

Section 27 Scenarios

1. The previous conviction for handling cannot be used. This is because OPPITZ is charged with theft and handling. Section 27 can only be used when the charge against the defendant is one of handling alone.

2. MATHAM's previous conduct can be admitted. It does not matter whether MATHAM was innocent or not. MATHAM had, within 12 months of the offence charged, been in possession of stolen goods.

3. The previous conviction cannot be admitted. The conviction was received over five years prior to the offence charged.

Have a look at the illustration of the rule under s. 27 of the Theft Act 1968 at the end of this section to assist your understanding.

See *Investigators' Manual*, para. 3.7.5

17.7 Conclusion

The offence of handling stolen goods is probably one of the more difficult subjects that you will cover in the Property Offences section. Therefore, study and revision of this subject demands care and attention to detail. Remember that there are several key factors to consider, particularly whether the goods handled are stolen and the state of mind of the defendant at the time of the handling.

17.8 Recall Questions

Try and answer the following questions.

- What is the definition of handling stolen goods?
- What is the *mens rea* required to prove an offence of handling stolen goods?
- What is the maximum sentence for an offence of handling stolen goods?
- The commission of which offences will make goods 'stolen goods'?
- When will 'stolen goods' cease to be 'stolen'?
- What are the relevant time periods relating to s. 27 of the Theft Act?
- What types of misconduct can be admitted as evidence under s. 27 of the Act?

17.9 Multiple-Choice Questions

Answers to these questions can be found in the 'Answers Section' at the end of the book. All explanations also include a reference back to the *Investigators' Manual 2022*.

1. HARDING offers to sell JONES a lawnmower for £30. JONES believes that this is a fair price to pay for the mower and buys it from HARDING in good faith. Several days later, a 'Neighbourhood Watch' newsletter is delivered to JONES, which features an article on recent thefts from sheds in the area. The stolen items are all listed including serial numbers. JONES checks his lawnmower and finds that it is stolen property. Instead of handing the mower to the police, he decides to get rid of it and approaches UXBRIDGE (a known 'handler') and asks him if he wants to buy the mower. UXBRIDGE offers him £20 and JONES accepts the money.

   At what point, if at all, does JONES commit the offence of handling stolen goods (contrary to s. 22 of the Theft Act 1968)?

A When he pays HARDING £30 for the mower.

B When he finds out the mower is stolen and does nothing about it.

C When UXBRIDGE hands him the money.

D The offence is not committed in these circumstances.

Answer _____

2. COWSER has been charged with an offence of handling stolen goods and has pleaded 'not guilty' to the charge. At his trial, the prosecution uses evidence admitted under s. 27 of the Theft Act 1968 with regard to a two-year-old previous conviction COWSER has for an offence of theft.

   What is the purpose of this evidence?

A To prove that he received, arranged or assisted in the disposal of the stolen goods.

B To prove that he knew or believed the goods to be stolen.

C To show that COWSER is of 'bad character'.

D To show that COWSER is dishonest.

Answer _____

3. BATT, ROBINSON and FARROW are drinking in a pub when they are approached by REVILL. REVILL tells the men that he has several Rolex watches for sale and asks them if they are interested. All three men say they are and REVILL produces several Rolex watches for them to examine. All the watches are fakes that REVILL bought and paid for on a recent holiday to Thailand to sell as the genuine article and make a tidy profit in England. BATT asks REVILL how much the watches are and is told '£300 to you'. BATT has heard that several identical watches were stolen in a robbery of a nearby jewellery shop and believes that the watches are stolen. ROBINSON and FARROW have not heard about the robbery but ROBINSON also believes the watches to be stolen. FARROW suspects the watches to be stolen. All three men give REVILL £300 and buy watches from him.

   Who, if anyone, has committed an offence of handling stolen goods (contrary to s. 22 of the Theft Act 1968)?

A Only BATT commits the offence.

B Only BATT and ROBINSON commit the offence.

C BATT, ROBINSON and FARROW commit the offence.

D The offence has not been committed.

Answer _____

Section 27 of the Theft Act 1968 Illustrated

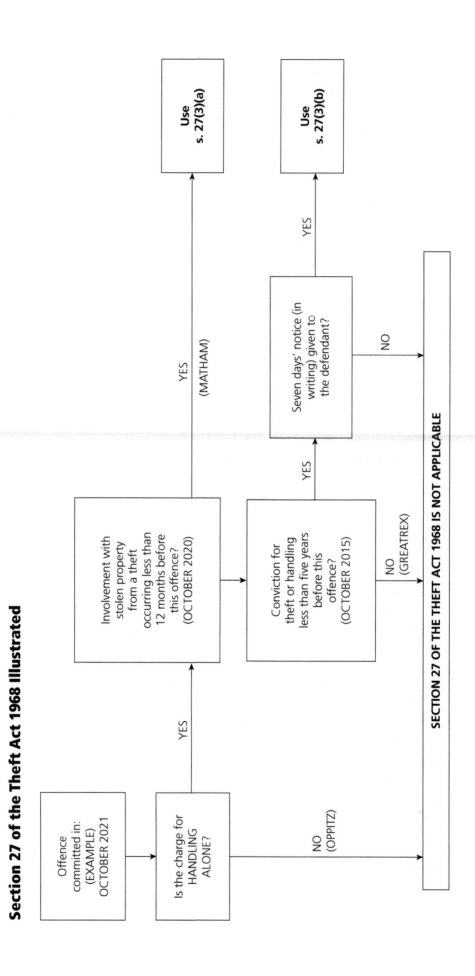

18 Fraud

18.1 Introduction

The Fraud Act 2006 takes a relatively simplistic approach to dealing with offences of fraud. However, this does not mean that understanding fraud offences automatically becomes an 'easy' task as a consequence. You must, once again, treat this area of law with respect—particularly as fraud questions are commonplace in the NIE.

18.2 Aim

The aim of this chapter is to provide you with an understanding of the issues surrounding some of the fraud offences contained in the Fraud Act 2006.

18.3 Objectives

At the end of this section you should be able to:

1. Outline the offences under ss. 2, 3 and 4 of the Fraud Act 2006.
2. Provide examples of how these offences could be committed.
3. Describe the offences under ss. 6 and 7 of the Fraud Act 2006.
4. Demonstrate your knowledge of the topic by completing the exercises in this section.
5. Apply your knowledge to the multiple-choice questions.

18.4 Fraud

18.4.1 Exercise—The Three Fraud Offences

The offence of 'fraud' can be committed in three broad ways. What are they?

1. _____

2. _____

3. _____

EXPLANATION 18.4.1

The Three Fraud Offences

Your answer should have included:

1. Fraud by false representation (s. 2 of the Act).

2. Fraud by failing to disclose (s. 3 of the Act).

3. Fraud by abuse of position (s. 4 of the Act).

It might assist you to remember FAD:

        F   False representation
        A   Abuse of position
        D   Disclose

18.4.2   Exercise—Conduct or Consequence?

Before you examine these offences in a little more detail, attempt to answer the questions in the following exercise.

ERWIN is examining an oil painting on display in an antique shop owned and run by HOWARD. HOWARD approaches ERWIN and asks him if he is interested in the painting, to which ERWIN responds, *'Yes I am.'* HOWARD states, *'Well, I'm afraid it will cost you a great deal as this is by John Gordan who I'm sure you know is a famous local artist.'* When HOWARD tells ERWIN the painting is by John Gordan, he is lying as he knows that it is not and is intending to make far more money on the sale of the painting than he should.

1. ERWIN knows that HOWARD's statement is a lie but he likes the painting so buys it from ERWIN at ERWIN's asking price. Is this an offence of fraud?
Yes / No

2. ERWIN does not rely on HOWARD's statement but actually arrived at the incorrect conclusion that it was a John Gordan painting from his own observations. Is this an offence of fraud?
Yes / No

3. As HOWARD tells ERWIN the painting is by John Gordan, ERWIN is intently examining the painting and is not listening to HOWARD. He does not hear HOWARD's comment and pays the asking price for the painting. Is this an offence of fraud?
Yes / No

EXPLANATION 18.4.2

Conduct or Consequence?

You should have come to the same conclusion in answer to all three of the previous questions and that is 'Yes' there is a fraud offence (by false representation in this case). The fact that ERWIN knows that HOWARD's statement is false, that he does not rely on HOWARD's statement or that he did not hear it, makes no difference as the fraud offence is one of conduct and intent and DOES NOT require a consequence—the offence is complete the moment the representation (or failure to disclose or abuse of position) is made.

18.4.3 Exercise—Common Elements in the Definitions

The definitions under ss. 2, 3 and 4 of the Fraud Act 2006 contain two very important common elements. What are they?

1. _____

2. _____

EXPLANATION 18.4.3

Common Elements in the Definitions

Those common elements are:

1. Dishonesty

2. Gain and loss

The good thing about these common elements is that you have already dealt with them and should therefore know and understand both of them.

18.4.4 Dishonesty

The test for 'dishonesty' for the purposes of fraud offences is that established in the case of *Barlow Clowes International (in liq)* v *Eurotrust International Ltd* [2006] 1 All ER 333. You have dealt with this test in the 'Theft' section of the *Investigators' Manual* and also this Workbook. It is no different in fraud.

18.4.5 Gain and Loss

Gain and loss in fraud, although referred to in the offences under ss. 2, 3 and 4, is specifically defined by s. 5 of the Act. This is a similar position to that you examined when considering the offence of blackmail. The beauty of this previous work is that if you understand 'gain and loss' for the purposes of the offence of blackmail, then you also understand it for the purposes of the offence of fraud because it is exactly the same. The key issue to remember is that 'gain and loss' is all about 'money and other property' and so, just like blackmail, fraud is an *economic* offence.

18.5 Fraud by False Representation

There is quite a lot going on with the definition of the offence of fraud by false representation under s. 2 of the Act but if you look at the title and consider our common elements you have the 'heart' of the offence:

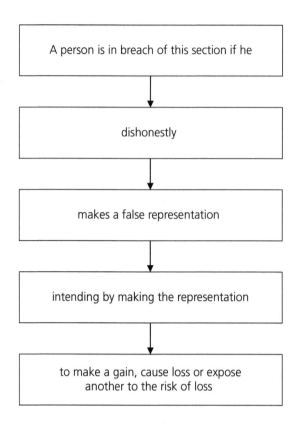

What is of critical importance when considering this offence are the words 'false representation'.

18.5.1 Exercise—False Representation

Consider the following comments on the term 'false representation' and answer the associated questions.

1. In order to be a 'false representation', the representation must be untrue. A representation will not be false if it is merely misleading.
True / False

2. A representation will only be false if the person making it knows that it might be untrue.
True / False

3. A false representation will always require some form of verbal communication to take place otherwise the representation is not made.
True / False

4. A broken promise is a false representation.
True / False

5. A false representation can be made to a machine.
True / False

6. If a false representation is made before, during or even after property has been passed to the victim, the offence will still be committed.
True / False

EXPLANATION 18.5.1

False Representation

1. False—a representation is false if it is untrue or misleading.

2. False—the person making the representation must know that it is untrue or misleading, or that it might be.

3. False—a representation can be express or implied and can be communicated in words or conduct. There is no limitation on the way in which the representation can be made.

4. False—a representation must be as to fact or law so a broken promise is not in itself a false representation.

5. True—there is no requirement for human involvement.

6. True—remember the offence is about conduct and intent so it does not matter when the representation takes place as long as the requisite intention accompanies it.

See *Investigators' Manual*, para. 3.8.4

18.6   Fraud by Failing to Disclose

Once again, you can include the common elements along with the title of the offence but you must remember that a person will only commit this offence if they are under a *legal duty* to disclose information.

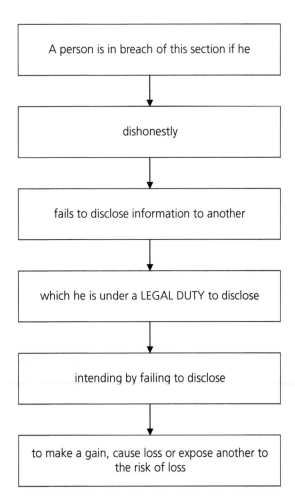

18.6.1 Exercise—Legal Duty

You are best to approach this from a common-sense perspective.

What kind of relationships do you think would create a 'legal duty'? Give three examples:

1. _____

2. _____

3. _____

EXPLANATION 18.6.1

Legal Duty

Perhaps you have included examples such as a solicitor with their client, an accountant with their client, a contract between persons involved in business, a relationship between the government and other persons or perhaps a doctor and patient or an insurance company and client.

These are good examples as these types of relationships are those envisaged by the Act (see the following).

A 'legal duty' might arise	Examples
From statute	The law creates the relationship so perhaps a government tax department and an individual
From the express or implied terms of a contract	A contract between persons involved in business
From the existence of a fiduciary relationship between parties	Accountant and client/solicitor and client
Where the transaction is one of the utmost good faith	Doctor and patient/insurance contract

The legal duty is not about a civil or moral duty but effectively one where a failure to disclose could lead to court action for damages or one which could allow a victim to change their legal position (the one they have found themselves in because of this failure to disclose).

See *Investigators' Manual*, para. 3.8.5

18.7 Fraud by Abuse of Position

Taking the standard approach to the definition, we can include the title, dishonesty and gain and loss along with the specifics of the offence.

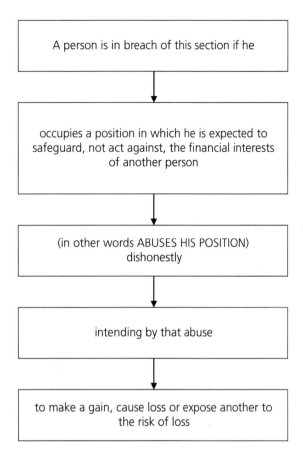

A person is in breach of this section if he

occupies a position in which he is expected to safeguard, not act against, the financial interests of another person

(in other words ABUSES HIS POSITION) dishonestly

intending by that abuse

to make a gain, cause loss or expose another to the risk of loss

18.7.1   Exercise—Abuse of Position?

Consider the following scenarios and decide whether there has been an abuse of position amounting to this offence—explain your reasons.

1. CARTER is the manager of a pub owned by a brewery. CARTER purchases several cheap barrels of beer from a friend of his and brings them to the pub. He attaches the barrels to the pumps at the pub and sells his own beer at a cheaper price than normal pub prices, making a profit for himself as a consequence.
Abuse of position?
Yes / No
Why / Why not?

_____

2. MILES works in a care home and is entrusted by TRANT (an elderly resident of the home) to look after her financial affairs. MILES takes a large amount of money from TRANT's account to bet with, hoping to win as a result. MILES wins, keeps the winnings and returns the money in full to TRANT's account.
Abuse of position?
Yes / No
Why / Why not?

_____

3. LANGHAM works for a company which sells shares in high-risk markets to wealthy customers. As the shares are invested in fragile markets, those markets need to be closely monitored so that the shares can be bought and sold at a moment's notice. LANGHAM is supposed to monitor those markets and sell shares quickly to minimise losses to customers but after an

argument with his boss he decides to play a computer game on his laptop all day intending by his lack of attention to the movement in the markets for customers and the company he works for to lose money as a result. Fortunately, the markets are quiet that day and the customers of the company suffer no loss.

Abuse of position?

Yes / No

Why / Why not?

EXPLANATION 18.7.1

Abuse of Position?

1. This is an abuse of position. CARTER is in a position where the brewery would expect him to safeguard their financial interests by selling their beer. He has abused that position by using the brewery's facilities to make his own profit.

2. This is an abuse of position. The fact that there is no contractual or legal relationship between MILES and TRANT does not matter as the position the person occupies may be the result of all sorts of relationships, even those within a family. MILES is clearly expected to safeguard TRANT's financial affairs and has exposed TRANT to a loss.

3. This is an abuse of position. It is important to remember that the offence can be committed by omission as well as by a positive act by the defendant.

See *Investigators' Manual*, para. 3.8.6

18.8   Possession or Control of Articles for Use in Frauds

18.8.1   Exercise—True or False?

Answer the following questions regarding this offence.

1. This offence can be committed anywhere except a person's home.
True / False

2. 'Possession or control' means that distance becomes important—you could not have 'control' over something 50 miles away from where you are.
True / False

3. Programs and data held in electronic form are covered by the term 'article'.
True / False

4. The offence covers articles that could be used in all types of fraud.
True / False

5. The offence would not cover a credit card that had been used to commit offences of fraud by false representation.
True / False

6. The offence would cover a person possessing a credit card reader intending to allow her friend to use it to commit fraud offences.
True / False

7. Possessing a forged passport to use in connection with, but not to actually commit, a fraud offence would be covered.
True / False

EXPLANATION 18.8.1

True or False?

The offence under s. 6 of the Act is very straightforward and can be summarised as follows:

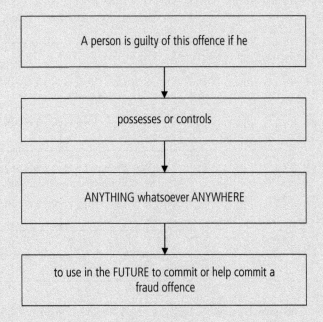

A person is guilty of this offence if he

↓

possesses or controls

↓

ANYTHING whatsoever ANYWHERE

↓

to use in the FUTURE to commit or help commit a fraud offence

1. False—this offence can be committed ANYWHERE at all, including a person's home.

2. False—distance is no object. You can control something 10,000 miles away.

3. True—in fact ANYTHING whatsoever is an 'article'.

4. True—s. 6 applies to ALL fraud offences.

5. True—this is the one limitation on this offence. The article has to be intended to be used in the FUTURE not the PAST (the card HAD been used).

6. True—the possessing or controlling takes place to enable that person or another to commit fraud.

7. True—in the course of or in *connection* with fraud.

See *Investigators' Manual*, para. 3.8.7

18.9 Making or Supplying Articles for Use in Frauds

This is another one of those 'catch all' offences where pretty much every kind of activity has been covered.

The word 'article' is used again and you should take the same approach to this as in the previous offence of possession or control of articles for use in frauds, i.e. an article is ANYTHING. Even an innocuous article is covered if the person making it or supplying it intends it to be used in some way in fraud.

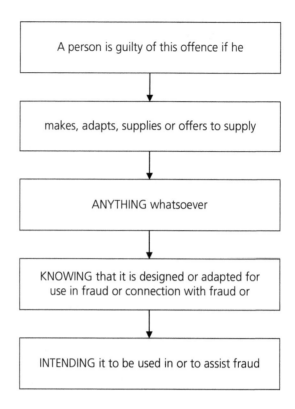

The situation with 'supply' and 'offer to supply' is exactly the same as it would be in relation to offences under the Misuse of Drugs Act 1971 and these activities are discussed in more depth in the 'Misuse of Drugs' section of your Manual and also this Workbook.

See *Investigators' Manual*, para. 3.8.8

18.10   Conclusion

Having completed this section of the Workbook, you should be able to identify the connections between the major fraud offences and, of course, their differences. You should also be able to see how other legislation can assist you to understand Fraud Act 2006 offences. You should pay particular attention to the examples given in this section of the Workbook as well as those in the Manual as they may figure in any questions on fraud in the NIE.

18.11   Recall Questions

Try and answer the following questions.

- What does FAD stand for?
- What is the most important thing you should remember about 'gain and loss'?
- What does 'dishonestly' mean for the purposes of fraud offences?
- What is a 'false representation'?
- What is the one limitation of the offence of possessing or controlling articles for fraud?

18.12 Multiple-Choice Questions

Answers to these questions can be found in the 'Answers Section' at the end of the book. All explanations also include a reference back to the *Investigators' Manual 2022*.

1. BRADNICK is struggling to pay her mortgage and she is cutting corners in every aspect of her life to save money. BRADNICK has parked her car in a pay-and-display multi-storey car park and, on leaving the car park, hands over her parking ticket to RICE who is working in the pay booth at the car park exit. RICE tells BRADNICK her parking costs £20. Attempting to get a reduction on the price of the car parking, BRADNICK says, *'I thought nurses like me only had to pay £5'* (BRADNICK is not a nurse). RICE is not fooled by BRADNICK and realises that she is trying to 'con' him. He tells BRADNICK that there is no such discount and the full fee needs to be paid. BRADNICK reluctantly pays the fee and drives off.

Considering the offence of fraud by false representation (contrary to s. 1(2) of the Fraud Act 2006), which of the following comments is correct?

A BRADNICK does not commit the offence because RICE was not fooled into thinking she was a nurse.

B BRADNICK has committed the offence.

C BRADNICK does not commit the offence because she did not obtain any financial gain from her activities.

D BRADNICK has not committed the full offence although this is an attempted fraud in the circumstances.

Answer _____

2. HAMMERTON is a financial adviser and has an oral contract with URWIN to provide URWIN with financial advice (the contract creates a legal duty for HAMMERTON to advise URWIN). Part of URWIN's financial portfolio includes £100,000 worth of shares in a Far East car manufacturing company. HAMMERTON is provided with information by the car manufacturing company that they are in difficulties due to a problem with a new car they have designed and, as a consequence, the share prices in the company are highly likely to drop significantly. HAMMERTON has never really liked URWIN and so, intending to cause URWIN to lose money on the shares, he keeps this information to himself. As it happens, the market does not react badly to the announcement by the car manufacturing company and the share price remains exactly the same.

Taking into account the offence of fraud by failing to disclose (contrary to s. 3 of the Fraud Act 2006), which of the following comments is true?

A The fact that HAMMERTON exposed URWIN to a potential loss in this way means that he has committed the offence.

B HAMMERTON has not committed the offence as the contract that he has with URWIN is not a written one.

C The offence has not been committed as no loss was actually caused to URWIN.

D HAMMERTON has not committed the offence as he did not intend to make a gain for himself or another.

Answer _____

3. VALE is a career criminal with a string of convictions for fraud-related offences. He intends to carry out a number of fraud offences in the near future and has assembled a variety of items to assist him in this task. He is sitting in the lounge of his house examining a number of blank forged credit cards he has obtained. He considers that they are of good quality and that he will actually be able to use the cards in fraud offences. VALE decides to use a machine he has in his car (which is parked outside his house) to stamp false details into the cards. He considers that he may need other items to assist him and remembers that he has several forged driving licences and passports in a storage unit 10 miles from his home. He decides that he will collect these items as a 'back up' to use if anyone challenges his identity when he commits the offences.

Considering the offence of possession or control of articles for use in fraud (contrary to s. 6 of the Fraud Act 2006), which of the following statements is correct?

A VALE commits the offence but only in relation to the forged credit cards as these are the only items that will actually be used to carry out fraud offences.

B VALE commits the offence in relation to the forged credit cards and the machine in his car but not the identification documents.

C VALE commits the offence in relation to all of the items (forged credit cards, stamp machine and identity documents).

D VALE does not commit the offence in this scenario.

Answer _____

4. ROTHWELL works for WebSaints, a computer software company. He has an argument with the owner of the company and feels insulted and undervalued and decides to leave the company. Before he leaves, he decides he will have his revenge on his employer in some way. In the week before he tenders his resignation, he is contacted by JONES who works for another computer company. JONES asks if WebSaints can do some work for his company which will mean a large income for WebSaints. ROTHWELL lies to JONES and tells him that WebSaints cannot do the work and he should try another company called Net Inc. which will do the work at a cheaper price, intending that WebSaints will lose money. ROTHWELL then clones a large amount of software owned by WebSaints with the intention of selling the software on to any buyer he can find.

In relation to the offence of fraud by abuse of position (contrary to s. 4 of the Fraud Act 2006), which of the following statements is correct?

A ROTHWELL commits the offence when he lies to JONES and also when he clones the software products.

B ROTHWELL commits the offence but only when he lies to JONES.

C ROTHWELL commits the offence but only when he clones the software products.

D The offence is not committed in these circumstances.

Answer _____

19 Criminal Damage

19.1 Introduction

Criminal damage in its 'simple' form is a very common offence. For the purposes of the NIE, you must not believe questions on it to be 'simple' as well. You also have to consider the more serious aggravated form of the offence as well as preparatory offences.

19.2 Aim

The aim of this section is to explain the law surrounding the offence of criminal damage and its associated offences.

19.3 Objectives

At the end of this section you should be able to:

1. Define the offence of simple damage contrary to s. 1(1) of the Criminal Damage Act 1971.
2. Identify potential defences to the offence of criminal damage.
3. Give examples of when property has been damaged.
4. Outline the terms 'property' and 'belonging to another'.
5. Define the offence of aggravated damage contrary to s. 1(2) of the Criminal Damage Act 1971.
6. State when an offence of threats to cause criminal damage contrary to s. 2 of the Criminal Damage Act 1971 has been committed.
7. State when an offence of having articles with intent to destroy or damage property contrary to s. 3 of the Criminal Damage Act 1971 has been committed.
8. Apply your knowledge to multiple-choice questions.

19.4 Simple Damage

19.4.1 Exercise—The Definition of Criminal Damage

Begin this section by writing down the definition of criminal damage. If it helps, there are some similarities between the phrases used in the definition of this offence and the offence of theft, and there are clues where that information may assist you.

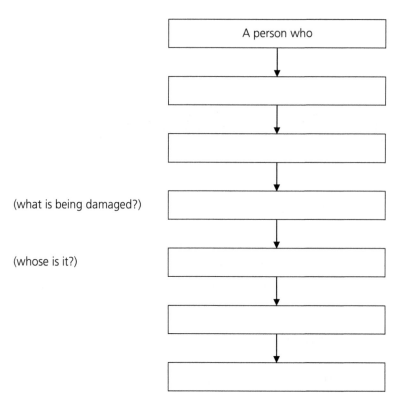

A person who

(what is being damaged?)

(whose is it?)

EXPLANATION 19.4.1

The Definition of Criminal Damage

Your definition should have included:

A person who

without lawful excuse

destroys or damages

property

belonging to another

intending or being reckless

as to whether any such property would be destroyed or damaged

You can see the similarities to the Theft Act 1968 in the previous definition and indeed the two Acts were meant to have connections. However, the terms used do not mean exactly the same as those in the Theft Act 1968. In order to understand the terms, we will examine each one briefly.

19.4.2   Exercise—Lawful Excuse

Examine the following scenario and consider the defence of 'permission' under s. 5(2) of the Criminal Damage Act 1971. Read the storyline and then deal with the situation at 1. Then use the same storyline but deal with the situations at 2 and 3.

Storyline

It is 10 am and COOPER is asleep in bed having worked a nightshift. His next-door neighbour's house alarm activates and this wakes COOPER. The alarm rings continuously and COOPER cannot get back to sleep. This is not the first time that this has happened and COOPER is extremely annoyed about the situation.

1. COOPER has complained to his next-door neighbour (HUDSON) about the alarm activating in the past, but HUDSON has done nothing about it. Believing that he has a right in law to do so, COOPER goes outside and puts a ladder against HUDSON's house wall. He climbs the ladder and smashes the alarm box using a hammer.
Do you think that COOPER would have a lawful excuse to commit this damage?
Yes / No
Why / Why not?

2. COOPER has complained to his next-door neighbour (HUDSON) about the alarm activating in the past. HUDSON has apologised and said he can understand COOPER's frustration and tells COOPER that he will get rid of the alarm. Believing that HUDSON would consent if he knew of the damage caused and the circumstances, COOPER goes outside and puts a ladder against HUDSON's house wall. He climbs the ladder and smashes the alarm box using a hammer.
Do you think that COOPER would have a lawful excuse to commit this damage?
Yes / No
Why / Why not?

3. COOPER picks up his phone and rings his next-door neighbour (HUDSON) to complain. HUDSON's nephew (who is using his uncle's computer to write an essay) answers the phone. COOPER complains about the alarm and HUDSON's nephew replies that if he is so annoyed by it he should do something about it himself. COOPER thinks that he was talking to HUDSON rather than his nephew and, believing HUDSON has consented, he goes outside and puts a ladder against HUDSON's house wall. He climbs the ladder and smashes the alarm box using a hammer.
Do you think that COOPER would have a lawful excuse to commit this damage?
Yes / No
Why / Why not?

EXPLANATION 19.4.2

Lawful Excuse

There is a link to theft with this part of 'lawful excuse' insofar as if the defendant believes that he has the consent of the person entitled to give consent, committing damage is permissible (see s. 2(1)(b) of the Theft Act 1968).

1. COOPER commits damage in this scenario and does not have a lawful excuse. Believing that you have a lawful right to damage property is irrelevant to criminal damage.

2. COOPER would have a lawful excuse in this scenario. This is because at the time of the damage he believes that HUDSON (the person entitled to consent) would consent if he knew of the circumstances of the damage.

3. COOPER would have a lawful excuse in this scenario. Although it is not actually HUDSON whom COOPER speaks to, he believes that the person entitled to consent to the damage (HUDSON) has given his consent.

19.4.3 Exercise—Protection

In the following exercises, consider the element of 'protection' under s. 5(2) of the Criminal Damage Act 1971.

1. TRECARN is married to the deputy warden of a block of flats for the elderly. TRECARN is not happy about the state of the fire precautions in the block of flats and believes that if they are not improved, the elderly residents will be at risk and could be injured. TRECARN decides to call attention to this inadequacy by setting fire to some bedding. The police are called and TRECARN is arrested for arson.
Do you think TRECARN would have a lawful excuse to damage the property?
Yes / No
Why / Why not?

2. Look at the previous circumstances regarding TRECARN. This time TRECARN's motivation is not to protect the lives of the elderly residents, but to show that the block of flats could be seriously damaged by fire.
Do you think TRECARN would have a lawful excuse to damage the property?
Yes / No
Why / Why not?

EXPLANATION 19.4.3

Protection

When you are considering the lawful excuse of protection you need to ask three questions:

i. Was the destruction or damage to property caused in order to protect property? If 'Yes' then,

ii. Was the property in immediate need of protection? If 'Yes' then,

iii. Were the means adopted reasonable having regard to all the circumstances?

1. In this scenario, TRECARN fails at the first question. The damage was caused in order to prevent harm to the elderly residents and not to protect property.

2. Even if the first question is answered 'Yes' as in this scenario, TRECARN fails at the second question as the property was not in immediate need of protection. This scenario is similar to the case of *R v Hunt* (1978) 66 Cr App R 105.

See *Investigators' Manual*, para. 3.10.2.6

19.4.4   **Exercise—Destroys or Damages**

The *Oxford English Dictionary* defines the word 'destroy' as to 'put out of existence by severe damage or attack'. There is no legal definition of the word and you should use your own common sense to tell you whether or not something has been destroyed.

The word 'damage' is, like the word 'destroy', undefined. However, case history has provided examples of when property will be 'damaged'.

Look at the following statements and decide whether damage has been caused.

1. BLAKE uses a marker pen to write a biblical quotation on a concrete pillar outside the Houses of Parliament.
Damage / Not Damage?

2. HARDMAN sprays human silhouettes on a pavement using water-soluble paint. The next rainfall will wash away the silhouettes.
Damage / Not Damage?

3. Graffiti smeared in mud on a wall by ROE.
Damage / Not Damage?

4. COX stuffs a blanket into a cell toilet and repeatedly flushes the toilet, flooding the cell in the process.
Damage / Not Damage?

EXPLANATION 19.4.4

Destroys or Damages

Examples 1 to 4 are all classed as damage. Generally, damage is something that can be perceived by the senses, i.e. you can see it. But this is a general rule. Please be aware that this is not always the case and remember that there does not necessarily have to be an economic cost to repair something for damage to be caused.

See *Investigators' Manual*, para. 3.10.2.1

19.4.5   **Exercise—Property**

This section is similar to the section on property for the offence of theft, but you should take care as there are some fundamental differences between the two definitions.

Using the same statements from the theft (property) section of the Workbook, decide whether the following are true or false in respect of criminal damage.

1. There are no circumstances under which land can be damaged.
True / False

2. The term 'property' does not include money.
True / False

3. Intangible property cannot be damaged.
True / False

4. The term 'property' includes human bodies.
True / False

5. Electricity is not property for the purposes of the Criminal Damage Act 1971.
True / False

EXPLANATION 19.4.5

Property

If you have read and understood this section in the *Investigators' Manual*, you will realise that statements 3, 4 and 5 are true and statements 1 and 2 are false.

1. Land cannot be stolen but it can be damaged.

2. Money can be stolen and damaged.

3. Intangible property can be stolen but it cannot be damaged. To damage something, the property must be tangible, i.e. you can touch the property subjected to the damage.

4. You cannot steal a human body (unless it has been altered) but you can damage a human body.

5. You cannot steal or damage electricity. This goes back to point 3; electricity is intangible.

See *Investigators' Manual*, para. 3.10.2.2

19.4.6 Exercise—Belonging to Another

Examine the following scenario and answer the questions that follow it.

Owing to escalating house prices, GRANT, DERBY and FLOWERS decide to buy a house together to get on the property ladder. After a short while, DERBY moves out from the house because of an argument with FLOWERS. As FLOWERS and GRANT do not have enough money to buy DERBY out, they remain in the house. DERBY is living in a flat and is desperate for money and, one night when FLOWERS and GRANT are out of the house, he lets himself in with a door key. DERBY removes a fitted oven and hob from the kitchen but in doing so damages the units and work surface.

Has DERBY committed criminal damage?
Yes / No
Why / Why not?

EXPLANATION 19.4.6

Belonging to Another

Having custody or control over something is a simple enough concept, but remember that you can damage property belonging to yourself if someone else has a proprietary right or interest in it. DERBY has bought the house with FLOWERS and GRANT and therefore the units and work surface belong to him. However, they also belong to FLOWERS and GRANT.

See *Investigators' Manual*, para. 3.10.2.3

19.5 Aggravated Damage

19.5.1 Exercise—Aggravated Damage Scenario

Read the following scenario and answer the questions relating to it. Although you will be able to use the information you have obtained from the 'Simple Damage' section of the Workbook to help you answer the following questions, be mindful that there are significant differences between the two offences.

ROBEY owns a large firm but business is bad and, as the financial situation becomes worse, ROBEY speaks to one of his employees, SIDWELL. ROBEY tells SIDWELL that he will go bankrupt and have to close the business unless SIDWELL can help him out. ROBEY persuades SIDWELL to overload the first floor of the business premises so that the roof will give way. The plan is that the first floor and the items stored on it will fall to the ground floor and everything will be destroyed, causing millions of pounds worth of damage. ROBEY tells SIDWELL that some workers on the ground floor might die from the cave in, but it will look more like an accident if that is the case. Over a period of days, SIDWELL places extremely heavy items on the first floor. However, the floor is stronger than SIDWELL believes and although a small part of the floor eventually gives way it only causes minor damage and no one is hurt. The plan comes to light and SIDWELL is arrested. The police interview SIDWELL, who states that he has not committed criminal damage because he had a 'lawful excuse' to commit the damage: ROBEY asked him to do it (permission).

1. Would this defence be allowed?

Yes / No

Why / Why not?

---

2. Would the defence of 'protection' be allowed in response to a charge of aggravated damage?

Yes / No

3. The actual damage caused by part of the roof caving in was minor. What effect will this have?

---

4. Does it make any difference that no one was injured as a consequence of the damage?

Yes / No

Why / Why not?

---

5. Imagine that SIDWELL was not involved and that the person responsible for the damage was ROBEY. What effect would this have and why?

---

6. What effect would it have if the only person working in the factory was ROBEY, and therefore when the damage took place the only life endangered was his?

EXPLANATION 19.5.1

Aggravated Damage Scenario

There are several significant differences between the simple and aggravated forms of criminal damage. These should have been highlighted by your answers.

1. The defence of 'permission' under s. 5(2)(a) of the Act would not be allowed. This is because the words 'without lawful excuse' in the offence of aggravated damage do not have the same effect as those in simple damage. An example of the type of 'lawful excuse' envisioned in aggravated damage might be where the defendant caused life-threatening damage but it was in self-defence.

2. The defence of 'protection' under s. 5(2)(b) would not be allowed for the same reason as in 1.

3. The fact that the actual damage caused was only minor has no bearing whatsoever on the offence.

4. The fact that no one was injured makes no difference. When you examine aggravated circumstances surrounding criminal damage, the question is, 'What was the potential for life to be endangered?'

5. This would have no effect as in the aggravated form of criminal damage; the defendant can damage his/her own as well as another person's property.

6. This would affect the scenario. The offence is committed when the life of another is endangered. If the only life being threatened is the defendant's, then there is no aggravated offence.

One other important point to bear in mind is that it is the damage itself that must endanger life. See *Investigators' Manual*, para. 3.10.3

19.6 Threats to Destroy or Damage Property

19.6.1 Exercise—Offence Committed?

Read the following scenarios and answer the questions.

1. BISHOP owns a house that is split into two bedsits. BISHOP occupies one bedsit and rents the other bedsit out to CARMICHAEL. Constant loud noise from CARMICHAEL's room has disturbed BISHOP's sleep. BISHOP knocks on CARMICHAEL's door and asks him to *'Quieten down'*, but CARMICHAEL ignores the request. BISHOP pushes a note under CARMICHAEL's door that states, *'If you don't turn that music down, I will burn your flat down right now and take you with it!'* BISHOP intends CARMICHAEL to believe the threat.

i. Has an offence contrary to s. 2 (threats to destroy/damage property) been committed?
Yes / No
Why / Why not?

_____

ii. Would an offence be committed if the note said, *'The next time you wake me up with that loud music, I'll burn your flat down and take you with it!'* (BISHOP intends CARMICHAEL to believe the threat.)
Yes / No
Why / Why not?

_____

2. Two friends, CASTLE and SPENCER, are standing in a pub having a drink. CASTLE has found out that SPENCER is having an affair with his wife and warns him to stay away from her. SPENCER just laughs and denies the affair. CASTLE gets upset and states to SPENCER that he is going to go outside to the car park to damage SPENCER's car, intending SPENCER to believe the threat. Unknown to CASTLE, SPENCER walked to the pub and had sold his car the previous day so the car cannot be damaged.
Has an offence contrary to s. 2 (threats to destroy/damage property) been committed?
Yes / No
Why / Why not?

_____

3. CLIFTON and ROBERTS are neighbours and have been having problems related to parking for years. CLIFTON regularly leaves his car parked across ROBERTS's driveway to cause him annoyance. CLIFTON parks his car across ROBERTS's drive when ROBERTS is expecting

visitors. ROBERTS sees this and comes out and states to CLIFTON that if CLIFTON does not move his car he will tip paint stripper on it. CLIFTON does not believe the threat from ROBERTS.

Has an offence contrary to s. 2 (threats to destroy/damage property) been committed?

Yes / No

Why / Why not?

EXPLANATION 19.6.1

Offence Committed?

1. i. An offence has been committed by BISHOP. This is because BISHOP has made a threat—intending that CARMICHAEL will fear that it will be carried out—to destroy or damage his own property in a way which he knows is likely to endanger the life of CARMICHAEL.

   You will see in the following scenarios that the crux of this offence is the intention of the person making the threat. If they make it intending the recipient to believe it, then the offence is committed.

   ii. As previously. It does not matter that the threat to cause the damage is one that may be carried out in the future.

2. An offence has been committed. Once again, it is the intention of the defendant that is important. It does not matter that the commission of the damage threatened is impossible.

3. An offence has been committed. It does not matter that the victim does not believe the threat.

See *Investigators' Manual*, para. 3.10.5

19.7 Having Articles with Intent to Destroy or Damage Property

19.7.1 Exercise—TUIBA and BRADBURN Scenario

Examine the following scenario and provide answers to the questions that follow it.

TUIBA and BRADBURN run a carpet-fitting business together. The two have an argument over how their business should be operated, resulting in the partnership being dissolved. Both men form their own respective businesses fitting carpets, with TUIBA forming a new partnership with LAKER. One afternoon, TUIBA and LAKER are driving to a warehouse when they see BRADBURN's car parked outside a leisure centre. TUIBA decides that he will get revenge against BRADBURN by damaging BRADBURN's car. TUIBA has a knife that he uses for fitting carpets in his jacket pocket and he intends to use this to scratch the paintwork of BRADBURN's car. He also has a hammer in the boot of the car he is driving and intends to ask LAKER to use this to smash the windscreen of BRADBURN's car.

1. Does TUIBA commit the offence under s. 3 of the Criminal Damage Act 1971?

Yes / No

Explain why / why not in relation to the knife and the hammer.

2. What is the 'Road Policing' connection to this offence?

_____

3. Would this situation change if TUIBA had put a hammer in his car boot intending to damage BRADBURN's car with it if he saw BRADBURN's car while he was driving around? Yes / No
Justify your answer.

_____

EXPLANATION 19.7.1

TUIBA and BRADBURN Scenario

1. TUIBA commits the offence. This is because the knife and hammer are in his custody or control and he intends to use (in the case of the knife) and cause (in the case of the hammer) them to damage BRADBURN's property.

2. 'Use it or cause or permit.'

3. It would not change. This is another offence that is all about the intention of the defendant. A conditional intent, for example to use an item if the need arose, would be enough.

Remember that this is custody or control and not possession.

See *Investigators' Manual*, para. 3.10.6

19.8 Conclusion

As you worked through this section of the Workbook, you will have been reminded that 'simple' offences do not necessarily live up to their names. You should possess a solid understanding of the four offences discussed and you should be able to identify when and which offences have been committed using your knowledge of the specific terms examined.

19.9 Recall Questions

Try and answer the following questions.

- What is the definition of 'simple' damage?
- Explain the term 'property' for the purposes of criminal damage.
- Give four examples of damage.
- What are the two defences to damage under 'lawful excuse'?
- Explain both of them.
- What is the difference between 'simple' damage and 'aggravated' damage?
- What is the central element of the offences under ss. 2 and 3 of the Act?

19.10 Multiple-Choice Questions

Answers to these questions can be found in the 'Answers Section' at the end of the book. All explanations also include a reference back to the *Investigators' Manual 2022*.

1. The employees of the company Jukes & Sons are on strike, but RATTLE (an employee of the company) has decided to keep working. TAYLOR (one of the strikers) is outraged by RATTLE's behaviour and visits RATTLE's house intending to intimidate him into joining the strike. TAYLOR has a revolver in his possession to accomplish this. TAYLOR speaks to RATTLE at his door but RATTLE ignores TAYLOR's threats, even when the revolver is produced, and he slams the door in TAYLOR's face. As TAYLOR walks away, he sees RATTLE standing behind a window in his lounge. TAYLOR shoots at RATTLE intending to scare him with a bullet shot from the revolver. The bullet shatters the window but misses RATTLE, who remains unharmed.

Has TAYLOR committed an offence under s. 1(2) of the Criminal Damage Act 1971 (aggravated damage)?

A Yes, because had a reasonable bystander been present, they would have seen the possible risk to life.

B No, as RATTLE was unharmed by the attack.

C Yes, as TAYLOR intended to injure RATTLE and damage was caused as a consequence of his actions.

D No, it was the bullet and not the damage to the window that endangered RATTLE's life.

Answer _____

2. HARRISON is dismissed from his job as a tool setter owing to an allegation of his being responsible for bullying his colleagues. He is so angry about his dismissal that he writes a letter to LINTON, the manager of the company, threatening to set fire to the factory some time in the following week. HARRISON intends that LINTON will believe the threat and worry about it, even though he has no intention of carrying out the threat. LINTON reads the letter and believes the threat.

Has HARRISON committed an offence under s. 2 of the Criminal Damage Act 1971?

A Yes, because he intended LINTON to believe that the threat would be carried out.

B No, as the threat was to set fire to the factory in the future.

C Yes, but only because LINTON believed the threat.

D No, as he had no intention of carrying out the threat.

Answer _____

3. ALINERI is a squatter and is standing outside the door of an unoccupied house he intends to squat in. ALINERI has a screwdriver in his coat pocket and, in the boot of his car (which is parked 10 metres away from the front door of the house), he has a crowbar. ALINERI intends to use both items to force the front door of the unoccupied house if the need arises.

Considering the offence under s. 3 of the Criminal Damage Act 1971 only, which of the following statements is correct?

A ALINERI commits the offence, but only in relation to the screwdriver as this is the only item he has with him.

B ALINERI does not commit the offence because he only intends to use the items if the need arises.

C ALINERI commits the offence in relation to both the screwdriver and the crowbar.

D ALINERI does not commit the offence because he has not actually used either item to attempt to damage property belonging to another.

Answer _____

PART 4

Sexual Offences

20 Sexual Offences

20.1 Introduction

Your examination syllabus covers some, but not all, of the Sexual Offences Act 2003. In this first section, you will examine some of the more common sexual offences, along with issues relating to consent and the terms 'sexual' and 'touching'. The fact that the 'Sexual Offences' section in your Manual is small in comparison to the other sections of the Manual should not be misinterpreted as meaning that this section is unimportant. There is a strong chance you will be asked a significant number of questions relating to this legislation.

20.2 Aim

The aim of this section is to provide you with an insight into ss. 1 to 4 of the Sexual Offences Act 2003 and their associated topics.

20.3 Objectives

At the end of this section you should be able to:

1. State when victims of sexual offences are entitled to anonymity.
2. Define the offence of rape contrary to s. 1 of the Sexual Offences Act 2003.
3. Explain the issues surrounding consent under ss. 74, 75 and 76 of the Sexual Offences Act 2003.
4. Outline the meaning of the terms 'sexual' and 'touching'.
5. Identify when offences under ss. 1 to 4 of the Sexual Offences Act 2003 have been committed.
6. Apply your knowledge to multiple-choice questions.

20.4 Anonymity

20.4.1 Exercise—Anonymity or Not?

Examine the following scenarios and decide:

i. whether the victim would be entitled to anonymity owing to the nature of the offence;
ii. whether the age of the victim impacts on anonymity; and
iii. if they are entitled to anonymity, how long would it be for?

1. MANSFIELD is a 32-year-old victim of an offence of rape.

Is MANSFIELD entitled to anonymity because of the nature of the offence?

Yes / No

Does MANSFIELD's age impact on anonymity?

Yes / No

For how long, if at all, would MANSFIELD be entitled to anonymity?

---

2. RILEY is a 14-year-old victim of an offence of sexual assault by touching.

Is RILEY entitled to anonymity because of the nature of the offence?

Yes / No

Does RILEY's age impact on anonymity?

Yes / No

For how long, if at all, would RILEY be entitled to anonymity?

EXPLANATION 20.4.1

Anonymity or Not?

The best approach to take with regard to whether or not anonymity will be provided is to presume that it will be. There is only one applicable time period—anonymity is for the lifetime of the victim/complainant. See *Investigators' Manual*, para. 4.1.2

20.5   Rape

20.5.1   Exercise—FORSYTH Scenario

Examine the following scenario and then answer the questions, giving a short reason for your answer where appropriate.

FORSYTH (a 27-year-old male) is in a pub when he sees STEWART (an 18-year-old female). FORSYTH introduces himself to STEWART and buys her a drink and they talk for a while. There are no seats available inside the pub so the two walk outside into a deserted garden area and continue to talk. Several minutes later, FORSYTH and STEWART begin to kiss and FORSYTH fondles STEWART's breasts with her consent. FORSYTH pushes STEWART to the floor so that she is kneeling down in front of him. He unzips his trousers and pushes his erect penis towards STEWART's mouth. STEWART says, 'No don't, I don't want to, I don't like oral sex.' FORSYTH ignores STEWART and pushes his penis into her mouth. Moments later, FORSYTH takes off his trousers and pants and forces STEWART to lie down. As he does this, STEWART says, 'Don't do it, you bastard!' FORSYTH pulls down STEWART's pants and attempts to put his penis in her vagina, but STEWART resists and punches FORSYTH in the face. FORSYTH retaliates and punches STEWART in the face several times. He tells STEWART he will kill her if she does not let him have sexual intercourse with her. STEWART believes FORSYTH and stops resisting. FORSYTH penetrates STEWART's vagina with his penis but does not ejaculate. Several minutes later, FORSYTH takes his penis out of STEWART's vagina, dresses and leaves.

1. What is the definition of rape?

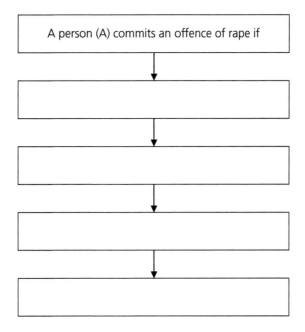

2. At what point, if at all, is the offence of rape first committed by FORSYTH?

3. The fact that FORSYTH did not ejaculate would cause difficulty for the prosecution if FORSYTH were ever charged with an offence of rape.

True / False

EXPLANATION 20.5.1

FORSYTH Scenario

1. The definition of rape is:

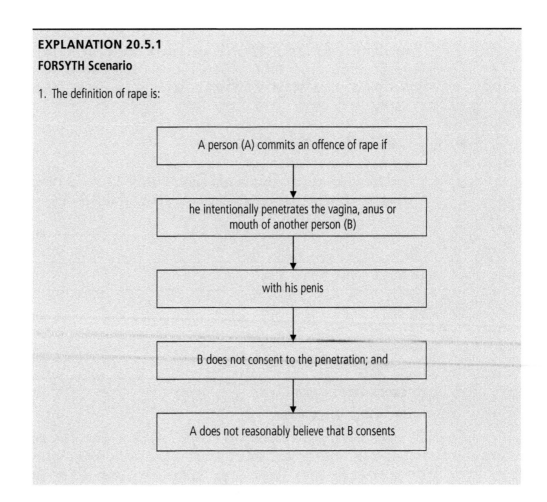

2. The offence is first committed when FORSYTH puts his penis into STEWART's mouth.

3. It is not necessary to prove ejaculation in a prosecution for rape. Try remembering the definition by using the mnemonic VAMPIRE:

V	Vagina
A	Anus
M	Mouth
P	Penis penetrated
I	Intentionally and with no
R	Reasonable belief in consent and
E	Either he or she does not consent to the penetration

This is the only offence where the offender must be male—*remember, rape can only be committed by a penis!*

All other sexual offences on your syllabus can be committed by both sexes.

20.6   Consent and Presumptions

Let's return to the scenario involving FORSYTH and STEWART.

STEWART leaves the pub in a state of shock. She makes her way back to her flat and, having given the incident considerable thought, she decides that she will contact the police and make a complaint of rape against FORSYTH. She visits her local police station and reports the offence. DS NORTHWAY and several officers on her crew deal with the case. One of those officers is TI LAPWORTH. TI LAPWORTH is instructed to obtain a statement of complaint from STEWART. STEWART gives an account of the incident at the pub to the officer.

20.6.1   Exercise—Issues Regarding Consent

Concentrate on the issue of consent under s. 74 of the Sexual Offences Act 2003. What should TI LAPWORTH be considering when STEWART tells her about the incident?

EXPLANATION 20.6.1

Issues Regarding Consent

TI LAPWORTH should note that, although STEWART was a willing partner at first, she did not consent to oral sex and was forced into the act. Sexual intercourse was obtained by threatening STEWART. Section 74 states that consent must be 'true' consent, not simply a submission induced by fear or fraud and that a person consents when they have the freedom and capacity to make that choice.

A statement of complaint is obtained from STEWART and she is medically examined to obtain evidence of the offence. DS NORTHWAY's team carry out a number of enquiries during which CCTV evidence from a security system at the pub is recovered. The CCTV is of high quality and shows the attack from start to finish. FORSYTH is identified from the footage and is arrested two days after the incident and interviewed about the offence. During the interview, FORSYTH maintains that STEWART had consented to oral and sexual intercourse with him and that he had not assaulted her.

20.6.2 Exercise—Conditional Consent

This aspect of 'consent' law has come about as a result of a number of high-profile case law decisions by our High Court.

Examine the below scenarios and consider whether consent is present.
1. GRAVE agrees to have sexual intercourse (penis to vagina) with PLATTER. GRAVE tells PLATTER that she is happy to have sex with him but makes it clear that he must wear a condom. PLATTER agrees but does not have a condom. He pretends to have put one on his penis and has sexual intercourse with GRAVE.
Consent present?
Yes / No
Why / Why not?

What if PLATTER originally wears a condom but during sexual intercourse feels that it is hindering his sexual performance, removes his penis from GRAVE's vagina, takes off the condom and then places his penis back into GRAVE's vagina (all the time GRAVE believes that PLATTER is wearing a condom)? Would this alter the situation?
Yes / No
Why / Why not?

2. THOMAS has split up with her husband because of his violence and sexual abuse towards her but during a meeting between the two she agrees to have sexual intercourse with her husband one last time on the express condition that her husband will not ejaculate inside her. Her husband has sexual intercourse with her and deliberately ejaculates inside her.
Consent present?
Yes / No
Why / Why not?

EXPLANATION 20.6.2
Conditional Consent

Consent does not exist in either set of circumstances. This has nothing to do with s. 75 or 76—it is purely an issue connected to s. 74 of the Act.
1. GRAVE has made it clear that she will only have sexual intercourse if PLATTER wears a condom—that is a condition of her consent. If PLATTER had said he would not wear a condom then GRAVE would not have had sexual intercourse with him. This is a condition as to the sexual act. If PLATTER agreed to use a condom but then did not or took it off, such behaviour would amount to an offence.

2. THOMAS will have sexual intercourse with her husband as long as he does not ejaculate inside her—that is a condition of her consent. If THOMAS's husband had said he was going to ejaculate inside her, then THOMAS would not have had sexual intercourse with him and again this is a condition as to the sexual act.

See *Investigators' Manual*, para. 4.2.4

20.6.3   Exercise—Rebuttable Presumptions

Consider the provisions under s. 75 of the Sexual Offences Act 2003 (Evidential Presumptions About Consent) and answer the following questions.

The existence of certain specified circumstances (under s. 75(2)) may allow the court to presume that the victim did not consent to the act and the defendant did not reasonably believe the complainant consented.

Rather than ask you to write down what these circumstances are, let's see if you recognise any of them in the following scenarios. Say whether the presumption can be made. We will start with FORSYTH.

1. FORSYTH was using violence against STEWART immediately before he had sexual intercourse with her.
The presumption can / cannot be made.

2. RABIN approached LAWLOR who was pushing a pram containing her two-month-old baby. RABIN produced a knife and told LAWLOR he would stab her child to death that instant if she did not have sexual intercourse with him. LAWLOR had sexual intercourse with RABIN.
The presumption can / cannot be made.

3. HUGHES has kidnapped EDGE and keeps him locked in a garage. HUGHES asks EDGE if he can have anal sex with him and EDGE replies 'Yes'. HUGHES penetrates EDGE's anus with his penis.
The presumption can / cannot be made.

4. HARPER goes to a party and has too much to drink. She goes into a bedroom and falls unconscious on a bed. KITSON enters the bedroom and decides to have sexual intercourse with HARPER while she is unconscious.
The presumption can / cannot be made.

5. COELLO is mute and because she is paralysed from the neck down she is confined to a wheelchair. INGLEY approaches her and asks her for sexual intercourse. When she does not reply, INGLEY takes her out of her wheelchair and has sexual intercourse with her.
The presumption can / cannot be made.

6. PICKFORD places a date-rape drug into ROBSON's drink, causing her to be stupefied. PICKFORD takes ROBSON to his flat and has sexual intercourse with her.
The presumption can / cannot be made.

EXPLANATION 20.6.3

Rebuttable Presumptions

In all the previous scenarios (1 to 6), the presumption could be made. This is a *rebuttable* presumption as the defendant does have the opportunity to challenge the presumption by producing sufficient evidence to raise an issue as to whether the victim consented, or as to whether the defendant reasonably believed the complainant consented.

Try to remember the circumstances of s. 75(2) by thinking 'Sex SLAVE'.

S   Substance to stupefy
L   Locked up (unlawfully detained)
A   Asleep/unconscious
V   Violence or fear of violence to that person or another
E   E-mobilised (physically disabled)

The final section dealing with presumptions about consent is s. 76 of the Act.

20.6.4   Exercise—Irrebuttable Presumptions

Examine the following scenarios and state whether a presumption under s. 76 would be drawn.

1. TIPPIN is a music teacher. He tells WIGLEY, one of his students, that if she has sexual intercourse with him it will improve her singing voice. As a result, WIGLEY allows TIPPIN to have sexual intercourse with her.
The presumption can / cannot be made.
Why / Why not?

2. JOHN and JAMES FELTHOUSE are twin brothers and have been seeing their respective girlfriends for six months. They decide it would be funny to exchange girlfriends for the evening. The brothers exchange girlfriends and have sexual intercourse with them, each pretending to be the other brother. The girlfriends are unaware that they have slept with a different brother.
The presumption can / cannot be made
Why / Why not?

EXPLANATION 20.6.4

Irrebuttable Presumptions

Think about s. 76 as the 'fraud' presumption; consent has been obtained because of a lie. The presumption would be made in both examples.

1. WIGLEY has been told that having sexual intercourse will improve her voice. She has been lied to as to the nature of the act.

2. The girlfriends have slept with the brothers because they have impersonated a person known personally to the complainant.

This presumption is *irrebuttable*.

Remember that the issues surrounding consent under ss. 74, 75 and 76 apply to all the offences under ss. 1 (Rape), 2 (Assault by Penetration), 3 (Sexual Assault by Touching) and 4 (Causing Sexual Activity Without Consent) of the Act.

See *Investigators' Manual*, paras 4.2.1 to 4.2.7

20.7 'Touching' and 'Sexual'

20.7.1 Exercise—FARREL Scenario

Before you examine the offences under ss. 2, 3 and 4 of the Act, you must understand the terms 'touching' and 'sexual'. Answer the following questions with regard to those terms after reading the following scenario.

FARREL (a 21-year-old male) and HALLARD (a 20-year-old female) are common-law husband and wife. They place an advertisement in a local paper stating that they have a second-hand designer wedding dress for sale. LLOYD (a 30-year-old female) contacts them and arranges to visit their house to inspect the wedding dress. The truth is that FARREL and HALLARD do not have a dress for sale. They have placed the advertisement in the paper in an attempt to lure a lone female to their house, where they plan to sexually assault and murder their victim. At the arranged time, LLOYD arrives and is shown into the lounge of the house by HALLARD. HALLARD asks LLOYD if she would like a cup of tea and LLOYD replies that she would. HALLARD makes LLOYD a drink and the two women talk about weddings for several minutes before LLOYD asks to see the wedding dress. HALLARD tells LLOYD that the dress is in a wardrobe in her upstairs bedroom and suggests that she view the dress there. LLOYD agrees and the two women go upstairs. HALLARD walks through the bedroom door followed by LLOYD. As LLOYD walks into the bedroom and past the door, FARREL (who has been hiding behind the bedroom door) approaches LLOYD from behind and places a chloroform-soaked rag to her mouth and nose. LLOYD struggles but is quickly rendered unconscious. When LLOYD wakes up, she is still in the bedroom and fully clothed but she is tied to a chair by her feet and hands and has been gagged. FARREL and HALLARD are both fully clothed and sitting on a bed watching her.

1. FARREL walks over to LLOYD and strokes her skirt. He does not actually touch her body. While he does this he says to LLOYD, *'Fancy a shag?'*
Is this 'touching'?
Yes / No
Why / Why not?

_____

_____

Is this 'sexual'?
Yes / No
Why / Why not?

_____

2. FARREL moves his hand onto LLOYD's leg and strokes her leg through her skirt saying, *'Go on, will you shag me?'*
Is this 'touching'?
Yes / No
Why / Why not?

_____

Is this 'sexual'?
Yes / No
Why / Why not?

---

3. HALLARD picks up a riding crop from the bed. She walks over to LLOYD and stands next to her. She rubs the end of the riding crop against LLOYD's breasts and says, *'I'm going to fuck you.'*
Is this 'touching'?
Yes / No
Why / Why not?

Is this 'sexual'?
Yes / No
Why / Why not?

---

4. FARREL takes off his jeans and masturbates his penis against LLOYD's arm (through her blouse). He does not say anything.
Is this 'touching'?
Yes / No
Why / Why Not?

Is this 'sexual'?
Yes / No
Why / Why not?

EXPLANATION 20.7.1

FARREL Scenario

1. This would be regarded as 'touching' and 'sexual'. This is because 'touching' has been held to include touching a person's clothing while they are wearing it (*R v H* [2005] EWCA Crim 732); it would be 'sexual' as, although this act is not sexual by its very nature (failing the first part of the definition of the term), it would fall into the second half, i.e. it becomes sexual because of the circumstances and FARREL's intention.

2. This would be regarded as 'touching' and 'sexual'. This is because the definition of 'touching' includes touching through anything (the skirt). It is 'sexual' for the same reason as point 1.

3. This would be regarded as 'touching' and 'sexual'. The definition of 'touching' includes touching with anything else (the riding crop). It is 'sexual' for the same reason as point 1.

4. This would be regarded as 'touching' and 'sexual'. It is 'touching' because the definition includes touching with any part of the body and through anything. It is 'sexual' because a reasonable person would always consider masturbation to be sexual by its very nature.

See *Investigators' Manual*, paras 4.3.1 to 4.3.4

20.8   Offences Under ss. 2, 3 and 4 of the Act

20.8.1   Exercise—Developing the FARREL Scenario

FARREL and HALLARD subject LLOYD to a horrific sexual attack lasting for a number of hours. At the end of the attack, they leave LLOYD naked, gagged and tied to a bed. They tell LLOYD that they will be back in an hour to further abuse her and then kill her. After FARREL and HALLARD leave, LLOYD struggles violently to escape her bonds. She manages to free one of her hands and from there she is able to remove her gag and free herself. She tries to escape through the bedroom door but it is firmly locked. She runs to the window and, pulling back the curtains, she bangs on the window and screams for help.

While LLOYD was being attacked, her fiancé, JARVIS, had become concerned for her welfare. He tried to ring LLOYD on her mobile phone but received no reply. LLOYD had told JARVIS where she was going and so JARVIS drives to FARREL and HALLARD's house. He sees LLOYD's car parked near to the house and, believing that LLOYD is still looking at the wedding dress, he decides to join her. As he walks towards the front door, he sees his naked fiancée banging on an upstairs window and hears her scream for help.

JARVIS forces the front door of the house and runs into the house and upstairs. He kicks open the bedroom door and finds LLOYD in the bedroom. She tells JARVIS what has happened and JARVIS gets her out of the house and contacts the police. The police attend and, after speaking to LLOYD and JARVIS, they lie in wait for FARREL and HALLARD to return. When they do, they are arrested.

LLOYD provides the police with a precise account of the incident, stating exactly what happened during her ordeal.

There follows a table listing the actions of FARREL and HALLARD. For each action, choose *one* offence you think has been committed; e.g. place a tick in column 2 for an offence of assault by penetration.

	Action	1	2	3	4
1	FARREL penetrates LLOYD's vagina with a vibrator				
2	HALLARD orders LLOYD to masturbate FARREL				
3	FARREL makes LLOYD penetrate HALLARD's vagina with her tongue				
4	FARREL penetrates LLOYD's vagina with his penis				
5	HALLARD penetrates LLOYD's vagina with a glass bottle				
6	FARREL penetrates LLOYD's vagina with his tongue				
7	FARREL penetrates LLOYD's anus with a vibrator				
8	HALLARD kisses LLOYD's buttocks				
9	FARREL penetrates LLOYD's anus with his penis				
10	FARREL penetrates LLOYD's anus with his finger				
11	FARREL forces LLOYD to penetrate HALLARD's vagina with a vibrator				
12	HALLARD penetrates LLOYD's anus with her tongue				
13	HALLARD forces LLOYD to penetrate her own vagina with her own fingers				
14	HALLARD penetrates LLOYD's anus with a knife				
15	FARREL compels LLOYD to lick HALLARD's vagina				
16	FARREL penetrates LLOYD's mouth with his penis				
17	FARREL fondles LLOYD's breasts				

EXPLANATION 20.8.1

Developing the FARREL Scenario

If you have your *Investigators' Manual* with you, you should turn to the pages dealing with the offences under ss. 1 to 4 of the Act. This may help you understand this exercise.

Section 1—Rape—Numbers 4, 9 and 16.

You should remember that this offence is triggered by the offender penetrating the victim's vagina, anus or mouth with his penis.

Section 2—Assault by Penetration—Numbers 1, 5, 6, 7, 10, 12 and 14.

As rape is the only offence that can only be committed by a man, this offence can be committed by FARREL and HALLARD. It involves the sexual penetration of the vagina or anus of the victim with a part of the offender's body, or indeed with anything whatsoever.

Section 3—Sexual Touching—Numbers 8 and 17.

You should have been able to identify these offences after the exercises in relation to both terms.

Section 4—Causing Sexual Activity Without Consent—Numbers 2, 3, 11, 13 and 15.

Where the offender(s) cause another person to engage in sexual activity involving some sort of penetration, the maximum penalty is increased from 10 years' imprisonment to life imprisonment.

Your completed table should look like the one which follows.

	Action	1	2	3	4
1	FARREL penetrates LLOYD's vagina with a vibrator		×		
2	HALLARD orders LLOYD to masturbate FARREL				×
3	FARREL makes LLOYD penetrate HALLARD's vagina with her tongue				×
4	FARREL penetrates LLOYD's vagina with his penis	×			
5	HALLARD penetrates LLOYD's vagina with a glass bottle		×		
6	FARREL penetrates LLOYD's vagina with his tongue		×		
7	FARREL penetrates LLOYD's anus with a vibrator		×		
8	HALLARD kisses LLOYD's buttocks			×	
9	FARREL penetrates LLOYD's anus with his penis	×			
10	FARREL penetrates LLOYD's anus with his finger		×		
11	FARREL forces LLOYD to penetrate HALLARD's vagina with a vibrator				×
12	HALLARD penetrates LLOYD's anus with her tongue		×		
13	HALLARD forces LLOYD to penetrate her own vagina with her own fingers				×
14	HALLARD penetrates LLOYD's anus with a knife		×		
15	FARREL compels LLOYD to lick HALLARD's vagina				×
16	FARREL penetrates LLOYD's mouth with his penis	×			
17	FARREL fondles LLOYD's breasts			×	

See *Investigators' Manual*, paras 4.2.1 to 4.3.6

20.9   Conclusion

Now that you have finished this section, you should be able to differentiate between the offences created by ss. 1 to 4 of the Sexual Offences Act 2003. You should be capable of identifying consent issues under the three appropriate sections and you should also be able to explain the terms 'sexual' and 'touching', which are of crucial importance to this category of offence. These abilities will assist you to answer questions on the subject in the NIE.

20.10   Recall Questions

Try and answer the following questions.

- Who is entitled to anonymity and for how long?
- What is the definition of rape? (Can you remember the mnemonic?)
- What does s. 74 of the Sexual Offences Act 2003 say about consent?
- List the six circumstances where a rebuttable presumption of consent may be raised by s. 75(2) of the Act.
- What would need to be proved for this section to apply?
- What does the law say with regard to surgically constructed body parts?
- What are the two circumstances where an irrebuttable presumption about consent can be raised?
- What does the term 'sexual' mean?
- What does the term 'touching' mean?
- What is the *actus reus* of an offence under s. 2 of the Sexual Offences Act 2003?
- When could you receive life imprisonment for committing an offence under s. 4 of the Sexual Offences Act 2003?
- What is s. 4 of the Sexual Offences Act 2003 about?

20.11   Multiple-Choice Questions

Answers to these questions can be found in the 'Answers Section' at the end of the book. All explanations also include a reference back to the *Investigators' Manual 2022*.

1. ABBOTT (who is 19 years old) is the victim of an offence of assault by penetration (an offence under s. 2 of the Sexual Offences Act 2003). DC COLES is investigating the offence and interviews ABBOTT. During the interview, ABBOTT expresses concern about her details becoming known to the public.

What response should DC COLES give?

A ABBOTT will be entitled to anonymity until she is 21 years old.

B ABBOTT will be entitled to anonymity until she is 24 years old.

C ABBOTT will not be entitled to anonymity.

D ABBOTT will be entitled to anonymity throughout her lifetime.

Answer _____

2. EMERY and her common-law husband JOYCE are both serial sex offenders. They kidnap PORTER while she is walking her dog in a park and drag her into a nearby hut where they sexually abuse her. During the attack, EMERY forces her fingers into PORTER's anus. Moments later, JOYCE forces his fingers into PORTER's vagina before forcing his penis into PORTER's mouth and ejaculating.

At what point, if any, is the offence of rape first committed?

A When EMERY forces her fingers into PORTER's anus.

B When JOYCE forces his fingers into PORTER's vagina.

C When JOYCE forces his penis into PORTER's mouth.

D The offence of rape is not committed in these circumstances.

Answer _____

3. MATELIN was born a male but has had hormone treatment to create breasts and has had gender reassignment surgery to replace the penis with a surgically constructed vagina. While walking along a street, MATELIN is approached from behind by SUTTON who pushes MATELIN into a nearby alleyway. SUTTON digitally penetrates MATELIN's surgically constructed vagina and then digitally penetrates MATELIN's anus.

Does SUTTON commit an offence of assault by penetration (contrary to s. 2 of the Sexual Offences Act 2003)?

A Yes, but only when he digitally penetrates MATELIN's anus.

B No, although the offence can be committed by either sex, the victim must be female.

C Yes, when he penetrates MATELIN's surgically constructed vagina.

D No, this offence can only be committed when penetration is carried out with something other than a part of the body.

Answer _____

4. WALTON has a fetish for feet. He gets a job at a shoe shop in order to satisfy his desires and obtains sexual gratification every time he touches a customer's foot when he is helping them to try on a pair of shoes. WALTON realises that shop customers would not consent to him touching their feet if they knew he was obtaining sexual gratification as a consequence.

Considering the offence of sexual touching (contrary to s. 3 of the Sexual Offences Act 2003) only, which of the following statements is correct?

A WALTON does not commit the offence because a reasonable person would not regard his fetish as being 'sexual'.

B The fact that WALTON obtains sexual gratification from the touching means that it is 'sexual' and as a consequence he commits the offence.

C The offence is not committed in these circumstances because WALTON has not touched a sexual organ or orifice.

D WALTON commits the offence because he did not believe that his victims would consent to the activity.

Answer _____

21 | Child Sex Offences

21.1 Introduction

This section deals with offences under ss. 9 to 15 of the Sexual Offences Act 2003, as well as legislation covering indecent photographs of children. Like all sections of the Sexual Offences part of your syllabus, it has been subject to questions on a very regular basis.

21.2 Aim

The aim of this section is to explain criminal offences relating to the sexual abuse of children.

21.3 Objectives

At the end of this section you should be able to:

1. Explain the offences connected with sexual activity with a child (ss. 9 and 10 of the Sexual Offences Act 2003).
2. State when an offence of sexual activity in the presence of a child (s. 11 of the Sexual Offences Act 2003) has taken place.
3. Identify key points from the offence of causing a child to watch a sex act (s. 12 of the Sexual Offences Act 2003).
4. State when an offence under s. 13 of the Sexual Offences Act 2003 (child sex offences committed by children or young persons) may be committed.
5. Outline the offence of arranging or facilitating the commission of a child sex offence (contrary to s. 14 of the Sexual Offences Act 2003).
6. Outline the offence of meeting a child following sexual grooming (contrary to s. 15 of the Sexual Offences Act 2003).
7. Identify the exceptions to aiding, abetting or counselling an offence involving or directed towards children.
8. Identify common factors relating to offences under ss. 9 to 15 of the Sexual Offences Act 2003.
9. Outline the offences connected with indecent photographs of children (s. 1 of the Protection of Children Act 1978 and s. 160 of the Criminal Justice Act 1988).
10. Apply your knowledge to multiple-choice questions.

21.4 Sexual Activity with a Child

21.4.1 Exercise—Several Scenarios

Examine the following scenarios and then complete the written exercises that follow them.

1. CLARKE (a 20-year-old male) approaches VICKERS (a 15-year-old female) in a cafe. The two strike up a conversation during which VICKERS tells CLARKE her age. CLARKE asks VICKERS if she would like to come with him to see his house and VICKERS agrees. At the house, CLARKE and VICKERS kiss each other and CLARKE takes all of VICKERS's clothing off. He inserts his finger into VICKERS's vagina with her consent.

   i. How old must an offender be to commit this offence?

   _____

   ii. There are two relevant ages regarding the victim. What are they and what is the requirement regarding the older of the two ages?

   _____

   iii. What effect will VICKERS's consent to the activity have with regard to this offence?

   _____

   iv. What would the situation be if VICKERS were 11 years old?

   _____

2. CLARKE (a 20-year-old male) approaches VICKERS (a 15-year-old female) in a cafe. The two strike up a conversation during which VICKERS tells CLARKE her age. CLARKE asks VICKERS if she would like to come with him to see his house and VICKERS agrees. At the house, CLARKE and VICKERS continue talking to each other and during the conversation CLARKE asks VICKERS if she would like him to put his finger in her vagina. VICKERS says, *'I don't know.'* CLARKE replies, *'Go on, you'll enjoy it once I've started.'*

   i. Think about what CLARKE has done. What offence does CLARKE commit in these circumstances?

   _____

   ii. VICKERS replies *'No'* and walks out of the house. Does it make any difference that no sexual activity has taken place?

Yes / No

   iii. Imagine that instead of just chatting in the cafe, CLARKE asked VICKERS to come to his house and have sexual intercourse with his friend, FINCH. What effect would this have?

   _____

EXPLANATION 21.4.1

Several Scenarios

1. i. The offender must be at least 18 (18\+).

   ii. The two ages are under 16 (–16) and under 13 (–13). If the victim is under 16, you have to show that the offender did not reasonably believe that the victim was 16 or over.

   iii. The fact that the victim (whatever their age) consents does not matter.

iv. You may have found this question difficult to answer, so do not worry if that was the case. It was included because it is an obvious question to ask when you study child sex offences and there is no answer contained in your Manual. If VICKERS were 11 years old, then it would appear that CLARKE has committed the offence under s. 9 of the Act. However, you may have realised that the activity would also constitute an offence under s. 2 of the Act (see previous section on 'Sexual Offences'), as all that would need to be proved is the intentional sexual penetration and the child's age. So which offence would be charged? Where a child is under 13, one of the relevant offences under ss. 5 to 8 of the Act would normally be charged. The penalties for these offences are higher, reflecting the fact that a child under 13 cannot legally consent to sexual activity. However, occasionally the offence might be used where the child is under 13. An example would be where a person is charged with the offence of sexual activity with a child, all parties believing the child to be 13 or over, and it then became known in the course of the trial that the child was actually under 13. The extension of the offence to children under 13 means that the trial could continue with the original charge when necessary.

2. i. CLARKE is encouraging VICKERS to engage in sexual activity that would constitute an offence under s. 9 of the Act. There is a specific offence of causing or inciting someone to commit the offence under s. 10 of the Act.

ii. No. Incitement (see 'Incomplete Offences' section) is all about trying to get someone to commit an offence. If VICKERS actually did something then the substantial offence would be committed. The offence exists to punish the pre-substantive offence conduct and so the fact that no sexual activity has taken place is immaterial.

iii. The offence would still be committed as the s. 10 offence is about incitement to commit the offence with the defendant (CLARKE) or a third person (FINCH).

In the process of completing exercises relating to ss. 9 and 10 of the Act, you will have unconsciously obtained information relating to the offences dealt with in ss. 11 and 12. As you continue, see if you can see these connections.

See *Investigators' Manual*, paras. 4.4.2, 4.3.6

21.5 Sexual Activity in the Presence of a Child

21.5.1 Exercise—Questions about the Offence

Try answering the following questions to form the basis of the definition of this offence. Your answers should have between one and four words in them (other than the answers to questions 6 and 7, where you will have more words in the answer).

1. What age does the offender have to be?

_____

2. What state of mind is required?

_____

3. What must the offender do?

_____

4. What kind of act must it be?

_____

5. What is the purpose of the act?

_____

6. He engages in the activity when?

_____

7. What has the offender got to know or believe?

_____

8. What age brackets must the victims fall into?

i. _____

ii. _____

EXPLANATION 21.5.1

Questions about the Offence

How far away were your answers from the actual definition of the offence?

> A person aged 18 or over (A) commits an offence if

> he intentionally

> engages in an activity

> the activity is sexual

> for the purpose of obtaining sexual gratification, he engages in it

> when another person (B) is present or is in a place from which A can be observed
> and
> knowing or believing that B is aware, or intending that B should be aware,
> that he is engaging in it and

> B is under 16 and A does not reasonably believe that B is 16 or over or
> B is under 13

21.5.2   Exercise—Section 11 Scenarios

Examine the following scenarios and decide whether an offence under s. 11 has been committed. Give a short reason for your answer.

1. GAUNT (a 25-year-old male) is standing outside a Portakabin, used as a changing room for under 16s who play football on a nearby field. GAUNT drops his trousers and, to obtain sexual gratification, he begins masturbating towards the Portakabin, believing that there are children inside who can see him. The Portakabin is in fact empty.
Section 11 offence committed?
Yes / No
Why / Why not?

2. COPELAND and his girlfriend BONE (both 37 years old) are having a picnic in a secluded area of a campsite. They both believe they are alone and cannot be seen and begin to have sexual intercourse together. Unknown to either of them, NICHOLLS (an 11-year-old) is watching them.
Section 11 offence committed?
Yes / No
Why / Why not?

3. THORNLEY (a 48-year-old male) is sitting in a steam room in a gym when PRICE (a 12-year-old female) walks in and sits opposite THORNLEY. THORNLEY pulls down his trunks and begins masturbating towards PRICE, believing she can see him and in order to gain sexual gratification. Unknown to THORNLEY, PRICE cannot see what he is doing because of the amount of steam in the room.
Section 11 offence committed?
Yes / No
Why / Why not?

EXPLANATION 21.5.2

Section 11 Scenarios

1. This would not constitute an offence, as you must show that a person under 16 is present or is in a place from which the defendant can be observed.

2. This would not constitute an offence because neither COPELAND nor BONE knew, believed or intended that a child should be aware that they were engaged in that activity.

3. This would constitute an offence as it is not necessary to show that a child was in fact aware of the activity in every case. If you work through the definition, you can see that THORNLEY has intentionally engaged in sexual activity for the purpose of sexual gratification when another person (PRICE) is present and believing that PRICE is aware that he is engaging in it.

See *Investigators' Manual*, para. 4.4.4

21.6 Causing a Child to Watch a Sex Act

21.6.1 Exercise—Basic Elements of the Offence

You should be able to answer the following questions based on your study of this section so far.

1. How old must the offender be?

_____

2. What age brackets do the victims fall into?

_____

The correct answers to the previous questions have been placed in the appropriate place within the definition of this offence (set out in the following), along with some hints as to the missing sections. Can you fill in the gaps?

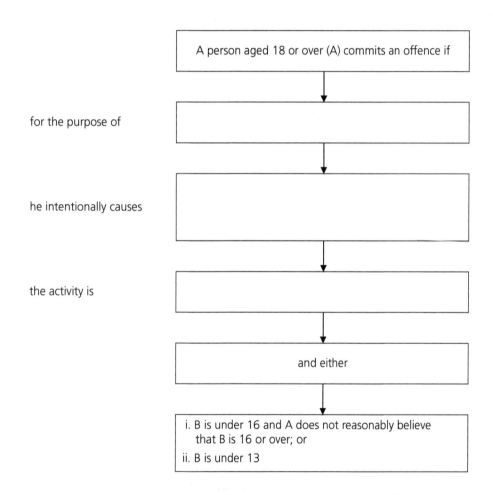

A person aged 18 or over (A) commits an offence if

for the purpose of

he intentionally causes

the activity is

and either

i. B is under 16 and A does not reasonably believe that B is 16 or over; or
ii. B is under 13

EXPLANATION 21.6.1

Basic Elements of the Offence

Your answer should have contained the following:

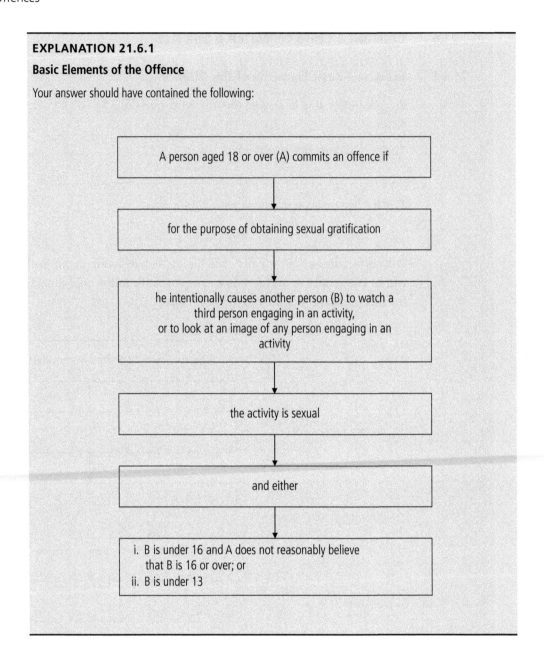

A person aged 18 or over (A) commits an offence if

for the purpose of obtaining sexual gratification

he intentionally causes another person (B) to watch a third person engaging in an activity, or to look at an image of any person engaging in an activity

the activity is sexual

and either

i. B is under 16 and A does not reasonably believe that B is 16 or over; or
ii. B is under 13

21.6.2 Exercise—Images

Concentrating on the activity of the third person and the word 'image', answer the following questions (take it that all the other elements of the offence are satisfied).

1. The activity that the child watches can be live or recorded.
True / False

2. There is a requirement that the child needs to be in close physical proximity to the sexual act.
True / False

3. Which of the following would or would not qualify as an 'image' for the purposes of this offence?

	Image	Not an image
A film		
A photograph		
A magazine		
A 3-dimensional sculpture		
A cartoon		
A computer-generated picture		

EXPLANATION 21.6.2

Images

1. True.

2. False. For example, an offender could show a child a live image via webcam where the actual activity is taking place hundreds of miles away.

3. All of these examples would qualify.

See *Investigators' Manual*, para. 4.4.5

21.7 Child Sex Offences Committed by Children or Young Persons

You will have seen that in all of the offences examined so far (ss. 9, 10, 11 and 12) the age of the offender is always 18\+. What happens when someone aged less than 18 commits one of these acts?

Section 13 deals with this situation by saying that the person will still commit an offence. However, the maximum sentence for an offender who is less than 18 is five years' imprisonment.

21.8 Arranging or Facilitating the Commission of Child Sex Offences

21.8.1 Exercise—MARCOU Scenario

Look at the following scenarios. Has an offence under this section been committed?

MARCOU operates a sex-tourism business. HOPE approaches MARCOU and asks him if he can arrange for a 14-year-old girl to be made available to him to have sexual intercourse with. MARCOU tells HOPE that he can, but the abuse will have to take place in Thailand. HOPE tells MARCOU to go ahead with the arrangements and MARCOU books flights and a hotel for HOPE, and also makes arrangements for a 14-year-old girl to be made available to HOPE when he arrives in Thailand. MARCOU makes these arrangements in the belief that HOPE will have sexual intercourse with the girl when he visits Thailand. A week before HOPE is due to fly out to Thailand, he is involved in a car accident and breaks his leg. He contacts MARCOU and tells him that he can no longer make the trip and to cancel all the arrangements.

1. Who, if anyone, has committed the offence under s. 14?

Why / Why not?

---

2. This offence can only be committed if the activities are to take place in the United Kingdom.
True / False

3. Arranging what 'relevant offences' would trigger the commission of this offence?

i. _____

ii. _____

iii. _____

iv. _____

v. _____

4. Does the fact that MARCOU only 'believed' that HOPE was going to have sexual intercourse with a 14-year-old girl make any difference?
Yes / No

5. HOPE never travelled to Thailand. What effect, if any, will this have on the case?

EXPLANATION 21.8.1

MARCOU Scenario

1. HOPE and MARCOU have both committed the offence. The title of the offence tells you a lot about it, but it is unlikely to be enough for you to answer questions.

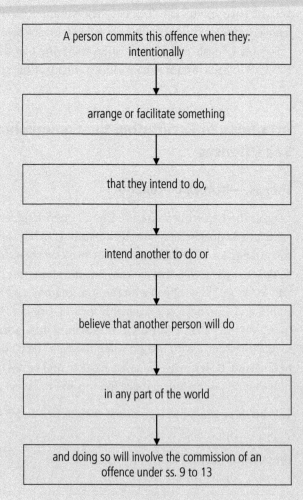

A person commits this offence when they:
intentionally

↓

arrange or facilitate something

↓

that they intend to do,

↓

intend another to do or

↓

believe that another person will do

↓

in any part of the world

↓

and doing so will involve the commission of an offence under ss. 9 to 13

2. False.

3. The five trigger offences are those that you have studied so far in this section of the Workbook, i.e. offences under ss. 9 to 13.

4. No—see the definition.

5. None at all. The offence is complete whether or not the sexual activity actually takes place.

See *Investigators' Manual*, para. 4.4.7

21.9 Meeting a Child Following Sexual Grooming

21.9.1 Exercise—HOLLIS and KIRK Scenarios

Study the following scenarios. Answer the questions and provide an explanation for your answers where you are asked.

1. HOLLIS (a 20-year-old male) has a full-time job working as a section supervisor in a supermarket. He is in charge of a number of staff, some of whom are part-time. One of the part-time workers is SUMPTER (a 15-year-old female), who works in the supermarket on Saturdays. HOLLIS is aware that SUMPTER has a 'crush' on him and one Saturday she approaches him and asks him to go to a works party with her on the following Friday. HOLLIS agrees to go with SUMPTER and intends to have sexual intercourse with her at the party. HOLLIS phones SUMPTER on Thursday night and they talk about the party. On the Friday morning, he phones her again and asks if he should take some condoms with him. SUMPTER tells HOLLIS that taking condoms will not be necessary as she will not have sexual intercourse with him; however, she will give him oral sex. HOLLIS travels to the party but SUMPTER does not turn up as she is unwell.

i. What age should the offender be?

ii. What about the age of the victim?

iii. How many times must the offender have met or communicated with the other person?

iv. Does the fact that SUMPTER made the initial contact have any bearing on the case?
Yes / No

v. The communication by the defendant with the other person must have some form of sexual content in it.
Yes / No

vi. What is a 'relevant offence'?

vii. SUMPTER did not turn up to the party. What effect(s) will this have?

viii. Does HOLLIS commit the offence?
Yes / No
Why / Why not?

---

2. KIRK (a 14-year-old male) lives next door to REDROW (an 18-year-old female). KIRK goes on holiday with his family to Spain for two weeks and REDROW is due to join them for the final week of the holiday. In the first week of his holiday, KIRK receives several text messages from REDROW telling him that she loves him and that she wants to have sexual intercourse with him when she arrives in Spain. KIRK sends several messages back to REDROW telling her that they do not have any type of relationship together and there is absolutely no chance whatsoever that they will have any sort of sexual contact. REDROW ignores these messages and, when she flies out to Spain, she does so with the intention of having sexual intercourse with KIRK.

i. Can a female commit this offence?
Yes / No

ii. The communications were sent from the United Kingdom to Spain. Does this make a difference?
Yes / No

iii. REDROW was travelling to Spain intending to have sexual intercourse in that country. Does this make a difference?
Yes / No

iv. There is no chance that REDROW could do as she intended. Does this make a difference?
Yes / No

v. Does REDROW commit the offence?
Yes / No
Why / Why not?

EXPLANATION 21.9.1

HOLLIS and KIRK Scenarios

1 i. 18\+

  ii. −16

  iii. ONE or more occasions.

  iv. None at all.

  v. False. There may be explicit sexual content in the communications, but there is no requirement that this must be the case. The communications could be completely inoffensive.

  vi. Any of the offences covered by Part I of the Sexual Offences Act 2003 (the sexual offences you have studied in your Manual).

  vii. It will have no effect. The intended offence does not have to take place as this offence is all to do with the intentions of the offender when meeting or travelling to meet the other person.

  viii. Yes. HOLLIS has communicated with SUMPTER on a least one previous occasion and travelled to the party with the intention of having oral sex with SUMPTER (an offence under s. 9 of the Act) who is under 16 years of age.

2   i. Yes. Remember that the only offence that cannot be committed by a female is rape.

   ii. No. The meeting or communication can have taken place in any part of the world.

   iii. No. The meeting can take place in any part of the world.

   iv. No. Remember that this is an offence that is all about the intention of the offender.

   v. Yes. REDROW has communicated with KIRK on one or more occasions and is travelling with the intention of having sexual intercourse with KIRK (an offence under s. 9 of the Act) who is under 16 years of age.

See *Investigators' Manual*, para. 4.4.7

21.10   Common Factors

s. 9 ↓	s. 10 ↓	s. 11 ↓	s. 12 ↓	s. 13 ↓	s. 14	s. 15
Offender 18\+ ↓	Offender 18\+ ↓	Offender 18\+ ↓	Offender 18\+ ↓	Offender UNDER 18 ↓	ANY AGE	Offender 18\+ ↓
Victim −16 ↓	Victim −16 ↓	Victim −16 ↓	Victim −16 ↓	Victim −16 ↓	Victim −16	Victim −16
Victim −13	Victim −13	Victim −13	Victim −13	Victim −13		

21.11   Exceptions to Aiding, Abetting or Counselling

In certain circumstances, a person acting in the interests of a child may appear to be aiding, abetting or counselling one of the offences in the 'Sexual Offences Against Children' section of your *Investigators' Manual*.

This will *not* be the case if the person is acting to protect, prevent or promote the:

   S   Safety of the child (protect)
   T   Transmitted sexual infection (protect)
   E   Emotional well-being (promote)
   P   Pregnancy (prevent)

and not for the purpose of:

   C   Causing or encouraging the sexual activity
   O   Obtaining sexual gratification
   P   Participation

See *Investigators' Manual*, para. 4.4.7

21.12   Indecent Photographs of Children

This section concentrates on the legislation in relation to indecent photographs of children under the Protection of Children Act 1978 and the Criminal Justice Act 1988.

Remember that a person will be a 'child' for the purposes of both of these Acts if it appears from the evidence as a whole that he/she was, at the material time, under the age of 18.

21.12.1 **Exercise—Section 1 of the Protection of Children Act 1978**

Answer the following questions relating to this legislation. Do not attempt to provide word for word answers; short notes/descriptions will be fine.

1. Apart from photographs, what other material is dealt with in this section?

_____

2. There are four ways that a defendant can commit the offence. What are they?

    i. _____

    ii. _____

    iii. _____

    iv. _____

3. There are two defences to this offence. What are they?

    i. _____

    ii. _____

4. The 'Marriage and other relationship' section provides a defence, but the defendant will have to satisfy four criteria. What are they?

    i. _____

    ii. _____

    iii. _____

    iv. _____

5. There are exceptions for criminal proceedings whereby a defendant is not guilty if he/she proves that:

    i. _____

    ii. _____

    iii. _____

6. Using the information you have from the previous answers to assist you, examine the following scenarios and decide whether the defendant has committed an offence. Give reasons for your answers.

    i. CUTLER is a delivery driver. He takes a sealed package from an office to the home address of GARGAN. He is stopped by the police as he walks towards GARGAN's house. The package contains indecent pseudo-photographs of children.
Offence committed?
Yes / No
Why / Why not?

_____

ii. FRIPP takes a photograph of his 17-year-old girlfriend, McQUEEN, with whom he is living in an enduring family relationship. The photograph is taken with McQUEEN's consent. In the photograph, McQUEEN is naked and sitting with her legs astride FRIPP's friend, LOGAN.

Offence committed?

Yes / No

Why / Why not?

EXPLANATION 21.12.1

Section 1 of the Protection of Children Act 1978

You will probably not have been able to answer all of the questions from 1 to 5, but you should have had some knowledge of the subject. If you had filled in these questions you would have a note form of the offence and defences for this offence.

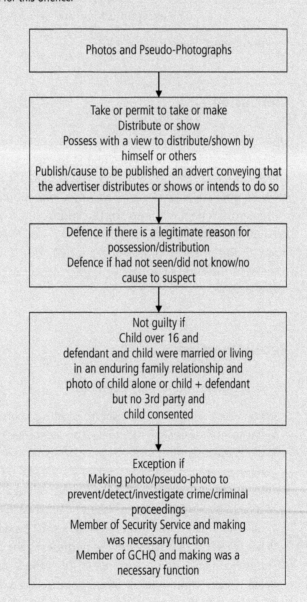

> With this information, you could answer the scenarios.
>
> 6. i. No offence. The material is indecent and CUTLER is distributing it, but he has a defence as he has not seen the pseudo-photographs.
>
>   ii. Offence committed. FRIPP has only satisfied three of the four requirements for a defence under s. 1A of the Act. As his friend LOGAN is in the picture, the offence is committed.
>
> See *Investigators' Manual*, paras 4.4.12.1 to 4.4.12.3

21.12.2 Criminal Justice Act 1988, s. 160

This is the same as the offence under s. 1 of the Protection of Children Act except:

It relates to *POSSESSION*

There is an extra defence—*photo/image sent to him without request and not kept for an unreasonable time*

The exceptions for crime/Security/GCHQ *do not apply*

See *Investigators' Manual*, para. 4.4.12.4

21.13 Conclusion

One of the major issues that candidates are concerned with regarding child sex offences under the Sexual Offences Act 2003 is the relevant ages for the offences. Having completed the exercises in this section, you should appreciate the similarities between some of these offences and, as a consequence, you should be confident regarding the age requirements. You should also see the connections with the previous section examining 'Sexual Offences', as the terms 'touching' and 'sexual' are significant components of many of the offences you have examined. You should now possess a good knowledge of most of the child sex offences applicable to the NIE syllabus (familial and protection issues aside).

21.14 Recall Questions

Try and answer the following questions.

- When would a person be exempt from aiding, abetting or counselling a child sex offence?
- What section deals with offenders who are under 18 years of age?
- What is the definition of the offence of sexual activity with a child under 16?
- What happens if a child consents to a s. 9 (Sexual Offences Act 2003) offence?
- What must you show to prove an offence of engaging in sexual activity in the presence of a child (s. 11 of the Sexual Offences Act 2003)?
- What is an 'image' for the purposes of a s. 12 (Sexual Offences Act 2003) offence?
- What is a 'relevant offence' for the purposes of the offence of arranging or facilitating the commission of a child sex offence (s. 14 of the Sexual Offences Act 2003)?
- What is the definition of the offence of meeting a child following sexual grooming (s. 15 of the Sexual Offences Act 2003)?
- What is the relevant age for the offence under s. 15?

- What is required if a defendant wishes to use the exception regarding marriage to a charge of possessing an indecent photograph of a child?
- What are the two defences to a charge of taking an indecent photograph of a child?

21.15   Multiple-Choice Questions

Answers to these questions can be found in the 'Answers Section' at the end of the book. All explanations also include a reference back to the *Investigators' Manual 2022*.

1. COLCOUGH (a 19-year-old male) approaches LEENEY (a 14-year-old schoolgirl wearing school uniform) while she is waiting for her mother to pick her up outside the gates of her school. COLCOUGH begins talking with LEENEY and after several minutes he asks her if he can fondle her breasts. LEENEY agrees but before COLCOUGH can do anything, LEENEY's mother arrives, picks her daughter up and drives off.

Which of the following statements is correct with regard to the offence of inciting a child to engage in sexual activity (contrary to s. 10 of the Sexual Offences Act 2003)?

A COLCOUGH does not commit the offence because LEENEY consented to the activity.

B The fact that there was no sexual activity between COLCOUGH and LEENEY does not matter; COLCOUGH has committed the offence.

C COLCOUGH does not commit the offence because he is under 21 years of age.

D COLCOUGH commits the offence and, because LEENEY is under 16 years old, the offence is complete.

Answer _____

2. MOORWOOD is a paedophile and derives sexual pleasure from masturbating in front of children. He visits a park and hides in some bushes near to a set of swings where SANDARS (a 14-year-old boy) is playing. MOORWOOD comes out from behind the trees, drops his trousers and begins masturbating.

With regard to the offence of sexual activity in the presence of a child (s. 11 of the Sexual Offences Act 2003), which of the following comments is correct?

A MOORWOOD must be at least 16 years old to commit this offence.

B Sexual gratification does not form part of this offence.

C The offence is not committed in these circumstances as SANDARS is over the age of 13.

D It is not necessary to show that the child was in fact aware of the activity in every case.

Answer _____

3. TURNER (a 45-year-old male) is in his study at his home and is using the internet to search for pornographic images. He is looking at a site where there are a number of still images of cartoon men and women having sexual intercourse. His nephew, MARTIN (who is 16 years old), walks into the study and sees the images. TURNER asks MARTIN if he would like to see some more of the images and MARTIN replies that he would. TURNER shows MARTIN more of the still cartoon images and obtains sexual gratification from showing them to MARTIN.

Considering the offence under s. 12 of the Sexual Offences Act 2003 (causing a child to watch a sexual act) only, which of the following comments is correct?

A TURNER does not commit the offence because the images are still cartoons and not real-life moving images.

B TURNER does not commit the offence because MARTIN is 16 years old.

C It does not matter that the images are still or that they are cartoons, TURNER commits the offence.

D The offence is not committed because TURNER was originally viewing the pictures on his own and did not intentionally show them to MARTIN in the first instance.

Answer _____

22 Preparatory Offences

22.1 Introduction

Although these offences are dealt with relatively quickly in your Manual, you will have realised by now that this is not indicative of your examiners' approach to the material. As preparatory offences are never far from the headlines, particularly the offence of administering a substance with intent, you can safely assume that questions on this area of the Sexual Offences Act 2003 may find their way into your examination.

22.2 Aim

The aim of this section is to give you a thorough understanding of the 'Preparatory Offences' found under ss. 61, 62 and 63 of the Sexual Offences Act 2003.

22.3 Objectives

At the end of this section you should be able to:

1. Define and explain the offence of administering a substance with intent (s. 61 of the Sexual Offences Act 2003).
2. Define and explain the offence of committing a criminal offence with intent to commit a sexual offence (s. 62 of the Sexual Offences Act 2003).
3. Define and explain the offence of trespass with intent to commit a relevant sexual offence (s. 63 of the Sexual Offences Act 2003).
4. Apply your knowledge to multiple-choice questions.

22.4 Administering a Substance with Intent

22.4.1 Exercise—A Series of Events

Examine the following scenarios and decide whether an offence has been committed or not. Give reasons for your answers.

1. DELEHAY is in a nightclub drinking from a bottle of beer. HURLSTON places GHB (a date-rape drug) into DELEHAY's bottle of beer without her knowledge, intending to stupefy her so that he can rape her. DELEHAY drinks the beer and passes out.

Section 61 offence committed?

Yes / No

Why / Why not?

---

2. KANSAL and RAVENHALL are in a nightclub drinking double vodkas. KANSAL is sexually attracted to RAVENHALL and thinks that RAVENHALL might be more likely to have sexual intercourse with him if he bought her triple vodkas. He suggests that they should have stronger drinks and RAVENHALL agrees. KANSAL buys RAVENHALL a number of triple vodka drinks, intending to make her more susceptible to his advances. Owing to the effects of the triple vodka drinks, RAVENHALL agrees to have sexual intercourse with KANSAL.

Section 61 offence committed?

Yes / No

Why / Why not?

---

3. TUCKWELL is working behind a bar in a pub when YASIN walks in. TUCKWELL has always liked YASIN but she has constantly spurned his advances. When YASIN asks for a coke, TUCKWELL puts rohypnol (a date-rape drug) into her drink. He intends the drug to overpower YASIN so that he can commit an offence of assault by penetration (contrary to s. 2 of the Sexual Offences Act 2003) against her. YASIN drinks the coke and becomes ill.

Section 61 offence committed?

Yes / No

Why / Why not?

---

4. RIPPON and YOUNG (two females) are attracted to SHELLAM (a male) who works in the same office as they do. One evening when the three are working overtime, RIPPON approaches SHELLAM from behind and places a cloth impregnated with chloroform over his face. SHELLAM falls unconscious to the floor. RIPPON has done this with the intention of enabling YOUNG to commit an offence of sexual touching (contrary to s. 3 of the Sexual Offences Act 2003) against SHELLAM.

Section 61 offence committed?

Yes / No

Why / Why not?

EXPLANATION 22.4.1

A Series of Events

Before the exercises are explained, it would be a good idea to refresh your memory in relation to the definition of this offence.

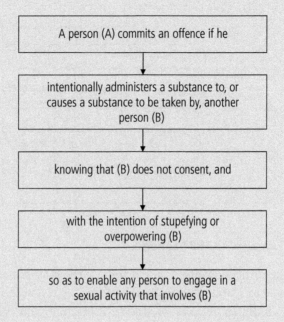

1. An offence has been committed. HURLSTON has intentionally administered a substance to DELEHAY intending to rape her.

2. An offence has not been committed. Although alcohol is a substance, for the purposes of this offence it has not been administered with the requisite intention, i.e. to stupefy or overpower. It would be an offence to add alcohol to 'spike' a drink where the victim did not know that they were consuming alcohol, or where the victim knew they were drinking alcohol but their drink was 'spiked'. It would not cover KANSAL encouraging RAVENHALL to get drunk so that KANSAL could have sex with her because RAVENHALL knew what she was drinking.

3. An offence has been committed. Remember that the reason for the substance being administered or being caused to be taken is to enable a person to engage in *sexual activity*, i.e. *any* sexual activity.

4. An offence has been committed. It is easy to become focused on date-rape cases, but remember that the substance can be administered in any way and not necessarily through a drink. The offence can be committed by a male or female and can be committed in order to enable some person (not necessarily the person who administered the substance) to engage in sexual activity with the victim.

See *Investigators' Manual*, para. 4.7.1

22.5 Committing an Offence with Intent to Commit a Sexual Offence

22.5.1 Exercise—What Do You Know?

Write down anything you know about this offence.

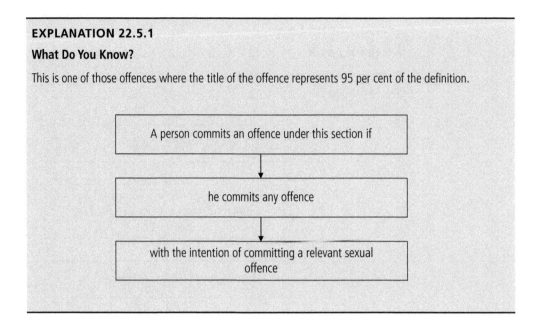

22.5.2   Exercise—BABB Scenario

Read the following scenario and use the information from the previous exercises to assist you to answer the questions.

BABB approaches GLADSTONE in a pub and begins chatting to her. Several minutes after they begin to talk to each other, BABB decides that he wants to have sex with GLADSTONE. However, it seems that he will be disappointed as, although GLADSTONE accepts a drink from him, she begins to talk to INMAN (another man standing at the bar). BABB feels insulted and annoyed by this rejection and decides that he will rape GLADSTONE at the first opportunity. BABB notices that GLADSTONE is wearing an expensive wristwatch and when the opportunity arises he manages to steal the watch from her wrist without her knowledge. His plan is that when GLADSTONE notices the wristwatch is missing, he will help her look for it and then suggest that he escort her to a nearby police station to report it lost. As soon as they are outside the pub, he will kidnap her and rape her. When GLADSTONE notices the wristwatch is missing, BABB offers to help her look for it. GLADSTONE thanks BABB but tells him not to bother as the watch was a cheap fake and she then leaves the pub with INMAN.

1. Would the theft of the watch qualify as 'any offence'?
Yes / No

2. What is a 'relevant sexual offence' and give an example of an excluded sexual offence?

_____

3. Does there have to be an immediate link between the offence committed and the relevant sexual offence?
Yes / No

4. What difference would it make if instead of stealing GLADSTONE's wristwatch, BABB waited for her to leave the pub and as she did he kidnapped her intending to rape her?

_____

5. GLADSTONE left without BABB even getting close to the commission of the planned offence of rape. What effect will this have?

6. Does BABB commit the offence?

Yes / No

EXPLANATION 22.5.2

BABB Scenario

As you will see, there is nothing complicated about this offence.

1. Yes, and for that matter so would absolutely any other criminal offence.

2. This is an area where it is better to remember the exception rather than the rule. If the intended sexual offence is not covered by the Sexual Offences Act 2003, then it is not a relevant offence. Your Manual gives a good example of this, stating that offences under the Protection of Children Act 1978 would not qualify. Therefore, committing a criminal offence with intent to take an indecent photograph of a child (s. 1 of the Protection of Children Act 1978) would not constitute an offence under s. 62.

3. No.

4. If the criminal offence is one of kidnap or false imprisonment, the maximum sentence is increased from 10 years to life.

5. None whatsoever. Remember that this offence and the offences under s. 61 (administering a substance with intent) and s. 63 (trespass with intent to commit a relevant sexual offence) are all preparatory offences. The whole point of these offences is to cater for behaviour that falls short of the intended end offence in the mind of the offender. If the offender actually had raped or sexually assaulted his/her victim before the preparatory offence was committed, then you would charge them with the substantive offence and these offences would be a complete waste of time.

6. Yes.

See *Investigators' Manual*, para. 4.7.2

22.6   Trespass with Intent to Commit a Relevant Sexual Offence

22.6.1   Exercise—A Definition?

What do you think the definition of this offence is?

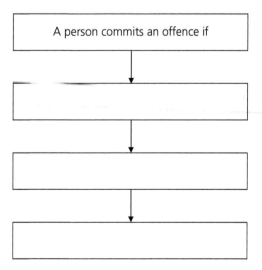

A person commits an offence if

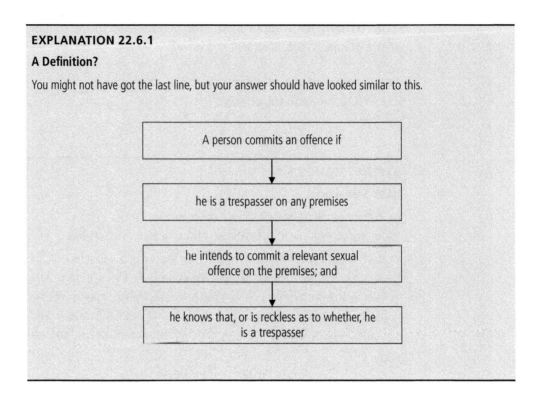

EXPLANATION 22.6.1

A Definition?

You might not have got the last line, but your answer should have looked similar to this.

22.6.2 Exercise—Further Points

Answer the following questions.

1. What is a 'relevant sexual offence' for the purposes of this offence?

_____

2. Which of the following would or would not be classed as 'premises' for the purposes of this offence?

Example	Premises	Not Premises
A semi-detached house		
A tent		
A Portakabin used as an office		
An abandoned houseboat		
A car		
The front garden of a private house		

3. A person is a trespasser if they are on the premises without the owner's consent.
True / False

4. This offence requires that the substantive sexual offence is at least attempted.
True / False

5. The defendant must intend to commit the relevant offence on the premises.
True / False

EXPLANATION 22.6.2

Further Points

1. A 'relevant sexual offence' for this offence is exactly the same as a 'relevant sexual offence' for the purposes of the offence under s. 62 of the Act (committing a criminal offence with intent to commit a sexual offence).

2. Your answers should have looked like this:

Example	Premises	Not Premises
A semi-detached house	×	
A tent	×	
A Portakabin used as an office	×	
An abandoned houseboat	×	
A car	×	
The front garden of a private house	×	

3. True.

4. False, this is a preparatory offence.

5. True. The premises where the offender is a trespasser must also be the intended location of the relevant sexual offence. If the offender is a trespasser in premises but intends to commit the relevant sexual offence elsewhere, the offence is not made out.

See *Investigators' Manual*, para. 4.7.3

22.7 Conclusion

Now that you have concluded this section of the Workbook, you should be conscious of the fact that there is more to these offences than meets the eye. Having said that, there is no need to make them out to be complex and lengthy affairs because that is plainly not the case. Completing this section should put you in a strong position to deal with any questions relating to these offences.

22.8 Recall Questions

Try and answer the following questions.

- What is a 'substance' for the purposes of s. 61 of the Sexual Offences Act 2003?
- What is the definition of the offence under s. 62 of the Sexual Offences Act 2003?
- What is a 'relevant sexual offence' for the purposes of ss. 62 and 63 of the Sexual Offences Act 2003?
- What does the term 'premises' mean?
- What is the definition of the offence under s. 63 of the Sexual Offences Act 2003?

22.9   **Multiple-Choice Questions**

Answers to these questions can be found in the 'Answers Section' at the end of the book. All explanations also include a reference back to the *Investigators' Manual 2022*.

1. FOXALL (an adult male) goes to a nightclub where he sees WALKER (an adult female) standing at the bar. He asks her if she would like a drink and she asks for an orange juice. FOXALL buys WALKER an orange juice but, before he gives it to WALKER, he asks a member of bar staff to add a double vodka to the drink. FOXALL's motive is to stupefy WALKER so that he can commit an offence of sexual touching (contrary to s. 3 of the Sexual Offences Act 2003) against her. WALKER does not notice her orange juice has been 'spiked' and after FOXALL has bought her three more 'spiked' drinks she becomes very drunk. She staggers towards the toilets and FOXALL follows her intending to fondle her breasts, but before he can touch WALKER she falls over. A member of staff comes to her aid and FOXALL decides to leave.

Does FOXALL commit an offence contrary to s. 61 of the Sexual Offences Act 2003 (administering a substance with intent)?

A No, as the offence of sexual touching has not been committed.

B Yes, but this is an attempt to commit the offence.

C No, as alcohol is not a 'substance'.

D Yes, in the circumstances all the elements of the offence are present.

Answer _____

2. HUBBALL (a 56-year-old male) wants to sexually assault a female (committing an offence of sexual assault by touching contrary to s. 3 of the Sexual Offences Act 2003 in the process). He is walking in a park when he sees PARTON (a 19-year-old female) place her bike against a tree and walk off into some nearby woods. HUBBALL decides to immobilise the bike so that it cannot be ridden and plans to sexually assault PARTON when she returns and is examining her bike. HUBBALL jumps on the front wheel of the bike to buckle it and smashes the chain mechanism.

Considering the offence of committing a criminal offence with intent to commit a sexual offence (contrary to s. 62 of the Sexual Offences Act 2003) only, which of the following statements is correct?

A HUBBALL commits the offence when he causes criminal damage to PARTON's pedal cycle.

B Sexual assault by touching is not a relevant sexual offence for the purposes of this offence.

C HUBBALL would only commit the offence if he committed an offence of kidnapping or false imprisonment.

D This offence is only committed when the criminal offence committed is one involving physical violence.

Answer _____

3. ROCHESTER breaks into a house owned by NICHOLL intending to steal property. ROCHESTER searches the house for any property worth stealing. While he is searching, he finds NICHOLL in the sitting room of the house and decides that he will kidnap her and take her to his own house where he will rape her. He grabs hold of NICHOLL who screams and fights back. ROCHESTER panics and runs away from the house.

Does ROCHESTER commit an offence in relation to s. 63 of the Sexual Offences Act 2003 (trespass with intent to commit a relevant sexual offence)?

A Yes, as he was a trespasser and intended to commit a relevant sexual offence.

B No, because he does not intend to commit the offence in the premises in which he is a trespasser.

C Yes, but he will have to attempt to commit the relevant offence.

D No, because when he entered as a trespasser he did not intend to commit a relevant sexual offence.

Answer _____

Sexual Offences Act 2003—Offence Summaries

Sexual Offences

Section 1
Rape
→
Section 5
Rape
Victim U13
→
Male offender
VAMPIRE
ss. 74, 75, 76 apply

Section 2
Assault by Penetration
→
Section 6
Assault by Penetration
Victim U13
→
Penetrating vagina or anus with anything
ss. 74, 75, 76 apply

Section 3
Sexual Touching
→
Section 7
Sexual Touching
Victim U13
→
Sexual touching without consent
ss. 74, 75, 76 apply

Section 4
Causing Sexual Activity
→
Section 8
Causing Sexual Activity
Victim U13
→
Intentionally cause sexual activity
Penetration = life
ss. 74, 75, 76 apply

Anonymity, Consent, Sexual, Touching and Conduct

Anonymity → Presume anonymity for life

Section 74
Consent → Must be 'true' no fear or force
Agree by choice
Freedom and capacity to choose

Section 75
Evidential Presumptions → Rebuttable
Sex SLAVE

Section 76
Conclusive Presumptions → Irrebuttable
Deception or Impersonate

Section 78
Sexual → Sexual by nature
May be sexual \ + circumstances or purpose
No exotic fetishes

Section 79
Touching → Any body part, with anything, through anything
Penetration is a continuing act

Criminal Conduct → No need for ejaculation
Surgically constructed = real

Child Sex Offences

Section 9
Sexual Activity with Child
↑ Offender 18\+ Victim U16 or U13
Consent is irrelevant if U13

Section 10
Inciting Section 9
↑ Offender 18\+
With defendant or 3rd party
No need for sexual activity

Section 11
Sexual Activity in Presence of Child
↑ Offender 18\+ Victim U16 or U13
For sexual gratification
Child must be there

Section 12
Causing Child to Watch a Sexual Act
↑ Offender 18\+ Victim U16 or U13
For sexual gratification
Watch 3rd person or image

Section 13
Child Sex Offence Committed by U18
↑ Same offences as ss. 9 to 12
Offender U18
Max five years' imprisonment

Section 14
Arranging or Facilitating Child Sex Offences
↑ Arranging or facilitating ss. 9 to 13
Any part of the world
No need for sexual activity

Section 15
Meeting a Child Following Sexual Grooming
↑ Offender 18\+ Victim U16
Met or communicated ONCE
Any part of the world for sex offence

Preparatory Offences

Section 61
Administer Substance with Intent

→

Any substance
Any sexual offence
Enable any person to engage in activity
No need for ulterior sex offence to take place

Section 62
Commit Criminal Offence with Intent to
Commit Sexual Offence

→

Any criminal offence
Any sex offence covered by SOA 2003
Kidnap or False imprisonment = Life
No need for ulterior sex offence to take place

Section 63
Trespass with Intent to Commit a Relevant
Sexual Offence

→

Premises = any structure or vehicle
Offence must take place in premises
Any sex offence covered by SOA 2003
No need for ulterior sex offence to take place

PART 5

Answers Section

Answers Section

1. *Mens Rea* (State of Mind) and *Actus Reus* (Criminal Conduct)

Answers to Multiple-Choice Questions

1. Answer **D** — The source of the intoxication can be drink or drugs (making answer A incorrect). Intoxication can be self-induced and still be relevant (to 'specific' intent cases), meaning that answer B is incorrect. Answer C is incorrect as a s. 18 wounding is a 'specific' intent offence. In the latter case, however, the courts will consider the known effects of the drug in deciding whether or not the defendant had formed the required *mens rea* necessary for the offence (correct answer D).

Investigators' Manual, para. 1.1.2.2

2. Answer **C** — The decision in *R v G & R* [2003] 3 WLR 1060 states that 'recklessness' will be considered on a subjective basis. This makes answers A and B incorrect (as B is objective recklessness). Answer D is fabricated.

Investigators' Manual, para. 1.1.3

3. Answer **A** — These facts are very similar to the case of *R v Smith* [1959] 2 QB 35. It is only in exceptional circumstances that medical treatment will break the chain of causation (*R v Jordan* (1956) 40 Cr App R 152), making answer C incorrect. Following the 'but for' test, the fact that LOVATT received poor treatment and was dropped several times on the way to the hospital will not affect GRICE's liability, making answers B and D incorrect.

Investigators' Manual, paras 1.2.6 to 1.2.7

4. Answer **C** — Drug dealers are not generally liable for the ultimate deaths of their victims (*R v Kennedy* [2007] UKHL 38), making answer A incorrect. You must take your victims as you find them, making answer B incorrect (*R v Blaue* [1975] 1 WLR 1411) and answer D incorrect (*R v Haywood* (1908) 21 Cox CC 692).

Investigators' Manual, para. 1.2.7

2. Incomplete Offences

Answers to Multiple-Choice Questions

1. Answer **D** — It does not matter that SALE and ALISON BURCOTT are unaware of the existence of each other—there is still a conspiracy between JOHN BURCOTT and SALE (correct answer D). It is worth noting that there would be no conspiracy between ALISON BURCOTT and SALE in these circumstances as they do not know of the existence of each

other (there is no meeting of minds between the pair). This makes answer A incorrect. An abandoning of the agreement altogether will not prevent a statutory conspiracy being committed, making answer B incorrect. Just because SALE happens to work at the bank will not prevent a conspiracy taking place, making answer C incorrect.

Investigators' Manual, para. 1.3.3.1

2. Answer **C** — At points 'A' and 'B', BLACKMAN's activities are 'merely preparatory'. At point 'C' he 'embarks on the crime proper' and has gone beyond mere preparation, making answer D incorrect.

Investigators' Manual, para. 1.3.4

3. Answer **A** — As a general rule, you cannot attempt a summary only offence. However, if the offence is a summary only offence solely because of a statutory limit imposed in some cases (e.g. criminal damage to property of low value or low-value theft), then the offence can be attempted, making answer B incorrect. You *can* attempt the factually impossible, making answer C incorrect. Answer D is incorrect, as MYCROFT's actions have gone beyond mere preparation.

Investigators' Manual, para. 1.3.4

3. General Defences

Answers to Multiple-Choice Questions

1. Answer **D** — In *R v Lee* [2001] 1 Cr App R 19, a case arising from an assault on two arresting police officers, the Court of Appeal reviewed the law in this area, reaffirming the following points:
- A genuine or honest mistake could provide a defence to many criminal offences requiring a particular state of mind, including assault with intent to resist arrest (*R v Brightling* [1991] Crim LR 364). This makes answer A incorrect.
- A defence of mistake had to involve a mistake of fact, not a mistake of law. Generally, it is no defence to claim a mistake as to the law because all people are presumed to know the law once it is made (making answer B incorrect).
- People under arrest are not entitled to form their own view as to the lawfulness of that arrest. They have a duty to comply with the police and hear the details of the charge against them (*R v Bentley* (1850) 4 Cox CC 406). This makes answer C incorrect.
- Belief in one's own innocence, however genuine or honestly held, cannot afford a defence to a charge of assault with intent to resist arrest under s. 38 of the Offences Against the Person Act 1861 (correct answer D).

Investigators' Manual, para. 1.4.2

2. Answer **B** — It is immaterial that HIMLEY is there and then threatened with serious physical injury (answer A) as duress is not available in answer to a charge of murder or attempted murder (correct answer B—also makes answer C incorrect). Answer D is incorrect as the defence could be used to answer a variety of charges, including one where serious injury had been caused to the victim (e.g. a s. 20 or s. 18 offence).

Investigators' Manual, para. 1.4.3

4. Entry, Search and Seizure

Answers to Multiple-Choice Questions

1. Answer **B** — When the detained person is in police custody at a designated police station, a s. 18 search is authorised by an officer of the rank of inspector or above, making answer D incorrect. Answer A is incorrect as the search can take place if the officer has reasonable grounds to suspect that evidence relating to the indictable offence for which the person has been arrested or to some other indictable offence which is connected to or similar to that offence will be on the premises. Answer C is incorrect because a theft of this nature is an either way offence which means that it is indictable.

Investigators' Manual, para. 1.6.5.3

2. Answer **A** — Section 32 allows an officer to search an *arrested person* for anything which might be evidence relating to the offence, making answer D incorrect. A search of the bedsit and communal lounge in the house can only take place if DC AHMED has reasonable grounds for believing (*not suspecting*) that there is evidence for which the search is permitted on those premises. Therefore, answers B and C are incorrect.

Investigators' Manual, para. 1.6.5.2

3. Answer **B** — Section 17 of PACE is a power to enter and search in order to arrest not to search for evidence, making answer D incorrect. The power can be executed by an officer in plain clothes in these circumstances, making answer A incorrect. Whether the occupier has been spoken with or not will not stop this power being used, making answer C incorrect.

Investigators' Manual, para. 1.6.5.1

4. Answer **D** — Section 19 is a power of seizure and does not provide a power to search, making answer C incorrect. The power can be used when a constable reasonably believes that the item has either been obtained in consequence of an offence or is evidence in relation to an offence he/she is investigating or any other offences and it is necessary to seize the item to prevent it being lost, damaged, altered or destroyed, making answer B incorrect. Answer A is incorrect as the power can only be used when the officer is 'lawfully' on the premises. DC DYER has been told to leave and is no longer 'lawfully' on the premises and is a trespasser and cannot then seize any property he may find.

Investigators' Manual, para. 1.6.8.1

5. Special Warnings

Answers to Multiple-Choice Questions

1. Answer **B** — Answers A and C are incorrect as, although the necklace was not found on DOOLEY's person or in or on his clothing or footwear, this would not preclude the giving of a special warning to DOOLEY in these circumstances. Answer D is incorrect, as it does not matter who gives the special warning to DOOLEY.

Investigators' Manual, paras 1.9.2.4 to 1.9.2.5

2. Answer **D** — Special warnings *do apply* to 'no comment' interviews, making answer B incorrect. Answer C is incorrect as the presence of a solicitor is immaterial as long as the suspect has had the opportunity to consult one. Answer A is incorrect, as SINGH was not arrested 'at a place at or about the time the offence was committed'.

Investigators' Manual, paras 1.9.2.4 to 1.9.2.5

3. Answer **A** — Sections 36(2) and 37(2) state that inferences can be drawn from 'special warnings' by a magistrates' court (enquiring into an offence as examining justices in deciding whether to grant an application for dismissal made by the accused under s. 6 of the Magistrates' Courts Act 1980), making answer B incorrect. This can be in respect of 'special warnings' under either s. 36 or s. 37 of the Act, making answer C incorrect. A defendant cannot be convicted solely on an inference drawn from a failure or refusal (s. 38(3)), making answer D incorrect.

Investigators' Manual, paras 1.9.2.4 to 1.9.2.5

6. The Regulation of Investigatory Powers Act (RIPA) 2000

Answers to Multiple-Choice Questions

1. Answer **C** — A CHIS is someone who establishes or maintains a relationship with another person for the covert purpose of obtaining information or providing access to information or who covertly discloses information obtained by the use of such a relationship. This will not cover members of the public who contact the police and supply general information to them, making answer A incorrect. Answer B is incorrect as the definition will not cover instances where members of the public have come across information in the ordinary course of their jobs and who suspect criminal activity and then pass that information to the police. However, once the police begin to direct the person, for example by asking them to develop the information in some way to enhance it, that person could then become a CHIS making answer D incorrect.

Investigators' Manual, paras 1.12.3 to 1.12.3.2

2. Answer **B** — Intrusive surveillance deals with surveillance on residential premises or private vehicles, making answers A and C incorrect as this is taking place in factory premises. The activity would be covered by the Act, making answer D incorrect, as this is a specific operation that is covert and likely to result in the obtaining of private information about a person.

Investigators' Manual, para. 1.12.4.2

3. Answer **A** — In ordinary circumstances, the authorising officer for directed surveillance will be of the rank of superintendent or above and the authorisation will last for three months beginning on the day on which the authorisation was granted.

Investigators' Manual, para. 1.12.4.1

7. Homicide

Answers to Multiple-Choice Questions

1. Answer **B** — The House of Lords ruled that the doctrine of transferred *mens rea* does not fully apply to an unborn baby, making answer D incorrect. The intention to kill or cause grievous bodily harm to JOAN cannot support a charge of murder in respect of the baby if it goes on to die after being born alive, making answer A incorrect. If the intention is to commit GBH to JOAN, and the baby is born alive but later dies from injuries received in the womb, it is manslaughter, making answer B correct. Answer C is incorrect as a consequence of this.

Investigators' Manual, para. 2.1.2

2. Answer **A** — The special defence of loss of control can only be used when the defendant is charged with the offence of murder, *not* attempted murder. This makes answers B, C and D incorrect. A consequence of a successful plea would be to reduce murder to manslaughter (not attempted murder to a s. 18 wounding), making answer C further incorrect. The consent of the DPP is not required to raise the defence, making answer D further incorrect.

Investigators' Manual, para. 2.1.3.2

3. Answer **D** — The sentence for manslaughter is life imprisonment (not mandatory), making answer C incorrect. Answers A and B are incorrect because to be guilty of manslaughter by unlawful act the defendant *must* have the required *mens rea* for the unlawful act. This question is based on the case of *R v Lamb* [1967] 2 QB 981, where the defendant was shown (in mirror circumstances to this question) not to have the required *mens rea* for assault and his conviction for manslaughter was quashed.

Investigators' Manual, para. 2.1.4.1

8. Misuse of Drugs

Answers to Scenario-Based Questions

1. Section 37 of the Misuse Drugs Act 1971 defines 'cannabis'. It states that cannabis means any plant of the genus *Cannabis* or any part of any such plant, except that it does not include any of the following products after separation from the rest of the plant:

- mature stalk of any such plant;
- fibre produced from mature stalk of any such plant; and
- seed of any such plant.

Mrs GRUNDY is only in possession of the seeds and commits no offence.

2. Section 6 of the Misuse of Drugs Act 1971 simply says that it shall not be lawful to cultivate any plant of the genus *Cannabis*. Cultivation is not clearly defined, but some form of watering or feeding would be more than sufficient. You may also wish to consider the offence of producing a controlled drug under s. 4(2) of the Act, as 'production' means producing by manufacture *or* by cultivation. The benefits of a charge under this section are simple; production is a drug trafficking offence and if found guilty the offender can be made the subject of a Drugs Profits Confiscation Order, allowing the court to seize any assets from his/her production activities. Another example of production is found in the making of 'crack' cocaine from normal cocaine hydrochloride. The process removes the salt part of the compound, thus creating a more potent drug. If you were able to prove a person's involvement in this, you would be able to consider the offence of producing a controlled drug as production is by manufacture, cultivation or *by any other method*.

3. Mrs GRUNDY is fully aware that the cake contains a controlled drug. The fact that it has been prepared in some other way for consumption is irrelevant. Putting the cannabis in a cake for consumption is no different to the more common method of including it with tobacco in a rolled cigarette for consumption. The term 'supply' means more than a simple transfer of physical control and includes distribution of a substance. Mrs GRUNDY has distributed the substance and the fact that her friend does not know is irrelevant.

4. Amphetamine (also spelt 'Amfetamine') is a Class B controlled drug under the Misuse of Drugs Act (MDA) 1971. However, when it is prepared for injection it is automatically reclassified as a Class A drug. Therefore, COLT is in possession of a Class A drug under the MDA 1971. This goes some way to explaining why amphetamine is listed under Class A and Class B in your *Investigators' Manual*.

5. COLT clearly possesses a controlled drug (morphine), as the tablets are issued to his mother and not to him. It does not matter whether the drug is illicitly produced or pharmaceutically produced; it remains a Class A drug under the Misuse of Drugs Act 1971.

6. COLT would have a defence to possession under s. 5(4)(b) in that 'knowing or suspecting it to be a controlled drug, he took possession of it for the purpose of delivering it into the custody of a person lawfully entitled to take custody of it and that as soon as possible after taking possession of it he took all reasonable steps to deliver it into the custody of such a person'. Therefore, as long as COLT had the authority of his mother to collect the tablets and he took them straight to her as soon as possible, he has a defence to possession.

7. Under s. 23(1) of the Misuse of Drugs Act 1971, a constable or other authorised person can enter the premises of a person carrying on the business of supplying controlled drugs, and demand the production of and to inspect any books or documents relating to the dealings in such drugs and to inspect any stocks of any such drugs.

8. No. Section 23(3)(a) and (b) of the Misuse of Drugs Act 1971 only allows for a Justice of the Peace to grant a search warrant if he/she is satisfied that there are controlled drugs on the premises or documents relating to any transaction or dealing in those controlled drugs. Therefore, any application to search for this machine would not be granted (under this particular section of this Act).

8. Misuse of Drugs

Answers to Multiple-Choice Questions

1. Answer **B** — In order to be in possession of anything, the common law requires the thing to be in the custody or control of the person plus the person has knowledge of its presence. If a drug is slipped into RUSH's pocket and he has no idea it is there, he is not in possession of it.

Investigators' Manual, paras 2.2.3 to 2.2.3.6

2. Answer **C** — Possession with intent to supply to an undercover police officer is an offence under this section, making answer A incorrect. Answer B is incorrect as, although

possession of this material is relevant to show that GARWOOD is an active dealer generally, it does not prove the offence. The presence of large sums of money can be used to prove the offence (*R v Wright* [1994] Crim LR 55) making answer D incorrect.

Investigators' Manual, para. 2.2.5

3. Answer C — Answer A is incorrect as the minimum period for such an order is two years (s. 33(3) of the Act). Answer B is incorrect as the offences covered by Travel Restriction Orders include the production and supply of controlled drugs (therefore including an offence under s. 4(3) of the 1971 Act). Answer D is incorrect as an offender may apply to the court that made the restriction order to have it revoked or suspended (s. 35 of the Act).

Investigators' Manual, para. 2.2.16

4. Answer D — Section 5 provides a defence to a person charged with an offence of unlawful possession of a drug, making answer B incorrect. It does not matter what type of drug it is or what classification it falls under, making answers A and C incorrect.

Investigators' Manual, para. 2.2.3.8

9.   Firearms and Gun Crime

Answers to Multiple-Choice Questions

1. Answer A — The firearm must be the means by which life is endangered and the fact that ROBE has possession of the firearm at the time of the offence is immaterial, making answer B incorrect. The fact that the victim of the offence is not injured makes no difference to the commission of this offence, making answer C incorrect. Answer D is correct insofar as the offence does not require the firearm to be produced, but option A supersedes this.

Investigators' Manual, para. 2.3.11.1

2. Answer B — This offence is 'absolute' but can only be committed if the defendant has with them a *loaded* shotgun, making answer A incorrect. This fact makes answer C incorrect as well. Answer D is incorrect because the offence is 'absolute' and knowledge is not required.

Investigators' Manual, para. 2.3.12.1

3. Answer A — Section 47 of the 1968 Firearms Act allows a constable who has reasonable cause to suspect a person has a firearm with him in a public place to require him/her to hand over the firearm for examination by the officer, making answers B and D incorrect. It does not matter whether the firearm is loaded or if the person who is requested to hand over the firearm has ammunition in his/her possession, making answer C incorrect.

Investigators' Manual, para. 2.3.13

4. Answer B — It does not matter what NORTH believes as this is an offence of intent—all that is important is that ZULFIKAR intended NORTH to believe that unlawful violence would be used against him by means of the firearm/imitation firearm, making answer A incorrect. The offence can be committed with an imitation firearm making answer D incorrect. An imitation firearm is anything that has the appearance of being a firearm whether capable of discharge or not—it does not matter that the case contains nothing at all, making answer C incorrect.

Investigators' Manual, para. 2.3.11.2

10. Racially and Religiously Aggravated Offences

Answers to Multiple-Choice Questions

1. Answer **A** — The offence of s. 20 (grievous bodily harm, Offences Against the Person Act 1861) is the only offence that could be racially or religiously aggravated.

Investigators' Manual, para. 2.6.1

2. Answer **C** — Under s. 28(1)(a) of the Crime and Disorder Act 1998, the demonstration of hostility will take immediately before, during or after the offence takes place.

Investigators' Manual, para. 2.6.3

11. Non-fatal Offences Against the Person

Answers to Multiple-Choice Questions

1. Answer **A** — A defendant commits an assault when he/she intentionally or recklessly causes another person to apprehend *immediate* unlawful violence, making answers B and D incorrect. Answer C is incorrect as an assault can be committed by words alone.

Investigators' Manual, paras 2.7.2.3, 2.7.2.4

2. Answer **B** — The injuries received by MATONI and the child will amount to an offence under s. 39 of the Criminal Justice Act 1988 (as they both receive what are clearly stated to be minor injuries) and not to a s. 47 assault (Offences Against the Person Act 1861) making answers C and D incorrect. Answer A is incorrect as THEAKSTON is liable for the injuries the child receives. This is because a battery can be committed indirectly (as per *Haystead* v *Chief Constable of Derbyshire* [2000] 3 All ER 890).

Investigators' Manual, para. 2.7.3

3. Answer **B** — Belief in your own innocence, even if it is thoroughly merited, is no defence to this offence, making answer C incorrect. The offence is committed when a person assaults any person (including members of the public) with intent to resist or prevent their own or another's arrest, making answers A and D incorrect.

Investigators' Manual, para. 2.7.16.1

4. Answer **A** — Loss of control is only a defence to murder, making answer D incorrect. The offence has not been committed as WEST did not intend either CRAIG or SARTIN to believe the threat.

Investigators' Manual, para. 2.7.17

12. **Child Protection**

Answers to Multiple-Choice Questions

1. Answer **B** — The fact that COLETO is the father of all three children will not afford him a defence as he has taken his children out of the United Kingdom without the consent of his ex-wife who has lawful custody of all of the children, making answer D incorrect. The relevant age for an offence under s. 1 of the Act is *under the age of 16.* This means that the offence is not committed with regard to ANTHONY who is 16 years old, but is committed with regard to PHILLIPPA (aged 14 years) and MARK (aged 12 years), making answers A and C incorrect.

Investigators' Manual, para. 2.9.2.1

2. Answer **A** — Answer B is incorrect as there is no requirement that the removal of the child from a person's lawful control be accomplished by the use of force or physical constraint. Answer C is incorrect as whether CURTIS has an ulterior motive for the removal is immaterial. In *R v Mousir* [1987] Crim LR 561, it was said that the phrase 'so as to' in s. 2(1)(a) of the Act is concerned with the objective consequences of the taking or detaining, and not with the accused's subjective motives. Answer D is incorrect as the consent of the victim is irrelevant.

Investigators' Manual, para. 2.9.2.3

3. Answer **B** — There are three defences available to an offence under s. 2 of the Act.

> (3) ... it shall be a defence for [the defendant] to prove—
>> (a) where the father and mother of the child in question were not married to, or civil partners of, each other at the time of his birth—
>>> (i) that he is the child's father; or
>>> (ii) that, at the time of the alleged offence, he believed, on reasonable grounds, that he was the child's father; or
>> (b) that, at the time of the alleged offence, he believed that the child had attained the age of sixteen.

As there are three defences, answer C is incorrect. Answer A is incorrect as the fact that DAY is not the father of the child does not necessarily mean he commits the offence (because of the other defences). Answer D is incorrect as PELL has removed the child from DAY's lawful control.

Investigators' Manual, paras 2.9.2.3 to 2.9.2.4

13. Offences Involving the Deprivation of Liberty

Answers to Multiple-Choice Questions

1. Answer **A** — An offence of kidnapping can be carried out by the use of force or fraud. When NICKLIN's wife is moved from the front of POYNER's house towards NICKLIN's car, the offence is complete.

Investigators' Manual, para. 2.10.2

2. Answer **A** — The use of force is not required for the offence of false imprisonment, making answer B incorrect. Answer C is incorrect as UDALL has moved ACTON from one point to another by the use of a fraud and the offence of kidnapping is complete at this point. There is no requirement for the victim to be taken to the offender's ultimate destination, making answer D incorrect.

Investigators' Manual, paras 2.10.1 to 2.10.2

3. Answer **C** — The offence of false imprisonment is committed when a person falsely imprisons another. The state of mind required to commit the offence is the unlawful and intentional/reckless restraint of a person's freedom. There is no need for force to be used on the person to commit the offence, meaning answer D is incorrect. There is no time limitation on how long a person should be detained in order for the offence to be committed, meaning answer B is incorrect. In *R v Shwan* [2007] EWCA Crim 1033, the court stated there was no reason why a householder should not be entitled to detain someone in their house whom they genuinely believed to be a burglar, providing a defence to the offence and making answer A incorrect.

Investigators' Manual, para. 2.10.1

14. Theft

Answers to Multiple-Choice Questions

1. Answer **D** — Section 2 of the Theft Act 1968 states that a person will not be treated as dishonest if he/she honestly:

- appropriates property in the belief that he/she has the right in law to deprive the other of it (answer A); or
- appropriates property in the belief that he/she would have the other's consent if the other knew of the appropriation and the circumstances of it (answer C); or
- appropriates property in the belief that the person to whom the property belongs cannot be discovered by taking reasonable steps (answer B).

A person *may* be dishonest notwithstanding that he/she is willing to pay for the property.

Investigators' Manual, para. 3.1.3

2. Answer **B** — If SMITH buys the car in good faith and gives value for it (i.e. a reasonable price) but then discovers it has been stolen, her refusal to return it to GOODALL will not, without more, attract liability for theft (see s. 3(2) of the Theft Act 1968). This makes answers A and C incorrect. Answer D is incorrect as the same property can be stolen on more than one occasion.

Investigators' Manual, para. 3.1.5

3. Answer **A** — This question relates to s. 5(3) of the Theft Act 1968, which states that where a person (DELACY) receives property from or on account of another (the mortgage funds from BOOTH) and is under an obligation to retain and deal with that property or its proceeds in a particular way (using the money for the mortgage), the property or proceeds shall be regarded (as against him) as belonging to the other (i.e. the mortgage money still belongs to BOOTH). The mortgage funds only ever belong to BOOTH, making answers B, C and D incorrect.

Investigators' Manual, para. 3.1.8

15. Robbery and Blackmail

Answers to Multiple-Choice Questions

1. Answer D — For there to be a robbery, there must be a theft. If FISHER honestly believes he has a right in law to the property then he is not dishonest. If he is not dishonest, then there is no theft. If there is no theft, then there is no robbery.

Investigators' Manual, para. 3.2.1

2. Answer B — Answer A is incorrect because this is a threat to use force at some time in the future (this would be a blackmail). The fact that RIHAN is deaf and blind is immaterial. LEWIN sought to put RIHAN in fear of being then and there subjected to force, and just because the threats are not heard or seen makes no difference. Therefore, answer C is incorrect as the threats were first made at point B.

Investigators' Manual, para. 3.2.1

3. Answer D — Blackmail is committed when the demand is actually made. It can be a written demand and in such a situation the demand is made when the letter is posted, making answers A and C incorrect. Answer B is incorrect as no special permission is required for a prosecution of blackmail.

Investigators' Manual, paras 3.3.1 to 3.3.4

16. Burglary and Aggravated Burglary

Answers to Multiple-Choice Questions

1. Answer D — Abstracting electricity is not theft, so at point A there can be no intent for the purposes of burglary. Once inside, REDGRAVE can only commit burglary in the garage by stealing or causing GBH or attempting either. Criminal damage is not a 'trigger' offence, so answer B is incorrect. TWOC is not theft as far as burglary is concerned, making answer C incorrect.

Investigators' Manual, paras 3.4.1 to 3.4.3

2. Answer C — At points A and B, BURTOFT has already entered the bedroom and not as a trespasser therefore she cannot commit burglary in the bedroom. Her intention to steal from the loft goes beyond a condition of entry and the moment she enters a separate part of the building she becomes a trespasser, making answer D incorrect.

Investigators' Manual, para. 3.4.1

3. Answer B — The rope is a weapon of offence as it is intended to incapacitate a person and comes within the WIFE mnemonic. WARREN actually has physical possession of the rope as well as an intention to use it to incapacitate a person and OAK has knowledge of its existence as well as access; so both men would be caught by the expression 'has with him' regarding this item. This means that both men commit an aggravated burglary in relation to the rope. Therefore, WARREN and OAK commit the offence.

While both men have the screwdriver 'with them', WARREN does not know of OAK's intentions regarding the sharpened screwdriver. The screwdriver is a weapon of offence to OAK (as he has sharpened it to use against HOLLAND, i.e. adapted and intends) but not to WARREN, to whom this is just a screwdriver. Therefore OAK commits aggravated burglary in relation to the screwdriver but WARREN does not.

Answer D says that both men commit the offence but OAK only commits it in relation to the screwdriver. This is wrong as he commits it in relation to the rope as well.

Answer B is right as both men commit the offence but WARREN only commits it in relation to the rope (and not the screwdriver).

Investigators' Manual, paras 3.5.1 to 3.5.2

4. Answer D — Although MARKER enters a building as a trespasser, there is no intention to commit grievous bodily harm, criminal damage or theft when he does so. He believes that he has a lawful right to the money that is owed to him and is therefore not dishonest—no dishonesty = no theft and no offence under s. 9(1)(a) of the Theft Act, eliminating answer A. MARKER does not commit a s. 9(1)(b) offence as this is all about doing something—steal or attempt to steal, commit or attempt to commit grievous bodily harm. Threatening LOVELL is not enough so answer B is incorrect. Criminal damage is not part of the s. 9(1)(b) offence, so answer C is incorrect.

Investigators' Manual, paras 3.4.1 to 3.4.5

17. Handling Stolen Goods

Answers to Multiple-Choice Questions

1. Answer D — When JONES obtained the lawnmower from HARDING he did not know it was stolen. To handle the goods, the defendant must know or believe they are stolen and this is not the case at point A. If the only person 'benefiting' from the defendant's actions is the defendant himself/herself, the element of 'assisting/acting for another's benefit' will not be made out (*R v Bloxham* [1983] 1 AC 109). This makes answer C incorrect. At point B, JONES has not even tried to dispose of the mower. Merely finding out you have bought stolen property does not make you a handler if you bought the property in good faith.

Investigators' Manual, paras 3.7.1, 3.7.6

2. Answer B — The purpose of admitting this evidence is for the purpose of proving that COWSER knew or believed the goods to be stolen goods.

Investigators' Manual, para. 3.7.4

3. Answer D — It does not matter what any of the men in this scenario believe or suspect or why they believe or suspect it—the fact is that an offence of handling cannot be committed unless the goods are stolen goods and the watches in the question, although fakes, have not been stolen.

Investigators' Manual, para. 3.7.1

18. Fraud

Answers to Multiple-Choice Questions

1. Answer B — The offence of fraud is all about the conduct and intent of the offender. BRADNICK tried to fool RICE and, although her trick was unsuccessful, it does not alter her liability—the offence is committed when she makes the representation (that she is a nurse) in an effort to gain a financial advantage. Whether it works or not is immaterial as the offence is complete when the representation is made, making answer A incorrect. The fact that BRADNICK did not obtain any financial gain from her efforts makes no difference as she intended to—intention alone does not require a result so answer C is incorrect. Answer D is incorrect as although an attempt fraud is possible, it will be rare and, as already stated, the offence is complete when the representation is made.

Investigators' Manual, paras 3.8.2 to 3.8.3

2. Answer A — Section 3 creates an offence of dishonestly failing to disclose information where there is a legal duty to do so—this question clearly involves such an obligation on HAMMERTON. Although the term 'legal duty' is not defined, it will include duties under oral contracts as well as written contracts, making answer B incorrect. Answers C and D are incorrect as the offence states that by failing to disclose, the offender *intends* to make a gain for himself or another or cause loss to another or to expose another to a risk of loss. It is the latter italicised comment which makes HAMMERTON guilty of the offence.

Investigators' Manual, para. 3.8.5

3. Answer C — The offence is committed by the person having possession or control of articles (control would cover the stamp machine and the identity documents even though they are, in the case of the identity documents, some distance away from VALE). The articles are to be used 'in the course of or in connection with' fraud. So the article does not have to be the actual means by which the fraud is carried out. Therefore all of the items are covered. The last point to mention is that although VALE is in his house this does not alter his guilt as the offence can be committed anywhere at all.

Investigators' Manual, para. 3.8.7

4. Answer A — A person commits this offence when they occupy a position in which they are expected to safeguard, or not to act against, the financial interests of another and they dishonestly abuse their position intending to make a gain for themselves or another or to cause loss to another. ROTHWELL intends WebSaints to lose money by failing to take up the chance of a crucial contract in order that a rival company can take it up at his employer's expense and commits the offence in doing so, ruling out answers C and D. When he clones the software products, he once again abuses his position and once again commits the offence, meaning that answer B is incorrect.

Investigators' Manual, para. 3.8.6

19. Criminal Damage

Answers to Multiple-Choice Questions

1. Answer **D** — When a defendant is charged with this offence, it must be shown that it was the damage that caused the danger to life. In *R v Steer* [1988] AC 111, a defendant fired a gun through a window pane. The court felt that, although the defendant was clearly reckless as to the damage his actions would cause, the two people standing behind the window pane were not put in danger by the damage but by the missile. Therefore, the court held that the defendant was not guilty of this offence.

Investigators' Manual, para. 3.10.3

2. Answer **A** — Section 2 of the Act (threats to destroy or damage property) refers to the offence as one of *intention*. The key element is the defendant's intention that the person receiving the threat fears it would be carried out. It is immaterial whether the threat is believed (answer C), whether the threat was to commit damage in the future (answer B) or whether the defendant actually intended to carry out the threat (answer D).

Investigators' Manual, para. 3.10.5

3. Answer **C** — This is an offence of intent, i.e. the damage need not actually have been attempted or committed, making answer D incorrect. A conditional intent, i.e. an intent to use something to cause criminal damage should the need arise, will be enough (*R v Buckingham* (1976) 63 Cr App R 159) making answer B incorrect. The term used in the definition is 'custody or control', which is far wider than 'possession'; there is no need to show that the defendant actually had the item with him, making answer A incorrect.

Investigators' Manual, para. 3.10.6

20. Sexual Offences

Answers to Multiple-Choice Questions

1. Answer **D** — Under the Sexual Offences (Amendment) Acts 1976 and 1992, victims of most sexual offences (including rape, assault by penetration, sexual assault by touching) are entitled to anonymity throughout their lifetime.

Investigators' Manual, para. 4.1.2

2. Answer **C** — The offence of rape can only be committed by a male, so answer A is incorrect. The offence can only be committed by penetration with the penis, so answer B is incorrect. The penetration by the penis can be to the mouth, anus or vagina, making answer C correct and answer D incorrect as a consequence.

Investigators' Manual, para. 4.2.1

3. Answer **C** — The sex of the victim is immaterial, making answer B incorrect. Penetration can be committed with a part of the body or anything else, making answer D incorrect. Section 79(3) of the Act covers the fact that references to a part of the body (e.g. penis,

vagina) will include references to a body part that has been surgically constructed, particularly if it is through gender reassignment. Therefore, the offence is committed when the surgically constructed vagina is penetrated by SUTTON.

Investigators' Manual, paras 4.2.1 to 4.2.2

4. Answer **A** — If the activity would not appear to a reasonable person to be sexual, then irrespective of the sexual gratification the person might derive from the activity, it will not be 'sexual'. Therefore, weird or exotic fetishes that no ordinary person would regard as being sexual or potentially sexual will not be covered. As the activity is not 'sexual', WALTON does not commit the offence, making answers B and D incorrect. Answer C is incorrect, as a sexual organ or potentially sexual organ does not have to be touched for the offence to be committed.

Investigators' Manual, paras 4.3.1 to 4.3.4

21. Child Sex Offences

Answers to Multiple-Choice Questions

1. Answer **B** — The fact that LEENEY consented to the activity is irrelevant, making answer A incorrect. Answer C is incorrect as the offence can be committed by someone over the age of 18. If LEENEY were under 13 then the offence would be complete, but as she is 14 years old the prosecution will have to show that COLCOUGH did not reasonably believe that LEENEY was over 16, making answer D incorrect.

Investigators' Manual, para. 4.4.2

2. Answer **D** — Answer A is incorrect as the offender for the offence under s. 11 of the Act must be aged 18 or over. Answer B is incorrect as sexual gratification is a required part of the definition. Answer C is incorrect as this offence applies to children who are under 16 years of age. Answer D is correct as it is not necessary to show that the child was aware of the activity in every case.

Investigators' Manual, para. 4.4.4

3. Answer **B** — The fact that the images shown to a child are still or cartoons is immaterial (s. 79(5)), making answer A incorrect. Although TURNER did not initially intend his nephew to see the images, he would commit the offence when he asked him if he wanted to stay (if MARTIN were under 16 years old). MARTIN falls outside the age group for this offence, making answer C incorrect.

Investigators' Manual, para. 4.4.5

22. Preparatory Offences

Answers to Multiple-Choice Questions

1. Answer **D** — Answer A is incorrect as this is a preparatory offence and there is no need for sexual activity to take place. Answer B is incorrect as the offence is committed when

the substance is administered to WALKER. Alcohol would be classed as a substance, making answer C incorrect.

Investigators' Manual, para. 4.7.1

2. Answer **A** — Virtually all sexual offences are 'relevant' offences other than those that exist under the Protection of Children Act 1978, making answer B incorrect. Answers C and D are incorrect as there is no limitation on the type of criminal offence committed. If the offence is one of kidnapping or false imprisonment, then the maximum sentence is increased from 10 years to life.

Investigators' Manual, para. 4.7.2

3. Answer **B** — The defendant must intend to commit the relevant offence *on the premises* in which he/she is a trespasser.

Investigators' Manual, para. 4.7.3